WE'RE ALL IN
THIS TOGETHER

RED GREEN

THE MAN BEHIND
THE CHARACTER AND
VICE VERSA

WE'RE ALL IN THIS TOGETHER

RED GREEN

THE MAN BEHIND THE CHARACTER AND VICE VERSA

Steve Smith in conversation with Mag Ruffman

ToolGirl Press
Mansfield, ON

Photographs in this book are used by permission from the collections of Steve Smith, Morag Smith, Dave Smith, Max Smith, Mary Muncey, Sandi Richardson, Mag Ruffman, Sue Mitchell, Daniel Hunter, Space Media, David Cremasco, Janice Holden, Peter Keleghan, John MacDonald (milk truck), Ken Morris, Jr. (vintage car) and Pier 21. The photograph of the Canada Bread sign is courtesy of the Canada Bread Company, Toronto. Professional production photos are used by permission of Roy Timms, Roy Timms Photography, Hamilton, ON, and Colin Kelly, Today's Faces, Hamilton, ON.

Photographs:
pp. ii-iii—Cast and crew, final season of *The Red Green Show*.
pp. iv-v—Three lads in a boat: a bucolic moment in the shooting schedule with Wayne Robson, Steve Smith and Bob Bainborough.
pp. vi-vii—Red Green with his stretch limo in a barnyard.
pp. viii-ix—Red Green in his amazing hose boat.
p. xviii—Steve and Dave's second car, a '54 Chrysler that they bought in 1962.

Publisher: ToolGirl Press, P.O. Box 167, Mansfield, ON L0N 1M0

Library and Archives Canada Cataloguing in Publication

Smith, Steve, 1945-
    We're all in this together : Red Green, the man behind the character and vice versa
/ by Steve Smith and Mag Ruffman.

ISBN 978-0-9810586-1-0 (bound).--ISBN 978-0-9810586-0-3 (pbk.)

    1. Smith, Steve, 1945-. 2. Red Green Show (Television program).
3. Television writers--Canada--Biography. 4. Television actors
and actresses--Canada--Biography. 5. Television producers
and directors--Canada--Biography. 6. Comedians--Canada--
Biography.
I. Ruffman, Mag, 1957- II. Title.

PN2308.S54A3 2008   791.45092   C2008-906181-0

Printed in Canada

Please visit www.WereAllinThisTogether.ca to find out what Steve is up to now.

DEDICATION

To you, because we're all in this together.

WE'RE ALL IN THIS TOGETHER

ACKNOWLEDGEMENTS

For their encouragement and enthusiasm, we are truly indebted to the following friends and colleagues, with apologies to anyone we have missed.

For their invaluable assistance in reading the raw manuscript, we wish to acknowledge Andrew Glinski, Sue Mitchell, Andrea Mathieson, Liz Foers, Outi Lloyd, Doreen and John Sipple, Jill Vandal, Laura Stratton, Bill and Trish Symons, Allan Horowitz, Gillian and Bill Danner, Jim Barry, Tom Farr, Brendan Kelly, Ted Ruffman and Daniel Hunter.

For their professional advice and encouragement on this project, we wish to thank Robert Mackwood, Seventh Avenue Literary Management, Vancouver, BC, and Brendan Kelly, Brendan Kelly Publishing, Burlington, ON, and Naples, FL.

We also gratefully acknowledge Sophie LaRochelle, 3M Canada, for her enthusiastic support, Leah Cherniak for offering her unique ideas about making a book, and Doyle Brown, Canada Bread, Toronto, ON, for finding the exact photo we needed, and in the nick of time.

Further appreciation and vast gratitude go to Harriet Cooper and Mavis Andrews, our editors, and to our design team—Paula Gaube, Dave Murray and Sue Mitchell—and to Jeff Lumby, Gordon Pinsent, Graham Greene, Peter Keleghan, Wayne Robson, Pat McKenna and Bob Bainborough for reading the advance copies.

We'd also like to thank Mary Muncey, and Morag, Max and Davy Smith for enabling us to include their thoughts and insights in the book.

For being an utterly indispensable friend and co-worker, we thank Sue Mitchell.

And for his unwavering faith in the project, for his wisdom regarding the creative process, for being a man of honour and for exuding well-being in the face of setbacks, we appreciate and thank Daniel Hunter.

C O N T E N T S

FOREWORD

PATRICK MCKENNA

After years of working with Steve, I feel like I probably know the man better than anyone. In fact, next to his wife, sons, extended family and friends, I am probably the person closest to him.

When Steve asked me to write the foreword for this book, I was thrilled. Then I read the book. Steve may have to change his name to Deepak Smith or Steve Chopra because his conversations with Mag have created an insightful and inspiring read.

Steve never speaks much about his childhood, but I got to read where, why and how he developed his wonderful sense of humour and self-discipline. Experiences that some of us would treat as personal injustices or social woes, Steve managed to learn from. He folded them into his life and moved forward.

I've often heard Steve quote one of his personal mantras—"Challenges are opportunities." Throughout the run of *The Red Green Show*, I witnessed numerous "opportunities" present themselves. Each time, I watched Steve *not* react to the current opportunity, but rather file it away somewhere until he had the proper time to deal with it. Eventually he would come back and say,

"Remember when such and such was a problem? Well, here's what we're going to do…." Sometimes his answers weren't to my liking—but they were always the fairest to the situation and the people involved. That's the thing with Steve—he believes in being fair and in keeping his word. And that's why I regard him as a mentor in my life, because at the end of the day, a person is only as good as their word.

Above all, Steve values the weight, rhythm and meaning of words. That's why his analogies, puns and double entendres land so squarely on the mark— he intended them to. It's also why he understands "Show Business" so well—he respects both words.

When we first started *The Red Green Show*, Steve's family would often come to the set to "check up on Pops"—but I noticed that when they said their goodbyes, it was all hugs and laughter. And these boys were teenagers then; teenagers who seemed to like their parents. Well, being a father of a young son myself, I was very impressed. Steve showed me a way of approaching parenting —with honesty, respect and laughter.

In these interviews, Steve comes across as an honest, deliberate and thought-provoking person—and that is exactly the man I have worked and laughed with all these years.

I'm sure that you will enjoy this book as much as I did—I give my word on it.

Patrick McKenna
November 2008

PREFACE

STEVE SMITH

I don't know if I was aware of it before these interviews started, but at some point early on in the process, it became clear to me that for this book to have any value to anyone, it would have to reflect how I *felt* about things rather than what I *knew* about them. The truth is, I do not have any extraordinary knowledge about anything. But maybe my emotional take on people and events could be of some use to others—even if it's only to reinforce their own feelings by rejecting mine. I'll still take credit for that.

This then became a book about my feelings, which opened some doors and closed others. Although I tried my best to remember the chronology and other factual details of events, I was more focused on how they impacted me emotionally at the time and how that affected my life going forward. So if I have some details wrong, that's unfortunate but of no great consequence in this context. Also, because this is a personal and singular viewpoint, I didn't seek opinions from others. I just tried to answer the questions as honestly and fully as I could.

I have to acknowledge the support and opportunities given to me by the people who are closest to me and have known me the longest, starting with my sweetheart, Morag, my two sons, and a whole pack of friends and family stretching back over the last 60-odd years. These are the people who created my environment and helped me adapt to it, and I thank them for that. And a special thanks to Mag for thinking this exercise was worthwhile and pushing me to do it.

My original goal for this book was to have two copies printed—one for each of my sons—so that they could improve the good, correct the bad, and make this a better world for all of their loved ones—including themselves. On the off chance that my perspective has value, I thought it would be nice to offer it to the world.

Steve Smith
November 2008

INTRODUCTION

MAG RUFFMAN

I've known Steve Smith since 1986 when he and his wife, Morag, hired me to work with them in their new TV variety series called *The Comedy Mill*. There were five of us in the cast, including Peter Keleghan (Ranger Gord on *The Red Green Show*) and Linda Kash (the Philadelphia Cream Cheese angel in TV commercials).

The five of us wrote, sang, rehearsed and performed together on TV for two years. We spent lots of weekends "writing" (read: drinking rum-based cocktails, playing charades and waterskiing) at Steve and Morag's cottage, and fell into the easy intimacy of co-workers.

When *The Comedy Mill* ended, we all spun off on diverse paths. Steve created and starred in *The Red Green Show*. Peter and Linda pursued their careers in Los Angeles. I spent seven years in a corset on *The Road to Avonlea*, a CBC/Disney series set in the early 20th century.

We all fell out of touch.

In 1989, a year after *The Comedy Mill* ended, I moved to California and got married. Ten years later, I moved back to Canada with my husband, Daniel

Hunter. We were busy with *A Repair to Remember*, a do-it-yourself TV series that I hosted. Eventually, we brought a couple of new show ideas to Steve's company, S&S Productions, and those shows were successfully produced under the S&S banner. Since Daniel and I were in and out of the S&S offices regularly, I'd sometimes bump into Steve and we'd catch up a little.

In the fall of 2003, I had a vivid dream that I was putting together a book where pieces of a huge puzzle formed into a story about Steve's unusual point of view and his unique way of thinking. I woke up from the dream feeling excited, but within seconds, realized that I had no experience in writing semi-biographical books about Canadian icons, so I dismissed the whole thing.

I had the same dream two more nights in a row.

Hoping to avoid having the dream a fourth time, I emailed Steve about the possibility of doing a book. Within ten minutes he replied that he was flattered but couldn't imagine there being any demand for a book about him. And that's where we left it.

The next spring, I ran into Steve at the S&S offices. We ended up sitting in the boardroom, talking about life. He told me a story about his father, and there was so much intensity in the story that, again, I thought of the book. How could there be no demand for a book about him? After all, Steve was entertaining at least a million people every week on CBC television in Canada, and countless others on PBS stations all across the United States. Steve's show had attracted a devoted fan base of 120,000 card-carrying, plaid-clad Possum Lodge members. There's something about Steve that people really connect with, and I was convinced they'd want to know more about him.

For some lucky reason that I still don't understand, Steve eventually agreed to talk to me about his thoughts and his life. We agreed that I would record the conversations and transcribe them, and then we'd see if it went anywhere.

We needed somewhere quiet to record the sessions. My husband, Daniel, suggested that we work on the 46-foot Chris-Craft houseboat where Steve does most of his writing. That was fine with Steve, so we agreed on a date to start.

Our conversations began in 2004, after Steve had made the decision to stop doing *The Red Green Show* once its fifteenth season finished taping in 2005.

I remember walking down the pier toward Steve's houseboat for our first session. I had typed up two pages of questions about Steve's early years. But as I plodded along listening to the easy rhythms of halyards clinking against masts, all of my preparation seemed strained. I wasn't even sure my questions were right. I'd known him for eighteen years and he was still a mystery.

We ended up having a sprawling, multi-year conversation about what has been important in Steve's life and what he's still looking forward to. The following chapters give you the highlights.

I'm hoping that this book feels like the sort of conversation you'd have with good old friends sitting around a campfire under a canopy of stars, with no subject off limits, and the topics rambling to the edges of this boundless universe.

Most of all, I hope you feel like you're part of the conversation.

Mag Ruffman
November 2008

P.S. Please visit www.WereAllinThisTogether.ca to find out what Steve is up to now.

WE'RE ALL IN THIS TOGETHER

CHAPTER ONE

BOYHOOD

FROM TOYS TO A HANDSHAKE

BOYHOOD

FROM TOYS TO A HANDSHAKE

THE RAMBUNCTIOUS BUILDER

MAG: *One thing I know about you is that you have a perfect memory. You remember names, dates, phone numbers, credit card numbers, even your driver's license number. I'm wondering, what's your earliest memory?*

STEVE: It was night. I was three years old and I was standing in my parents' bedroom at 250 Strathmore Boulevard in the east end of Toronto. The room was at the front of the house. I can remember standing there with windows all around. From their bedroom window, you could see the Canada Bread sign in the distance somewhere. It was a long ways away. Well, everything is a long ways away when you're three.

And the sign would flash "Canada." Then "Bread." And then it would go "Canada Bread." I just thought, "Well, there's nothing cooler than that."

And I would watch to see if it ever did anything different. But it was always "Canada." Then "Bread." Then both—"Canada Bread"! Always, after I brushed

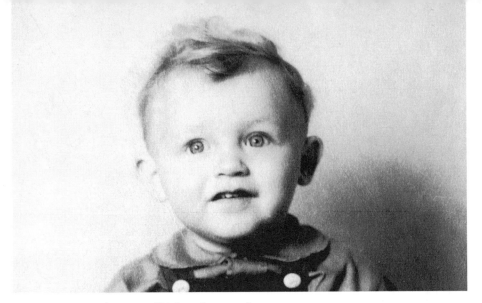

Steve in 1946, revealing one of his brand new teeth.

my teeth and got ready for bed, I'd go right there and watch that for a while. It kind of calmed me down.

MAG: *Why did you have to calm down?*

STEVE: I was rambunctious. I wasn't a docile kid. I had lots of energy. If there was something going on, I was usually somewhere near the centre of it.

MAG: *And you could read at age three?*

STEVE: I think I could read. I could make out those words on the sign. It wasn't just lights. Of course I had an older brother and whatever he could do, I could do an hour later.

MAG: *What sorts of things were you curious about as a kid?*

STEVE: I was more drawn to how *things* worked than how people worked. I was always more interested in toys and machines. Even now I'll look at something and I'll try to figure it out, try to see what makes it work. You know that Rube Goldberg guy? I just thought his stuff was phenomenal. I thought it was pure art.

Back then we had Meccano sets. If you were really rich, you had the Meccano set that had a little motor so you could do pulleys and gears and you could make a crane or whatever. Instead of just building a static structure, you could do kinetic stuff.

Of course we had mini-bricks. And we had primitive remote control cars and planes. But I just liked anything that had some kind of cause-and-effect type of machinery. I really liked that one thing would do this, and another thing would do that, making this first thing do *that*.

I always found that stuff really interesting because it was really a way of stealing time. I could get that thing done over there by doing something here, without doing this and this and that. And it all happens simultaneously!

So I've always liked machines. I mean, what's better than a car? Nothing. You have climate control. You have a full complement of musical entertainment. And now some cars even have TVs in them. You have luxury furnishings, you have all kinds of things to twirl and press. And if you don't like where you are, you can take it somewhere else. That is the ultimate. A car is the ultimate.

Rube Goldberg was an American artist famous for cartoons depicting complex machines that perform simple tasks in indirect, convoluted ways, similar to every device ever invented by Red Green.

Dave and Steve, ready for an outing in 1950.

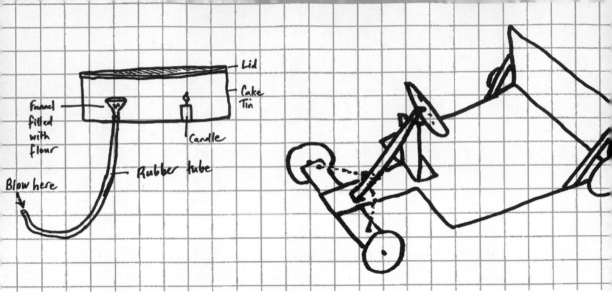

Labels in diagram:
Lid
Cake Tin
Funnel filled with flour
Candle
Blow here
Rubber tube

Above Left: Schematic diagram of a cookie-tin flour bomb, not to scale. *Above Right:* Basic soapbox car design, hand-drawn from memory by Steve.

MAG: *What was your favourite thing to do when you were a little kid?*

STEVE: I was very active. I liked adventures. Like in sports, I'd be out there till you couldn't see, playing baseball or football or hide 'n seek or whatever. I wasn't a kid who sat inside reading a book or watching television.

We had so much fun building soapboxes, little cars. You'd get a baby carriage and take the wheels off it. The guy across the street had an older brother who showed us how we could get a steering wheel from a wrecker for two bucks. You'd put the steering wheel on a broom handle, and then the front axle would just be a board with the baby carriage wheels on each end of it.

And if you ran the rope from the board through a screw eye on each side of it, wrapped the rope three times around the broom handle and then put a nail in the middle of the three-times-around, that would give you your steering. It was pretty cool. If you got the rope tight enough, there wasn't a whole lot of play in it. There was always a *little* bit of play, which you didn't actually realize till you were coming down a hill.

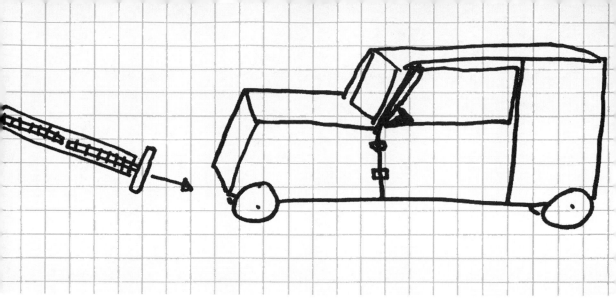

The soapbox car made from a giant refrigerator/freezer box with detail of double axle attached using U-shaped fence nails.

We had these monstrous hills, which have shrunk considerably over the years, but they were huge back in those days. I remember one Saturday, one of the gang had gotten a new refrigerator/freezer and *we* had the box. Well, holy cow.

We built the hugest-of-all-time soapbox car out of this refrigerator box. We had a windshield. We had doors. We didn't have an axle long enough so we had to use two—an axle on each end of the board, with the wheels out the side.

So off we go. I have this mental picture—one guy sitting inside driving it, the other four of us pushing it along down the street as we went toward the hill. And then we all got in. Well, we didn't all get *in*, but we were all involved. There were three of us inside, and two guys on the roof. Until the first bump. Then there was only one guy on the roof and the other guy had fallen onto the hood, so that whoever was driving couldn't see. Then we get into this side-to-side oscillation. We're all yelling "Left! Go left! Go LEFT!" because the guy who's driving can't see. Then the oscillations get bigger and bigger until we flip over into the ditch.

The whole thing was probably a ten-minute deal. If you had looked out your front window you'd see five boys go by with this huge soapbox car. Then if you listened you might hear yelling and a bit of a muffled crash. And then you'd see five guys, limping back, each carrying a different piece of the car. It was great.

MAG: *What else did you like to do?*

STEVE: We used to make these bombs. Out of flour. You get a cookie tin with a lid on it. You drill a hole in the bottom of the cookie tin. You put a rubber hose up through the hole into the bottom of the cookie tin. Then you put a funnel in the hose. So, that's sitting inside the tin. And you fill the funnel with flour. Now you put a candle inside and you light it. You put the lid on the can. Now you blow on the hose and the flour goes into particles and explodes. And I'm telling you, the flame would go up about ten feet high. Blow the lid off ten feet in the air. You do that at night and it's like "Canada Bread"!

I was drawn to that kind of stuff. That was fun for me. It was probably stupid and dangerous. I don't think it was really *that* dangerous. It wasn't dynamite, it was just flour. Nobody ever got hurt. And nobody ever went home bored.

The very sign on Danforth Avenue, circa 1948, that captured the attention of a certain three-year-old every evening.

FIRST KISS AND OTHER ADVENTURES

MAG: *What other sorts of activities appealed to you?*

STEVE: We used to go hiking. We'd pack a lunch and just go. And never go to the same place twice. We were explorers. We'd be gone all day, every day, all summer.

MAG: *Who did you go with?*

STEVE: My friend Richie Farnsdon who lived across the street. And the girl next door, Gail Roper. She was a hottie. When I was maybe seven, I kissed her. No, I might've been eight. I might've wanted to wait a year. We were in the garage one day and it was just one of those things, you know. It just happened. We had a little kiss.

That total fearlessness about the unknown— just go and do it.

I thought, "Well, that's it. She kissed me. We're an item." Then I found out that she had also kissed Richie Farnsdon. Nobody kisses Richie Farnsdon! So, I thought, "Well, Gail's just a kisser, that's all *that* is." That was a bit of a letdown, but I always liked her.

Anyway, this is when we lived in the Kingsway. There was that whole area down by the Humber River that, at that time, was completely undeveloped. There were just fields and fields and fields. So, you had a river, some waterfalls, lots of bulrushes and away we'd go on a hike. That was great.

MAG: *Did you spend the whole time hiking or was there a lot of crouching beside ponds and looking for rocks and stuff?*

STEVE: Well, we'd see animals and try to follow them and then find where they lived. It's amazing what you come across when you're hiking like that. You know, you take those milkweed plants and open them up and they go all over the place. Or you see a tree and it's just like, "Let's just climb it." If it was climbable, you'd climb it. And you'd have a little knife and you'd have to do something with your knife, so you'd put a little notch in the tree. Otherwise there's no point in bringing a knife.

MAG: *Anything else?*

STEVE: Yes, I had the same approach to tobogganing in the winter. And not to do it alone. Like, for me to go on a hike by myself...absolutely not of any interest. It was that small-group thing. Seeing things together.

But the soapbox cars—that was always a fantastic adventure, too. I mean, you build this thing and to a kid...like you get in it and you've got to be doing a hundred miles an hour down a hill with no brakes and *some* steering, and that was it. If you lived, it was, "Let's go again!"

MAG: *In either case, it was the unknown that attracted you. How fast can we go down the hill, or how far can we go across the fields.*

STEVE: Yeah. That was great stuff. That total fearlessness about the unknown— just go and do it.

MAG: *Was there ever in your early life any adventure you turned down or turned away from?*

STEVE: Sure. Skiing. I just never took up skiing. I thought skiing was over the line. That was like jumping out of an airplane for me.

MAG: *So racing down a hill in a dodgy soapbox car with no brakes was okay, but going down a hill on skis—which you can actually steer—was not okay?*

STEVE: Well, I wouldn't go down a ski hill in a soapbox. You know, when they build the roads there's some respect...

MAG: *...for gravity.*

STEVE: Exactly. Plus, I knew a lot of kids who rode in soapbox cars and I never saw them in a cast. And I knew kids who went skiing and a *lot* of them were in casts.

MAG: *No respect for terminal velocity.*

STEVE: No. I wasn't trying to defy death or dismemberment in anything that I did. If I thought that the probability was that I was going to get hurt badly, I didn't do it. I didn't think I was going to get hurt in the soapbox car or tobogganing, but I thought I was going to get hurt skiing. So, that was an adventure I turned down.

I wouldn't go parasailing or hang-gliding or anything like that because in my estimation there's a line. You can cross that line and survive, but that's dangerous because that means you're just going to start moving the line.

If I'm going to be brave—I don't think I'm a very brave person—but if I *am* going to be brave, I'm going to save it for something where it's got some real value for me…like a big, life-changing negotiation or something where you need a lot of courage. I'd rather use it for that than going straight down the icy side of a mountain, hoping for good news at the bottom.

SOMERSAULTING TO GREATNESS

MAG: *Do you remember when you first discovered that you liked entertaining people?*

STEVE: When my brother, Dave, was in kindergarten, if you had a younger brother or sister who would eventually be coming to school, you got to bring them. So, he presented me and I did a somersault for the whole kindergarten class.

That actually became a pattern for Dave and me. We'd put on shows just for the family, like if my grandparents came over. By now I was seven and Dave

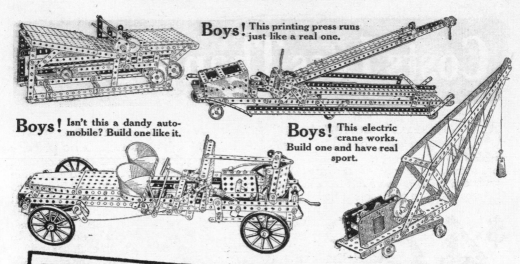

Boys! This printing press runs just like a real one.

Boys! Isn't this a dandy automobile? Build one like it.

Boys! This electric crane works. Build one and have real sport.

was eight. And he'd have the whole show organized. He was the emcee and he'd introduce me, but first he'd get them all to stand for the singing of *God Save the Queen*. It wasn't even *O Canada* back then. My grandfather would take about fifteen minutes to get out of his chair and stand for *The Queen*.

Then we'd do a little variety show. They were short. I think the long ones went ten minutes, and at least half of that was when we played the anthem. I would sing and maybe we'd tell a joke or do a little skit together. The songs were always dead serious. *Faith of Our Fathers*, or something almost hymn-like—*The Battle Hymn of the Republic*.

MAG: *Do you remember any of the jokes you and Dave did together?*

STEVE: Well, if it was a back and forth thing, it would be a knock-knock joke. Like, knock knock. Who's there? Gunther. Gunther who? (lisping) Gunth are dangerouth weaponth.

We'd be hysterical, and there'd be a lot of blank looks out in the audience.

Those little shows we did at home were kind of our version of the Junior Red Cross program we had at school. Once a month, the teacher would conduct a meeting in the classroom and collect a nickel from every kid for the Red Cross. And there'd be an entertainment component. If you could do something for the Red Cross, you were expected to do it—recite a poem or sing a song or tell a story.

When I was a kid I was kind of a singer. I remember my Grade Six teacher getting really upset one time because I didn't want to sing a song. Her point was that if you have that ability, if you have that gift, you don't have the right not to share it.

I thought it was better not to have the gift. I felt it should be my choice. I didn't think that because I *could* sing, I should have fewer choices than a person who *couldn't* sing. The person who couldn't sing didn't even get asked; you never found out whether or not they wanted to sing. I had to actually stand up and give my point of view, which I thought was quite private.

MAG: *Where did you get the idea that what's going on in your brain is so private? Most kids don't have that boundary.*

STEVE: I think it's probably that I would escape to it so much that it was like my own little fort, so I had to protect it from intruders. Because it was my escape hatch.

MAG: *For avoiding anything you didn't want to see or do?*

STEVE: Yes, and I didn't really want to share it with everybody. And then to have that opinion judged. Well, wait a sec, let me get this straight—I have an ability, so therefore I'm going to be punished for it? This was in front of the whole class when the teacher said that I had to do this, and that it wasn't right for me not to share.

Now this was a teacher I had for three years in a row. Her name was Ruth Purdy. She was terrific. I mean, that out-of-context example was based on a pretty good relationship so she could say stuff like that. It didn't hurt my feelings, but it also didn't necessarily change my opinions. She knew *that* too.

THE GIFT THAT KEPT ON GIVING

MAG: *How did you come to have the same teacher three years in a row?*

STEVE: At that time, they were running an experiment in Toronto. They were going to start a program for gifted kids, so they came around and tested all the kids in Grades Three to Seven. I got picked as a gifted kid when I was about to start Grade Six, and then we had Ruth Purdy through Grades Six, Seven and Eight.

And I'll tell you why I got into that gifted school. My brother, Dave, is only fourteen months older than me, but for some reason he thought that qualified him to be the third parent. I already told you he took me to kindergarten that time. He was always very good at school.

So what he would do was…and I'm not talking *one* year; this happened for a few years until he finally got the message. On the first day of summer holidays, it's eight o'clock in the morning and somebody's shaking me.

"What the hell's going on?"

"Come on, Steve, you gotta get up, we're all set."

"What do you mean we're all set?"

"We're all set up downstairs."

"*What's* all set up downstairs?"

"I'm going to teach you everything I learned this year so that when you go to school in the fall, you'll already have it nailed."

"WHAT?"

I go downstairs. There's a blackboard. I've got a little desk. I said, "Get outta here! I just *finished* a year of school! I'm goin' outside. I'm gonna play!"

But he would teach me. He would tell me the stuff he was learning. So, I had a preview all the time. When I got to the next grade, it wasn't that I was smart, it just wasn't anything new. Dave should have gone to the gifted school, not me. There was some horrible mix-up there.

If you don't keep your word then we can't survive as a species because there's no solid ground anymore.

MAG: *You left your regular classmates behind and started Grade Five in a brand new school?*

STEVE: Right, and that was another thing—where's the good news here? Suddenly I'm not going to school with any of my own friends. I've got to get on this school bus with a bunch of nerds. I never considered myself a nerd, and these kids were goofballs. I mean there were a couple of them that I considered normal, but many of them were these egghead goofballs who played chess all the time. They could tell you everything about the War of 1812, but they couldn't throw a football.

So, I was getting on the bus early in the morning, and coming home late at night. After about a month of that, all of the friends that I used to have had made other friends and were doing other things. Then they carried the gifted program into high school. At that point we moved to Brantford, and I was so happy to get out of that program. I knew there was no way that Brantford would have a gifted program.

MAG: *You said earlier that even though you had a run-in with your teacher about the Red Cross show, the two of you had a good relationship. Can you give me an example of why you liked her?*

STEVE: Recently the teacher's union wanted me to do an article about a significant teacher I'd had and I picked Ruth Purdy—she would let me speak out in class. That was very odd; nobody was allowed to speak out in class except me. I could say anything I wanted.

MAG: *What did you say?*

STEVE: Anything I wanted. She told me that when I did speak out, it was usually funny and it was rarely disruptive. It was mostly a way of making things more interesting. I wasn't doing it in a way that undermined what anyone else was doing. It would just be something that struck me funny. So I was allowed to do that.

MAG: *Do you remember the very first time you spoke out?*

Be sure you are right, then go ahead.
—Davy Crockett

STEVE: I remember the teacher writing on the board during an English lesson. It was about tenses of verbs. She had written "Persons in tense" and I yelled out, "Indians!" And everybody laughed. It wasn't anarchistic. It was just goofing around.

And I think that really helped me later because that's been reaffirmed for me when I've been able to make people laugh. So, it's not a surprise for me. I still really enjoy it, but I'm not as tentative as I would have been if I hadn't had that early support. That was an acknowledgement of some ability that comes naturally and is fun for me. I enjoyed people laughing.

Later in life I thought, "Wow, that really planted a seed that wasn't there before." I'm not sure I would have pursued it at all without that encouragement. You don't know because you can't go down two paths at the same time. But I do think back on that as being a pivotal time.

MAG: *Would you say that your teacher made you feel special or isolated?*

STEVE: I think both. She used to call me "Puck." I was different. I wasn't Hamlet, or anyone heroic. I was just doing my own thing and having fun. I didn't take that nickname as an insult, but it definitely did make me feel different. I *am* different. I'm not like anybody I've ever met, which is okay. I'm sure it's okay with the people I've met too.

WILL OF IRON, WORD OF HONOUR

MAG: *In Grade Six you were saying, "No, I won't perform for the Red Cross thing." You already had a certain amount of confidence at that point.*

STEVE: I suppose that was confidence. I was stubborn, but I guess stubbornness comes out of confidence. You really think you can get things to go your way just by using your will.

MAG: *When do you first remember being aware of your will?*

STEVE: I think it was something I was conscious of pretty early. I can probably go back to Grade One or Two—being six or seven years old—and deciding that I was going to go tobogganing, and I was going to go down a certain hill. And that was it. I made that decision and I was going to see that through.

When I got there and that hill was either steeper or icier than I remembered, I just went ahead anyway because I thought it was really important to go ahead. I can remember consciously doing that. I didn't really care that much about the

Crockett, David, 1786-1836, Am. pioneer, b.Limestone, Tenn., known as Davy Crockett: self-taught. Served in Creek War, 1813, under Gen Jackson: magistrate of lawless community founded on shoal creek, Tenn. Then candidate for state legislature; elected 1821 and 1823. In 1826 was elected by Gen. Jackson's party to U.S. House of Rep.; served until 1830; defeated then; re-elected 1832. After 1830 opposed Jackson, and therefore later left Tenn. for Tex., which was revolting against Mex. Was one of six survivors who surrendered Alamo after long seige, all of whom were then shot down by Santa Anna's order. Autobiography was pub. Philadelphia, 1834. A shrewd, brave, whimsical backwoodsman, with motto: 'Be sure you are right, then go ahead.'

outcome. I thought that whatever the outcome was, even if it was negative, it wouldn't be as negative as me not doing something that I had set my mind to do.

I've always had this thing that there's some ground zero level for me. I'll let you push me to a certain point and then, there's no more. You're now at bedrock.

It throws people sometimes. I think I give off this kind of wishy-washy or easy-going thing, but I'm just easygoing in the areas that I decide to be. I've had it happen where somebody will push me and I'll push back and all of a sudden they're thinking, "Where'd this come from? Who's *this* guy?" Well, this guy was always there; it's just that your behaviour has forced the receptionist to turn you over to the manager.

I've always had that, even when I was a kid. There was what I was prepared to do and what I wasn't prepared to do. And there wasn't too much that you could do, I didn't think, to change that. I didn't think an external force could ever change it. I'd have to see some logic or some motivation to change it myself. It wouldn't be through external force or coercion or bribery. I've been that way forever.

Take playing on the street. I was going to go outside and I was going to play football on the street until it got dark. And it didn't matter. I mean, a hurricane could come through and you'd have to come and grab me and bring me in. I was going to stay out there until it got dark 'cause that's what I'd decided to do.

MAG: *What created this ethic that you were going to do something no matter what? Was there some experience you can remember when you felt a loss that prompted this to become a lifetime pattern?*

STEVE: I think that seed got planted from the positive side rather than the negative. In my upbringing, there wasn't any negative motivation for me to go another way. Certainly from my experience of going to movies and watching TV and reading books and the way we were taught in school, there was a moral code that was presented as worthy and that would help you define yourself. The guys who were heroes had a high moral code.

So I thought, "Well, if I have a high moral code, I could become a hero and I could feel good about myself." I really have always wanted to feel good about myself.

MAG: *Did you have any heroes?*

STEVE: Davy Crockett had a huge effect on me—"If you're sure you're right, then go ahead." I just thought, "Holy cow. That's how I feel." You know, I'll take some time to think about it, but if I think I'm right, it's going to be really, really tough to stop me. I'm going to have to prove *myself* wrong. You're not going to be able to do that on my behalf.

At that time there was a whole thing in movies and television shows that I really responded to, which was, you've got to keep your word. If you don't keep your word then we can't survive as a species because there's no solid ground anymore. It was Roy Rogers, John Wayne...all those cowboys. None of the "white hat" guys would ever break his word, break his

Dave and Steve nattily attired and ready to emcee their homestyle variety show. *Opposite:* A coonskin cap and a biography of Davy Crockett taken from the 1957 *Webster's Encyclopedic Dictionary of the English Language*.

promise. There was never any contract or anything; there are no lawyers in a Western.

One thing I try to be very careful about is giving my word. I don't give it easily. It upsets some people that I won't commit to something. When I do commit, I don't go back, or at least I try not to. I'm sure I have gone back on my word in my life, but that really bothers me. I work hard on keeping my word if I give it.

FIT TO BE TRIED

MAG: *When you were a kid, was there anything you were afraid you would regret in life?*

STEVE: You know, as a kid…probably not much at the public school level. In high school, I really felt that I probably was screwing up my future by not laying down a very good academic foundation for myself. Even in terms of going on to university.

But the thing was, nothing ever felt like it fit for me. So, from that perspective, I wasn't being presented with opportunities that I was missing. It's not like they talked about all these various professions or careers or interests and I went, "Oh yeah! That's what I want to do." They didn't present anything that I really felt drawn to.

MAG: *What did you want to be when you grew up?*

STEVE: I wanted to be a teacher. I think a lot of kids do. I just thought that'd be kind of a neat thing. I've always liked being in a protected area. I don't like being in an unfamiliar environment. And it seemed to me that once a teacher goes in and closes that door, that's their territory and they pretty much know within reason what's going to go on in there. They can control their environment.

MAG: *How did you envision your future at that age?*

STEVE: I've always thought of myself as really alone. A lone person. I've never thought of myself as part of a team. Whenever I would daydream as a kid, projecting forward, it was always me doing something alone. I wouldn't daydream about being the President of General Motors or anything like that. I could never see that. It's just too frantic an environment.

You know, I can remember when I was maybe ten, I was thinking about the Millennium, the year 2000. And I was thinking, "Am I going to be alive? Yeah, probably. How old am I going to be? Well, I will turn fifty-five in the year 2000."

And then I took a whole afternoon trying to imagine what my life would be when I was fifty-five. That was like the other side of the moon for me. That completely blew my mind. I had nothing to base it on. I didn't have nearly enough information. And you know how, as you get older, you worry more about the future and the uncertainty with health and everything else? Well, I always think back to that day, when I was ten. It totally freaked me out thinking of myself at fifty-five and I had no idea what would happen. But it turns out I didn't *need* to know. So now I don't worry about sixty-five or seventy-five. I've never been a guy who was any good at looking ahead.

I totally believed that there was magic, that there was some power you could tap into if you knew the trick.

Some people are good at looking ahead. Like, when I was going to school, I used to be funny on the bus. And one day a kid who sat behind me, Robert Sager, said, "I'm going to be watching you on television one day." I was probably eleven or twelve. I phoned him a few years ago. He's some big doctor in Toronto now, and I said, "Man, you were right," and he said, "Told ya!"

To me, so much happens so fast that you couldn't possibly look that far ahead. I love my life right now because I have so many things that happen in one day. I said to my wife, Morag, the other day, "It used to be that if I knew I was doing something on the 25th of June, from the 1st of June on, all I could think of was the 25th. How many more days?" Now, I don't even think about it until it's the 24th because every day seems to have lots of stuff in it. I love that. I love having lots of stuff going on, lots of stuff to do.

It's ridiculous to imagine that I could project forward through thousands of days filled with stuff and figure out what's going to be at the end of it. I think my main thing was, "Am I going to be alive with my current behaviour?" I figured I would be. I knew my grandfather was older than fifty-five even then. So I figured I had a shot.

MAG: *Do you remember when you felt the most alive in your life?*

STEVE: You know when you say that, my memories go back to being on the water in a boat. I remember being at a friend's cottage and I was probably eleven or twelve. His uncle had this old wooden sailboat with canvas sails. I'd never sailed before. And we were out there sailing on this very narrow river, so you're just tacking forever. And I thought, "This is just the greatest."

To me, sailing is a miracle anyway. There are no motors running or anything. And you seem to be going *into* the wind. It's like, the wind is having the *exact*

Below Left: Steve's great aunt Mary, perpetrator of garish gift underwear. *Below Right:* Ever pragmatic, young Steve added an arrow in case Auntie Mary wasn't clear on the concept of school photos.

Love to
Auntie
Mary
from
Steve →

1954   CANDID BY *Hardy* · KINGSWAY

opposite effect on you than what it intended. And I thought, "That would be a great thing if I could do that with life."

MAG: *You thought that? At eleven?*

STEVE: I did. Like, just to take something—something that's trying to push you back—and be able to use it to move yourself forward. I thought, "This is just phenomenal." I felt very alive then.

That experience was probably the first physical representation I'd seen of a force that seemed impenetrable…something that was pushing you back that could actually be used to move you forward.

You hear about these karate and judo things—where you use your opponent's own weight and force to help you. I thought, "Well, that's the same thing."

It made me feel like there may be a way to do that same thing when you're confronted with something. I thought it was empowering. I remember that day and just thinking, "This is impossible. It never occurred to me that this was possible, and because *this* is possible…there must be a billion things that are possible that I don't even know about yet. Hell, I'm only eleven! "

A BRIEF TRAGEDY

MAG: *Do you remember the first time you were ever humiliated?*

STEVE: There was a bread man who pulled my pants down. Now, this is worse than you could ever imagine. First of all, my grandmother was born in England and she had a sister who would send us Christmas gifts from England. I don't know if you've ever had a Christmas gift from a great aunt in England, but there are some very scary categories in relation to clothing. The only up-side was that I would never see this aunt. She would never know. We didn't have Polaroid cameras or anything, so as far as she was concerned, I was wearing that purple and yellow sweater to school every day.

Anyway, when I was seven or eight she sent me some odd underwear. It had a bizarre pattern on it—hearts or something. I don't remember what it was, but it was something I was never going to wear in this current lifetime. So, this pair of underwear goes into the underwear drawer in the Absolute Last Ditch category.

Well, I wasn't good…I mean I didn't over-wear my underwear, but I wasn't good at necessarily getting it into the laundry hamper. It wasn't *on* me, but it wasn't *in* the hamper either.

Wouldn't you know it, one day I looked in my underwear drawer and there's only one option—the English underpants. So, that's what I'm wearing, and that's when Mr. Breadman decides, "I know what I'll do. I'll pull his pants down."

I'm standing in a circle of my friends, he walks up, FOOF, down go my pants. I'm standing there and they're all thinking I wear those underpants everyday. Oh man, that's pretty humiliating. He was probably a pervert or something.

Why would he do that? Why pick on me? It seemed so random and so totally unmotivated. It wasn't like I was a smartass to this guy. I'd never spoken to him in my life. The one day I had those underpants on. Boxers with patterns on them. I wouldn't be surprised if they had a belt.

Mainly, I just couldn't believe it. Why would he do that? He didn't even know me. He just saw a group of kids and I was standing there—FOOF!

That was humiliating. I think I ran home.

GOD, MAGIC AND FORCES UNSEEN

MAG: *I gather you've always had a pretty rich inner life. What was your concept of God as a kid?*

STEVE: My grandmother—my mother's mum—was a Christian Scientist and she had survived a very difficult childbirth. She considered that it was all done

Above Left: The Christian Science Church under a condominium. *Above Right:* Steve's maternal grandmother, Nan, who "made things magical."

through Christian Science.

So until probably twelve or thirteen years of age, we went to the Christian Science church on High Park Avenue, north of Bloor Street. And that was a different kind of thing. It was never forced on me, and I never fully embraced the religion. But there was an aspect that your mind is very important, and that you can change a lot of things just through the way you perceive them.

I really believed that. I didn't necessarily think you could heal a broken bone. But I thought you could make yourself healthy with your mind. I thought you could make yourself as healthy as you could possibly be with your mind, and then let medicine close the rest of the gap if it was still unsatisfactory. But don't *start* with the medicine.

I've very rarely in my whole life taken any medicine. I might have an aspirin every six months or something. I really believe firmly that you can make yourself healthy using your mind. If I start feeling sick I assume I'm doing something wrong. Either I've made a decision that I'm not happy with, or I'm taking a path that doesn't suit me. So getting sick is my way out? Wait a minute. Let's just figure out where the problem is and let's deal with that. And then let's see how you feel.

Usually when I do what I think is the right thing, I feel better. And if it turns out that I was wrong, it doesn't destroy me because at least at the time, I did what I thought was right. When I do something that I'm pretty sure is the wrong thing but I'm doing it for expediency, I can hardly get out of bed the next day. I mean, who are you *now*, Steve?

Anyway, a friend of my grandmother's was a Christian Science practitioner in England. So it was definitely a big thing in the family. I don't know if you've ever been to a Christian Science service but they just read. They read from the Bible and then they read from Mary Baker Eddy's book, *Science and Health with Key to the Scriptures*, which was her interpretation of that stuff. Then I would go downstairs to the Sunday school and we'd just have a discussion group. I liked that.

My grandmother would say, "You've just got to know the truth about it." That was Christian Science in nine words—"You've just got to know the truth about it."

Whenever she'd see me upset about something, or if I wasn't feeling great, or something was off, she'd tell me that. That stuck with me.

MAG: *Did you believe in magic when you were young?*

STEVE: Absolutely. Loved magic. We had little magic tricks that we would do. Actually, magic tricks make you *not* believe in magic. But we were the Wide World of Disney generation, so Tinker Bell and all that...somebody could wave a magic wand and make things happen. I totally believed that there was magic, that there was some power you could tap into if you knew the trick.

I've stopped believing in "magic" but I still believe there's a power you can tap into. I don't know quite what it is. I don't think things happen *only* scientifically and logically. I think they *do* happen scientifically and logically—but then there's something else. I've had too much evidence to the contrary, where something will happen that's just impossible. The probability of what just happened is just impossible—some force had to have made that happen.

I base my life on cause and effect. So, if I need to believe something, I will. I see it this way—if I don't believe this, I will not be able to function or move forward. I think it's really important to move forward, so I'll say, "I need to believe this in order to move forward." Then I will believe it.

And I think that there's a lot of that in people believing in myths—and maybe being completely wrong—but they're more comfortable believing in something, even something they know could be wrong, than to be left with no beliefs, which absolutely paralyzes them. I think there's an element of that in me.

BECOMING YOUR OWN PERSON

MAG: *Do you remember the first time in your life that you were deeply moved by something?*

STEVE: You know, I don't get emotionally moved very often. I think I save it all up and then something will really nail me. Like, when my father died, I was just useless. For a long time.

But when I was a kid…probably my earliest connection to something I thought I just couldn't live without was seeing a Laurel and Hardy movie. For some reason, I just loved those two guys, they were huge for me. It was beyond funny for me. I just wanted them to be in my family. And their comedy—just such a joy, such a warm joy to it. Oh my God, I could just bask in it. Go into the theatre and just lose myself in it.

And in the Fifties…some of the really early television shows. I was never a

Sid Caesar fan and Red Skelton was somebody I didn't find particularly funny, but he just had such a love of people. There was so much love coming out of him. I really liked that. It was very comforting for me. I liked to be in that environment. That wasn't lost on me. There were a few guys like that. I always preferred Art Carney to Jackie Gleason. Jackie was kind of a cold, self-serving fish. Carney was the warm guy.

As far as being moved by anything on a personal level…well, there was Gail Roper but then she kissed Richie Farnsdon. That was over in a hurry.

MAG: *I'm so sorry. But at least you've put it behind you now. Apart from your romantic disappointments, what was your general mood when you were young?*

STEVE: I was a happy kid. I didn't let anything bother me that much. I was oblivious to things that would make other kids unhappy. I've always just kind of been in my own world. If I was upset about something, I had ways of getting myself around to feeling okay. I had things that I really enjoyed doing, and friends I really enjoyed being with. So I would do something I really liked with somebody I really liked, and I would soon be able to put whatever was bothering me away.

Like we'd ride bikes and we'd try to do what they do in the rodeo. We'd come speeding along on our bikes and then swing both legs off and jam our heels into the gravel so we were skidding. And then we'd lean on our bikes like we were wrestling a steer to the ground. Well, you can't be doing that and feeling angst about whether or not you ate your beans for dinner. There was just an unlimited supply of fun.

Funny things would occur to me too. I remember coming home from school really late. I was little—seven or eight years old—and for whatever reason, I had a bag of peanuts. So, everybody's sitting at the dining room table, wondering where the hell I am. And I come walking through the front door with a bag of peanuts. I didn't make any eye contact at all, just said, "Did anybody see any squirrels in here?"

They all just burst out laughing and nobody could be mad.

MAG: *How were you as a judge of character when you were a kid?*

STEVE: Not good. I had that adventurous side, so I was drawn to adventurous people. Like the tough kids. We had two tough kids on our street. One of them had Wellington boots and smoked and he was about eleven. He was the guy who showed me how to make the flour bomb. We got along great.

We had another kid. He had a BB gun and he would shoot at kids. He shot out his neighbours' windows while they were on holiday. I would never do that,

The brothers with their new baby sister, Vicki, circa 1955.

and I was never his friend.

I was drawn to somebody who was an individualist and maybe a bit of a renegade, but within the confines of not destroying society. Somebody who was just really more about making a statement on his own behalf, rather than trying to bring down everybody else's sense of what was right.

In school, I would tend to make friends with the rougher guys. I didn't like the academics or the whole nerd thing. I didn't want any part of that. It just felt like a lack of individuality to me. Those guys all looked like some watered-down version of their own fathers. If we already have your father, why would we need you?

So, I was drawn to people who were more their own person. At least in my mind, they seemed to be that way. I don't know whether they were or they weren't.

But number one, I was drawn to what we were *doing*. If we were going to throw a ball around…I mean, I didn't care; I'd throw a ball around with Jack the Ripper.

But as far as going around in a gang of people, I wouldn't want to be hanging around with a bunch of dorks.

Also I liked girls. I wanted to attract girls.

GIRL TROUBLE

MAG: *Okay—what about girls?*

STEVE: I liked girls. I always liked girls, even from an early age. There was a girl named Mary Bye. She got in bed with me when I was in Grade Five. In bed with me.

MAG: *Isn't that young to be getting in bed?*

STEVE: Not for Mary, apparently. She just came over. We were both nine. She just thought it would be nice to cuddle. She had her ballerina costume on. And I thought, "You know, this is not a bad hobby."

Then there was Gail Roper, who kissed Richie Farnsdon in her garage… but I've gotten over it.

MAG: *Sure you have.*

STEVE: Apparently not. I've always liked girls, even though I was shy with them, especially as a teenager. I didn't go out with a lot of girls. I just really liked them from afar. There were always pretty girls around. And when you're a twelve-year-old boy going through puberty…I can't believe I survived that. I'm very, very fortunate.

I remember taking a girl out when I was maybe thirteen or fourteen. We'd moved to Brantford and I asked a girl out. She liked me. I thought she'd probably go out with me and she did. She was in Grade Nine and I was in Grade Ten.

We went to the school dance. We went through the front door. She took three steps and projectile-vomited about ten feet down the hall. I took her home. What could you do?

So, that was my first major date. Just me and the girl, not a gang or anything. I think she was just really nervous or she was coming down with something. Anyway, I really felt bad for her. I took her home and her parents were all upset. I'm sure she survived it. I think that was my only date for that whole year at Brantford.

FRATERNAL INSTINCTS

MAG: *You might not have had early success with girls, but from things you said before, it sounds as if you had a good relationship with your brother, Dave. Apart from spending summers learning what he wanted to teach you, what else did you do with your brother?*

Steve's first job was delivering fresh milk on Saturday mornings for Silverwood's Dairy.

STEVE: On Saturdays, my brother would help the milkman deliver milk. When he first started he'd get paid a quarter a day, then after a while fifty cents, and he kept working it up for years. Finally, after two or three years, he said to me, "Would you like to do something like that?"

"Yeah, alright."

The milkman Dave worked for knew another guy from a different dairy. The two of us didn't want to be with the same dairy because we wanted to work the same territory close to home. So, my brother was delivering for Borden's and I was delivering for Silverwood's. But I *started* at two bucks, which was what my brother was at after three and a half years.

Then after delivering milk in the morning, my brother loved going to the movies on Saturday afternoons. He would always try to get me to go with him. I hated going because I could be outside playing baseball. If the show was at night, okay, but I'm not spending a Saturday afternoon sitting in a theatre.

At this point we lived in the Kingsway. The Kingsway Theatre is still there. We had to catch the bus at a certain time or we wouldn't get to the movie. So he'd ask, "Do you wanna go?"

"Nah, I don't wanna go."

He had to leave or he was going to miss the bus. He'd be walking up the street and he'd keep yelling back at me, "You sure you don't?"

"Nah, I don't wanna go." I'd be out there playing ball.

And I'd wait till he got *way* up the street, right to the corner, and I'd say, "Yeah, okayyyyy." And I'd go running after him and we'd barely make the bus.

So we'd go to the movie. They serialized these two-reelers—twenty-minute movies that would run before the feature came on. There might even be two of them. There'd be Hopalong Cassidy or Roy Rogers or Gene Autry, and then a couple of cartoons and then whatever the feature was. I think it was a quarter for all of that.

MAG: *Earlier you said your brother was like a third parent. Why did you need a third parent?*

STEVE: I didn't. My grandmother lived with us. I already had a third parent. Dave was a fourth parent. I had so many damn parents. Maybe I needed them all.

I think Dave likes to feel responsible for people. He likes to do it in a really offhand way, so most people don't even realize that he feels that way.

But my brother and I always got along. He had his own set of friends. It's not that we shared friends or anything, so we didn't have any jealousies. And especially once we split schools, I had a whole set of friends that he didn't know at all. So, that was always good.

It was kind of neat that we both had our areas. Like, he was always right. He always knew stuff and did smart things. He would never make a bomb out of a cookie tin. He'd know that's just a stupid thing to do. I got lucky and didn't hurt myself. He didn't have to get lucky because he would never do anything that stupid.

His actions were always straight on. He'd do his homework. He did really well on all of his tests. He was well liked at school. He was always a leader at school. We'd call him "The Prof" because he was carrying a briefcase to school in Grade Six. He was President of the Student Council in high school, all that stuff. And I was happy that he did that.

He even ran a business between high school and college. The company he worked for had one arm of their business that had lost a whole lot of money,

The Kingsway Theatre today, awaiting its future.

and they just handed it over to him. He was just a high school kid and there were airplanes involved and everything.

He ran that business and turned it around and it was great. He's always excelled in that area. He wasn't into sports or music, and I did okay there. So, I think that took away a lot of the competition. And I don't think our parents set any territories like, "You have to excel at this," so that made it easier. That's still true today. He and I have totally separate strengths. It really helps.

MAG: *Do you have any other stories about you and your brother?*

STEVE: My brother and I slept in the same room with bunk beds. I can remember having built a crystal radio and using the bunk bed springs as an aerial. We were supposed to be asleep, but we'd be listening to the Jack Benny Show. I was terrible. I was always dinkin' around. Dave was up in the top bunk. So, he'd just want to go to sleep and I'd do one of those kicks and he'd tell me to quit. And then my dad would come up the stairs. I'd hear him coming up. I knew how many stairs there were.

So, he'd come in, and he'd be mad. "Stop it! Go to sleep right now! If I hear one more peep out of either one of you…"

Then out he'd go. And I'd count the steps, right? He was a big man. I figured he probably wouldn't come back up. So, when he'd get to the bottom step, I'd give a little peep. Just "peep."

Up he comes. By the time he got upstairs, my brother was already in the bathroom. So I took the heat.

MAG: *What was the heat like?*

STEVE: Oh, he spanked me, you know, spanked my bottom. And when it was over, my brother would come out of the bathroom and my dad would say, "And that goes for you too!"

MAG: *Can I just go back for a second? When you would say "Peep" at the bottom* *of the last stair, you* knew *you were going to get walloped right?*

STEVE: Yeah. But it was just too *good*. It was just too perfect. Like, if it was in a movie, you'd just think that was the funniest thing.

Dave would say, "You idiot!" Then he's gone to the bathroom. Now the question is, if I was alone in that room, would I have done it? The answer is no. I was only entertaining Dave. And *I* thought it was funny too. It *was* funny! My father should have laughed.

MAG: *Maybe he did.*

STEVE: Maybe, but he was over it by the time he got to the top of the stairs.

A FATHER'S INFLUENCE

MAG: *Did you ever ask your parents for advice about stuff?*

STEVE: Every dinner my father was quick to point out how to live, especially if we asked stuff like that. One did not have to ask. I can't remember *ever* asking. And I'm not good at listening to that kind of thing, so I wouldn't ask because I wouldn't even listen to the answer.

MAG: *Did you ask anyone at all for advice when you were growing up?*

STEVE: I honestly don't think I did. I never felt short of advice. Like I say, my dad was really into the advice business big, although he had very few clients. So, it was kind of like I was full. By the time I got up from the dinner table, I was full in oh, so many ways.

I *would* look at somebody whose life I respected and who seemed like they were making a difference. Who looked happy themselves. Then I would try to see what it was about their life that made them that way, rather than go to somebody who's bitching all the time and ask him how'd he get so darn happy.

"What's your secret? Let me have some of that!"

MAG: *Can you give me an example of an everyday family moment, like a meal?*

STEVE: Well, uh, quiet. For most of the people at the table. If I could put myself back into the headspace of me sitting at the dining room table…Don't initiate any conversation because there's just going to be trouble. There's going to be something you're going to say that's going to start a situation where you're going to be told the way to think in that particular area.

And then you have two options. One is to pretend that you agree. And the other is to start a huge argument that will be seen as absolute anarchy. So you just don't talk. It creates room for other people to talk. I don't remember any of us talking very much. My dad pretty much dominated the whole thing. He'd been at work all day and he'd come home and talk.

MAG: *What else do you remember about your dad?*

STEVE: My father was the disciplinarian, but he was very busy. He worked a lot of hours and he was very wrapped up in what he was doing and he always had things on his mind. So he couldn't be bothered. He would try to discipline me a bit, but eventually he'd give up.

He liked his job. He really enjoyed being a salesman, so he would talk about that. He'd have some theories on neighbours and that kind of thing. I don't remember us having a lot of friends or good relationships with the neighbours. I mean everybody loved my mum, she had no problem, but he was difficult. And Mum would try to have neighbours over and then after they left, for the next week all we'd hear from Dad was how miserable the neighbours were—"Those stupid people"—it wasn't great.

And I didn't like the way my father treated my mother. My mother is the most gracious person you'd ever meet. She just makes everybody very comfortable. It's not her thing to look for ways to be confrontational. But my dad was very dismissive. Very chauvinistic. He'd come home, dinner's ready.

Then he'd pass comment on whether it was any good or not. I was always uncomfortable. And as I got older and became more aware of it, I got more and more uncomfortable.

I don't like friction. I don't like friction between people. If you've got a problem, deal with it. Get to it, find out what it is, and then move forward. "Move forward" may mean you're going to resolve it and you're not going to do that anymore, or you're not going to be together. But just the day in, day out, grinding each other down into some smaller version of what we were supposed to be…that doesn't seem like a very good option.

So, mainly I remember just sitting there quietly at the dinner table. It sounds horrible but dinners were short. A lot of the rest of the day was okay. I think kids adapt. Like when you get a needle at school, it doesn't hurt as much if you don't look at it.

MAG: *What would have happened if you hadn't gone along with what your dad wanted?*

STEVE: My dad always said, later in life, that I was the only one who would argue with him and he really liked that. I don't remember arguing with him at all, but I think I give out a vibe…I think people find me a little reserved and it makes them uncomfortable that this is a guy you can only go so far with, and then that's going to be it. He's not just going to go along with you. Some people don't like that.

I'm guessing that's probably what my dad was thinking. He'd look at me and think, even though I may not be saying anything, that I was giving him a big fat "yeah right" with that look.

MAG: *Were there things you did with your family that made you feel connected?*

STEVE: Sometimes we'd rent a cottage for part of the summer. So in the summer we would just be a normal family. Everybody just seemed to be relaxed there. I know my dad was always very relaxed at the cottage. He seemed to really enjoy it. My brother still loves a cottage. He's got a cottage now and he just loves it. So those were great times. We'd go out and be in the water all day. I remember those as being really good family outings.

MAG: *Do you have any other family memories?*

STEVE: My father's parents had a hobby farm, about ten acres, for most of the time I knew them. It was in Colborne, which is east of Toronto. We'd drive out—it might even have been every other Sunday—and have family dinner with them. And the dynamic between my dad and his parents and his brother was just…it was just unbelievable. They'd be arguing with whatever each other said. The way my dad spoke to his mother was just offensive to me. My grandfather wasn't as harsh to my grandmother as my father was. His own mother.

I thought it was really weird. And my dad and my uncle were very competitive. If one was doing something, the other one had to top it.

I would stay away from the group. My grandfather had a den. I'd go back there and look at his lamp and turn it around because it had a picture on it. But it just had to be exhausting for my mother.

My mother's mother and my mother came from an entirely different background. My mother was an only child and I think it was a very peaceful household.

When Dad married my mum he moved in to my grandmother's house and then sold the house. He was being a big shot on somebody else's dime. I didn't know this until years later. I always thought he had bought my grandmother's house from her.

Instead, my dad sold the house, moved us all to the Kingsway, then to Brantford, then to Streetsville, then to Mississauga, and then a year after that he left us all. My mother ended up in a two bedroom apartment in Streetsville. My sister and my grandmother slept in one bedroom, my mother slept in the other, and I slept on the living room couch. And this is while I was at teacher's college, and working too.

But I was never upset. I knew I could find a life.

MAG: *Was he affectionate with you guys?*

STEVE: No. Absolutely not.

I remember when I was about thirteen, I took a plane to Detroit. We had real close friends of the family in Detroit—we called them "aunt" and "uncle." I went down to stay with them for a few days.

My dad took me to the airport. When I was about to get on the plane, he shook my hand. It brought tears to my eyes. That was the only show of affection I'd ever experienced till then. Never a hug or anything like that.

He was standing right there. I had put my hand out first because I didn't know what to do. And he shook my hand.

That handshake. I remember it. I can visualize it right now. I can remember.

Opposite: Steve at age 13.

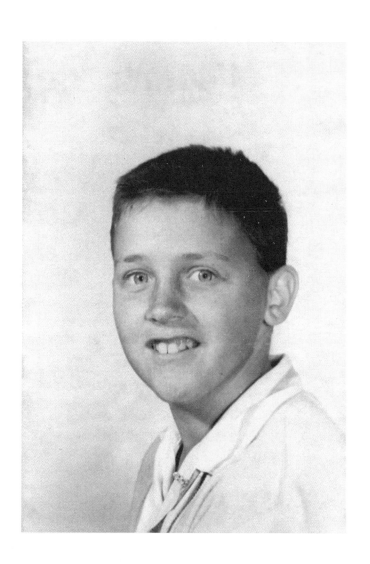

Remarkable Teachers

Steve Smith's Remarkable Teacher: Ruth Purdy

"THERE'S no way I would have gone into the entertainment business if it wasn't for Ruth Purdy. There's no way," says Steve Smith, better known as Red Green to legions of devoted fans of duct tape and homespun humour.

Steve Smith was born and educated in Toronto and until the end of Grade 5, attended Park Lawn Public School in Etobicoke. Then one day he wrote a test. "I didn't know what they were testing for," he says now. "I either scored really high or really low in some way that qualified me to go into a strange environment with a lot of other kids who had scored the same way."

In fact, he scored high and qualified for classes for exceptional children. Beginning in 1956 and for the next three years—for Grades 6, 7 and 8—Steve Smith attended Wedgewood Public School in the Kingsway area with Ruth Purdy as his classroom teacher.

Smith remembers the incredible sense of freedom that he encountered in Purdy's class.

"The idea was that we were supposedly given a little more free rein and I had never experienced anything like that. In fact, she made a rule that students couldn't talk out in class—except for me. It was her way of acknowledging that I didn't upset the class and I didn't upset her, and it would sometimes make things more entertaining."

Smith says it was the first time that his tendency to see things differently didn't put him at a disadvantage. "I've since been able to turn it into an asset, but that was the first indication I had that that was even possible for me."

"I remember that time as an acknowledgement that it was okay to think differently from other people. That in certain environments it was welcomed. That's a much bigger lesson than the times tables or historical events, or anything like that, because it changed my approach to life."

Purdy had had a varied career in small-town Ontario, becoming principal of a junior high school near Cobourg before moving to Etobicoke. Smith remembers that she had taught K to Grade 8 in a one-room schoolhouse. "So I think she was drawing on that experience and was right up to speed on child psychology."

"I always thought her job was especially hard because we all felt like prisoners at first. I know when I first started there, I was resentful. For five years I had walked to school with my friends and now I was getting on a bus every morning, watching them walk to school while I'm with a bunch of people who don't share any of my interests or my background. And once you do that for a month, by the end of the day when you go home, your friends have found other friends."

School up to that time had been very conformist, he says. "Suddenly, I was in this environment where it was all totally an individual endeavour. This was a revelation to me. It was like university—university in Grade 6."

Although he took advantage of the freedom to express his sense of humour in class, Smith says he was still quite shy and it was Ruth Purdy who helped him to like being centre stage.

"If the class was going to do a play or something, I was never one who volunteered. But one year she came and asked me to be the lead in a play, and that was probably Grade 7 at that point. I didn't want to do it but I didn't say no. I was flattered to be asked, and sometimes you say 'yes' when what you mean is 'thank you'," Smith says with a laugh.

"I can remember her saying to me when I was hesitant to do it, 'You have a gift in that area and you have to share it. That's why you have the gift. If you have the gift and don't share it, that's a terrible crime. It means the gift was given to the wrong person.'"

Smith doesn't remember either he or his family having any idea that these new experiences might lead him to his current fame. "It isn't something your family would push you into. They want you to be able to support yourself, 'cause they want to be off the hook," he says, laughing.

Smith took another aptitude test in high school. "I scored very high in the physical sciences and in entertainment. And the guidance counsellor said, 'Well what you want to do is push the physical sciences', and I said 'Well, what about this entertainment?' He said, 'Oh, you can't make a living at that.' Of course, what he meant was, *he* couldn't make a living at it," says Smith with a laugh.

Nevertheless, he did make use of his aptitude for science when—having found little satisfaction in a string of jobs—he earned a teaching certificate at Lakeshore College in Toronto and taught science to Grade 6 students in Oakville. But the world of entertainment still lured him.

Starting with a rock band in the early 1970s, he eventually made his way into comedy and this spring, his first movie, *Duct Tape Forever* was released in Canada and the U.S.   ◤

Steve's tribute to his favourite teacher, Ruth Purdy, published in *Professionally Speaking* magazine, September 2002.

A FEW WORDS FROM MARY MUNCEY...

My mum sort of took Steve over because he came so soon after David. Steve's always been a very affectionate person and he needs that one-to-one, and that's what my mother gave him. She was an amateur actress, so that might be where he gets it. She was in local plays and really enjoyed that. And she had a wonderful memory like him.

When he was around nine or ten I noticed he would have very different ideas about things. Nobody in my family was that way. They were all practical. He was a dreamer. I sent him out one day for a loaf of bread from the truck that came around the street. I gave him the money and he went out to the truck, but he forgot what he was going for. He saw the sign on the truck, "Pies and Cakes," so he came in with a cake. I said, "This isn't what I wanted."

Steve with his mother, Mary Muncey.

"Oh well," he said, "I figured you'd rather have a cake." And I knew he'd forgotten.

But he always charmed you. He always got around you with his sense of humour. Dave was always the serious big brother. And then Vicki —she came along seven years later— and they were playmates. They got along great.

And then when he and David would put on little variety shows, he used to sing *The Battle Hymn of the Republic*, with forty verses. It would go on and on. We'd be ready to say, "Enough!" But my aunt would say, "No, no, don't stop him. Let him finish." You know, those extra verses about "John Brown's body lies a-mouldering in the grave." Oh dear.

My mum had a lot of hats. When she went out, Steve would go up into her bedroom and assemble all her hats. We had a big, three-storey house in the Kingsway and all the kids would come into the backyard. He'd open up the window and put on one hat after the other and say some things—it was like a passing parade. The kids thought it was terrific. My mother had a turban that Steve named "Ali Baba"—he had names for all her hats. My mum never knew.

The kids all liked him. There was a rapport there because he was bright and he was interesting. He didn't mean to be funny, it just sort of came out of him. We'd be laughing so hard, we'd beg him to stop.

When he was in public school, he'd sit and look out the window and be so bored. The teacher thought he would be better having special training of some kind, something to challenge him. They tested him and he had quite a high IQ, so he went into a school for gifted children. It isolated him from his friends; they thought he didn't want to bother with them. That was the only part he didn't like about going to that new school.

The school was like Montessori is now; you could be free and say what you wanted. I remember the teacher said to him, "You know, you have a gift for entertaining, and if you don't use it, it's given to the wrong person."

He was different. One time in his early teens he said to me, "Some of the kids think I'm weird." I said, "No, you're not weird. You just see a funny side of things that other people just don't see."

I've never felt I had to worry about him—I thought he had enough intelligence to find something he'd be comfortable with, which he did. Steve's son Davy has that same easygoing way, an outgoing, fun personality. Davy sees things that other people don't quite see. It's imagination. You can't turn it off.

And Steve thinks he's just ordinary. He doesn't have much ego.

The time I saw him happiest was when he met Morag. They have a wonderful relationship. Morag's always been so supportive. It was an amazing relationship —still is. It's never changed. They're always like they're just courting still.

The worst thing that could have happened was for me to succeed in something I wasn't interested in.

CHAPTER TWO

PUBERTY TO PARENTHOOD

FROM SCHOOL TO STAGE

PUBERTY TO PARENTHOOD

FROM SCHOOL TO STAGE

THE GEEK FACTOR

MAG: *You said you were lucky to make it through puberty. What kind of teenager were you—and what did you most want to change about yourself?*

STEVE: I think I was afraid of being a geek. I wasn't geek-like, but I had geek tendencies. One of my biggest fears was being kind of a nerdy, brainy techno goofball. I wasn't athletic enough to be an athlete. I was okay. I mean, I could throw and catch a ball and all that stuff. But I wanted to be cool.

And I really thought I wasn't. I was always small and I had skipped a grade, so I was that much smaller. And then I was sent off to that brainy school, so you've got a little, twerpy, nerdy guy at a brainy school. Good luck. Every bully in the world wanted to kill me. But I could make them laugh.

So, I think geekiness was my biggest fear. My brother was pretty geeky. He took a briefcase to school in Grade Six, for God's sake. Didn't bother him. He was on the corporate track in those days. But for me, it was like—no, no, no.

And through high school…I knew the roughest guys. I didn't hang out with them, but in school I was one of them, without really being one of them.

MAG: *But you were an outsider. You didn't actually* belong *to a group.*

STEVE: No. They were making choices that I didn't think I'd be comfortable with, behaviour-wise. And yet I didn't want to be a geeky goof either. I wanted to be a contender. You know, kind of like…a sleeper. Remember those cars they used to have? It would look like a normal car but it would have a really souped-up engine. And there was no indication until the light turned green—

MAG: *And then they're gone.*

STEVE: Yeah. That's neat.

MAG: *That's what you wanted to be in high school.*

STEVE: That's what I've wanted to be in *life.*

MAG: *Okay. So what was it really like for you as a teenager?*

STEVE: Well, in the first three years of high school, I was at three different schools, so that made it tough. In Grade Nine I went to my local high school, but I'd been out of the local school system for three years, so I'd lost touch with all of my friends.

Streetsville is a small suburb in the Greater Toronto area, just west of Mississauga.

Then I moved to Brantford and I was really lost because those kids all knew each other. And then I ended up in Streetsville, which was a similar thing. So, that didn't help.

MAG: *So, Grades Nine, Ten and Eleven—new school each year?*

STEVE: New school each year. And like I said, I was little and I was odd. I wouldn't blame those things on making me feel kind of separate. I think that a different kind of person would have gone into those environments and within a month would have made a circle of friends. But it didn't come naturally or easily to me, so I didn't really work on it.

In each of those schools, I had one or two friends and that was pretty much it. Everybody else, I would make them laugh, just so they thought, "Okay, he's okay."

No matter how far I fell in any part of my life, there was a landing area and I would be okay.

But I didn't really work myself into any kind of social environment there. And even with girls—I went to one dance in Grade Nine, but I didn't go out with a lot of girls. For the rest of high school I'd have a girlfriend for a month or maybe two months, and then after a while I'd have another girlfriend. I wasn't dating five or six girls at a time.

I remember watching Dick Clark's *American Bandstand*…and he said, "You've got to enjoy high school; these are the best years of your life."

And I went, "Wha-a-a-t? You better be lying!"

Generally, I've found that people who thought their years in high school were the best years of their lives, haven't done that well. I just couldn't wait to get out of high school.

MAG: *If high school was so bad, what kept you going?*

STEVE: The thing that kept me going through all those things—like Grade Eleven on—was that I could see myself surviving. I could work in a factory. I had summer jobs doing that and I was okay. I could stand on an assembly line and tighten that one bolt a thousand times a day, because there were so many things going on in my mind that I didn't need my job to be my stimulus. And I was only a kid then.

Those guys in factories, they do okay. I could have a place to live, I could have a car. And, in many ways, the idea of having a mindless job was very appealing to me because my employer didn't get my mind. My mind was *my* territory, and I didn't want to give that to anybody for minimum wage.

That gave me a lot of strength and power, and I could get through whatever

I had to get through because I knew what ground zero was for me. That no matter how far I fell in any part of my life, there was a landing area and I would be okay. I could think, I could function and I could probably do enough to sustain myself. And I thought, "You know what? That's good enough for me."

I didn't have the drive to be a millionaire or king of the world or to be hugely successful. I didn't want to give up my "Self" for anything. I would keep my life at a lower level rather than give up my Self and look like a real winner.

That became very important in school.

DO NOT ATTEMPT TO REAPPLY

MAG: *After high school, did you go straight into university?*

STEVE: I enrolled in Engineering at the University of Waterloo. My grandfather gave me my university tuition, so I didn't have to earn money the summer between high school and college. I just worked on a farm and I got paid, but not much, maybe forty bucks a week. The farm was run by a single guy named Alan Trainor. He was probably thirty-five. It was his father's farm, about 150 acres. He had dairy cows and he had wheat and hay. I was there primarily to help him with the harvest.

I realized that it didn't matter how funny you were when that hay wasn't getting in.

And he had so many neat things on the farm…little machines that he'd made.

Like he had to pump the water up from a well into a water tower, and that would feed into the barn. So he had a switch that was attached to the gas engine that ran the pump. He'd start the pump and then he'd go out and work in the field.

When the water tower got full, it would overflow over a pipe, and the water would run down into a can. When the can got heavy, it would pull a string and that would turn the pump engine off.

So I said to him, "Well, okay that's great, but how do you ever get the thing to turn on again?"

Well, there was this little hole in the bottom of the can. So the water would eventually drain out and it would go back to its starting position and then you could start the motor again. There were all kinds of little gizmos like that.

MAG: *What were your chores on the farm?*

STEVE: We were baling hay. He'd brought me in for that purpose and I was totally useless. I was completely useless. And he knew right away, but I was a little longer realizing it. I wasn't big enough and I wasn't strong enough. The job came through the friend of a friend. Alan had never even met me.

Morag had no use for me at all, but she was competitive enough that if her girlfriend liked me, she'd maybe take a run at it.

It was a hard job and I was kind of a scrawny kid. I just couldn't handle it. And I remember maybe the third or fourth night, I was very uncomfortable, feeling useless.

Alan went into town, and I went with him. There was another guy he knew that could help out. We found him and this guy was just hammered out of his mind. So that wasn't going to work out. He said to the guy, "If you're feeling better in the morning, come on around."

The guy never came around. But I did. It was that feeling of being useless. I realized that it didn't matter how funny you were when that hay wasn't getting in. Within two days, I was doing the job.

MAG: *After that summer on the farm, you started university. How did that work out?*

STEVE: I flunked out. That was a bleak comeuppance. I really thought I could fake it through because I could fake it pretty good. I was quick on my feet. But I didn't do the work at university. I was smart enough to figure out what they were talking about in class and I could ask questions and I could actually even make some points, say some things so everybody thought, "Hey, that's pretty smart." But I never did the work when it came to exams or assignments.

Drafting was one of my courses. I didn't do any of my drawings. Didn't do the work. And then when they sent me the report card, it was a piece of computer paper with all these horrible marks on it and "Do not attempt to reapply for at least one year." Even the computer kicked me out of school. Then I had to tell my parents. That was bad.

MAG: *Did anything good come out of that year at university?*

STEVE: Yes. I enjoyed my work term at Canadian General Tower, which was a vinyl factory in Cambridge. I worked in the maintenance department, so I'd be doing everything—machining, welding, carpentry, electrical, steam fitting —the whole deal. And I'd be one of the guys. These guys all worked with their hands and they had their own vocabulary. When you see how smart these guys are and the skills that they have…it's a lot harder to disrespect someone you actually know.

I never wanted to excel at anything, but I sure didn't want to fail.

We had to fix steam leaks without shutting the equipment down. So you make a mistake there, and it's bad. I've got a lot of respect for those guys. I think that went into my psyche too. All of these things have come out in *Red Green*. When I do something, the guys who do it know that I know what I'm doing—I've done it before. I learned how to get along with guys like that. I felt more comfortable with blue-collar people than I ever did with the executive types.

The biggest difference I found was that the blue-collar guy, warts and all, was never pretending to be something else. I knew exactly who I was talking to. The guy I was talking to today would be the same guy I'd be talking to tomorrow. Maybe it's the fact that his life doesn't change much, so he doesn't have to adapt to a lot of different things. But I just found that guy much more reliable than an executive whose demeanour can go through a hundred and eighty degrees, depending on what meeting he's coming out of.

I really felt from an early age, like eighteen or nineteen when I was experiencing that stuff, that the blue-collar guy was much more in control of his life than the executive was. I don't know if that's true or not, but I always felt that.

BROKEN WORD

MAG: *What happened next?*

STEVE: My father and I had an incident when I was nineteen. This was after I'd flunked out of university. I was working to save up to go to Lakeshore Teachers' College. My father had advised me to put my money into an investment account. He had a mutual fund business at the time and he had an account that the fees had been paid on. He felt I'd get a lot better return than I would at the bank. So every payday I would give him a cheque.

When it came time to pay my tuition, I went to him for my money. He asked me if I had receipts for the money I'd given him. Then he said, "What about all those toys I bought you?" I didn't know what he meant. He explained that after all the money he'd spent raising me, he considered us even.

I got a part-time factory job working the night shift while I went to Teachers' College during the day, and I arranged to pay my tuition over several months. But the money was the easy part to get over.

MAG: *Your father's behaviour must have really upset you. Do you feel like you changed after that experience?*

STEVE: I can't help but think that it made me much more cautious of people. If there was somebody who had the characteristics that I didn't like in my father, I couldn't get away from them fast enough. I had no use for them. I wouldn't be nice to them or curry favour from them, even if it might help my career. If they were that kind of person, I didn't care. I'd live with less success. I'd live without whatever they could give me access to rather than have to deal with them. So I think that was the biggest change.

But, you know, I don't think it was negative. It did change things, but…it wasn't even a setback now that I think about it. I mean, what came out of that was a huge step forward. I really took responsibility for myself starting that day. And maybe I never would have otherwise. Who knows?

Above Left: Steve's high school graduation photo—an inscrutable expression borne by a young man setting out to seek his fortune. *Above Right:* Morag, who graduated from high school a year after Steve, wouldn't begin her lifelong romance with Steve until he called her looking for a place to rehearse his band.

But for years it was my festering sore inside. I don't have any of that now, not even a wisp of it. There's none of it left, not even a scar there.

MAG: *Well, I don't know. After all, a scar is reinforced tissue. That experience reinforced what you* do *believe in.*

STEVE: Yes, because that was him breaking his word—which was huge for me. It made me see how important keeping your word is, and how rare it is.

Since then, when people have given me their word, I have really hoped that they're going to keep it. And I act like I'm expecting them to keep it. But inside, I'm not *that* surprised when they don't. So, I really treasure somebody who does.

But those haven't been negative things for me. Probably saved me from being a little bit naïve, because I do tend to trust people. They think I trust them more than I really do, because I'll give them lots of leeway. I'll give them every chance to do the right thing, but I'm going to be okay whatever they do. I'm not as vulnerable as they think I am.

THEN ALONG CAME MORAG

MAG: *You were married not too long after you had the falling out with your dad, right? At what point did you start your courtship with Morag?*

STEVE: That actually started when I was in Grade Twelve. I hadn't dated a whole lot in high school. I had probably gone out with six different girls and I felt I'd seen the full range of girlship. Morag had a girlfriend who had a crush on me and she kept sending me love letters. But they were in Morag's handwriting, which I thought was just ridiculous. I guess this girl would dictate to Morag. And I knew Morag's handwriting because she was always doing posters in school. Everybody knew her handwriting.

Now, Morag had no use for me at all, but she was competitive enough that if her girlfriend liked me, she'd maybe take a run at it. So Morag invited me to her sixteenth birthday—a dance at the golf course. Her family was into golf pretty big. But she gave me the wrong directions, so I got to the dance at eleven-twenty and the dance was over at eleven-thirty. I was hopping mad.

Things that I'm missing, well, she's got 'em in spades. We're a tag team.

MAG: *You must have been three, four hours late.*

STEVE: Yeah. They were *bad* directions. "Turn right here. Now, it'll feel like a really long way, but it *is* there." This was out in the country—there were no numbers. There were no cell phones. Anyway, I got there really late.

I hardly even knew her. But I remember we had the last dance, might've had two dances. And we went for a little walk. And I just found that she was the only girl that I could really have conversations with. I'd talk to her and we'd go back and forth. She was smart and funny.

At that time, she was sixteen, I was seventeen. I maybe went out with her one more time. I really felt that she'd make a great wife but a lousy girlfriend.

MAG: *What are the criteria for a great wife and a lousy girlfriend?*

STEVE: Well, I think to be a great girlfriend you've got to be completely irresponsible. Just ready to do anything at the drop of a hat. Like go to Wasaga Beach—"Let's just go!" instead of, "We've got a garden to look after. We've got bills to pay. We can't afford to do that." That's a wifely thing to do. I'm not talking about the love relationship. I'm just talking about a certain...you know...there are certain people who get together and it can be dangerous because you need a control, sort of a governor.

It wasn't that we decided to have kids, but we decided not to do anything not to have kids, and just see what happens.

And I just thought, "I don't really want a governor right now." I didn't see that as a negative thing, it was just a timing issue. I tried explaining that to her, but it didn't go well.

And I've got to tell you, Morag was really popular in high school. It wasn't like she went out with me for two weeks and then that was it for her. She had lots of boyfriends.

MAG: *How did you two ever get back together?*

STEVE: By now I've flunked out of university and I've got a job in Toronto working in product development at Maple Leaf Mills. A couple of other guys in the lab played instruments, so we formed a band called *The Gamblers* around June of '65, and we needed a place to practise. And I'm thinking, Morag's mother was a Girl Guide pack leader. They had the Girl Guide Hall in Streetsville, and it just sits there for at least six days a week.

So I called Morag. She'd just gotten off the phone with her boyfriend. She'd just hung up and there I was asking her about this hall. First of all, she was shocked that it was me because she hadn't heard from me in a couple of years. And her mother wasn't a Girl Guide leader anymore, but the woman who *was* doing it was Shirley Granger.

"Pronounced Grann-ger," said Morag.

So I said, "How do you spell that?"

She said, "G-R-A-N-G-E-R."

I said, "Well, that's Grayn-ger."

She said, "No, it's Grann-ger."

I said, "Really? And it's the Lone Rann-ger?"

She starts laughing hysterically and within ten minutes we're going out on a date. She said to me later, "You know, I'd just spent an hour on the phone with my boyfriend, and that five-minute phone call with you was way more fun."

Then we went out on our first real date. We went to a movie. It was *Dr. No*, that James Bond thing. I got lost again because we got talking. We got to the theatre not later than the movie started, but close. And it was full. It was at the Odeon at Bloor and Jane. And they had smoking loges in those days, way upstairs in the balcony.

A smoking loge was a section of seats in a raised mezzanine at the back of the theatre where patrons could smoke through-out a movie.

So we're way up in the back and the projector is three feet away. And this is our first date. In the first scene in the movie, there's a guy walking down the street, and three Chinese guys just blow him away. Then a hearse comes around the corner, guys jump out, grab the body and throw it in the back.

We're watching the action and she says to me, "Pretty efficient funeral service in that town."

And I said, "Yeah, stiff competition."

Well, that was it. That sealed the deal. On the way home I took her to the Dairy Queen and asked her what she would like. She said she wanted a Dilly Bar. And I said, "Well, you know I can get eleven of those for the price of ten and save myself some money." That meant ten more dates, so she thought that was great.

THE IDEAL GIRL

MAG: *What happened after those ten dates?*

STEVE: It was one of those things where, a couple of months into it, this was now the right time for me. And Morag and I were in love. We were going to elope.

The elopement was scrapped in favour of a more traditional wedding.

We got it all set up. We rented an apartment in Oakville. Neither one of us used to go to church much—at that point I never went at all—but we went down to the Anglican Church in Oakville. It was a nice-looking church, so we walked in and talked to the guy and he said he was glad to do it.

We were going to elope on a Saturday, but the minister advised us, "On the Thursday night of that week, get your parents together and tell them your plans. Then they at least have the option of attending."

So, that's what we did on the Thursday night. We sat them down, and they just went crazy. Not in a good way.

And when they found out that Morag wasn't pregnant, they *really* went ballistic. Not my mum as much, but Morag's parents. Because they said, "Well, everybody's going to *think* you're pregnant anyway!" What a mess.

Morag and I went and sat in the car, and I said, "You know, this wedding has nothing to do with us. Why don't we just accept that and do whatever they want? We still love each other and we're getting married."

So we put the wedding off for a couple of months. By then I had finished Teachers' College. I started teaching in the fall of '66 and we got married on Remembrance Day, November 11th of that year.

We had the ceremony in the church in Streetsville, and everybody came. But the wedding for us, because of that—all the romance went out of it that night when we told our parents our plan to elope and they weren't happy about it. We just went through the wedding. We did what we were supposed to do. Had the rings and said the things.

Eloping was where the romance would've been for us. We didn't even make any of the decisions about the wedding. And Morag had dyed her hair. I didn't even know who was coming down the aisle. And she was half an hour late.

So she's late. I'm waiting. I'm standing there thinking, "What's going on?" And then this person comes down the aisle with a white dress on. "Who the hell is that? Oh geez, that's Morag."

I said, "What'd you do that for?"

She said, "I don't know." She was just fed up.

But here we are, still in love forty-one and a half years later.

MAG: *What were you looking for? How did you know that Morag was your ideal girl?*

STEVE: I didn't. It was a process of elimination. The light went on for me when I could talk to Morag about things. And she would respond in a way that encouraged me to talk more and share my real inner thoughts. I had never experienced that before. I'd never connected with anyone intellectually before. Or emotionally.

I mean, you're a kid and the hormones are raging. There's always the physical attraction. That's easy. But usually when it came down to the talking it was…crrrrr.

But Morag and I could talk about the stuff that I thought was really important, things that were important in life.

Brother Dave clocks the newlyweds.

MAG: *Like?*

STEVE: A moral code. How do you have a successful life? How do you survive this thing? How do you want to be thinking at the end of the trip? Where do you want to live? Why? What kind of people do you like? What kind of people do you stay away from?

We just have a lot of good fits. And then the biggest part of our relationship— it's really why it's worked so well—is that we're very complementary emotionally. Things that I'm missing, well, she's got 'em in spades. We're a tag team.

CLASS ACTION

MAG: *Okay, now you're newly married and that's going well. What about the teaching?*

Answering the call of pedagogy—Steve's graduation photo from Lakeshore Teachers' College.

STEVE: Well, if I'd put into teaching what I ended up putting into entertainment, I think I could have been a good teacher. But I just didn't make the effort. It's like all the way through school I just never made the effort. I thought I was lazy and maybe I was. I was unmotivated. I wasn't going to put my money on that horse.

When I look back now, I think the worst thing that could have happened was for me to succeed in something I wasn't interested in. Because then it would have been awfully hard for me to leave it.

I taught for two years. And teaching wasn't a good fit for me, so I had an uneasy feeling about that. I just felt I could do more.

There was something that happened when I was teaching—a realization that this was now my *life*. And I didn't like it. So, I decided that I was going to find something that I enjoyed doing, and put a lot of work into making a living at it, rather than find some way of earning money and then put a lot of work into making myself enjoy it. That was a huge thing for me.

I left teaching without even applying for a permanent teacher's certificate because I didn't want the safety net of having a teaching profession that I could fall back on if my other things didn't work out.

FINDING THE FIT

MAG: *So you quit your teaching job. What was your plan for the future?*

STEVE: Morag was teaching and she was making enough money that we could survive. And I wanted to see if I could go back to university and actually pass. I had never passed anything in my first experience at university.

Between the end of teaching in June and the start of university in September, I got a job as a mailman. This was the perfect job for me. At six-thirty in the morning I sort a bunch of mail for half an hour and then I'm gone and you don't see me until six-thirty the next morning. Like...I can *think*. As long as you're not trying to get into my mind, I'm happy. Because there are a million things going on in my mind all the time. And as long as I can enjoy that movie and watch it every day, I don't need a big office. I never have.

If you're going to go into something and you're expecting success, then you better be pretty realistic about what you're bringing to it.

MAG: *How did it go for you at university when you went back the second time?*

STEVE: I did great. I went to McMaster and in my first year I think I had a seventy-five average. I got into Honours the second year, and then I quit at Christmas. I was just uncomfortable in that environment. It wasn't taking me anywhere I wanted to go. I was kind of at odds, thinking, "This is wrong."

Then I got a job at Boston Gear and I was a salesman selling power transmissions and stuff like that, and that was another situation where it just was not a fit for me at all. So I was eliminating.

MAG: *But during that time—you've just spent a day doing something you don't like, and you go home. What kind of mood are you in?*

STEVE: Oh...good. All the time these things were happening, we'd be performing in the band on weekends, and that was a satisfying outlet.

MAG: *Was that the same band you put together with the lab technicians at Maple Leaf Mills after you flunked out of university the first time?*

STEVE: No, this was a new band called The Unpredictables. This was Morag and me, my sister, Vicki, and her boyfriend, and a couple of other friends from high school. What happened was, there was a coffee house in Streetsville and they had advertised for local talent. So we put together a group and learned three or four songs, and we went down and auditioned. We got the job, so we'd work Friday, Saturday and Sunday nights.

I would arrange the vocals. I was the leader of the band and kind of managing that business. It was entrepreneurial and it was creative. It had some status to it. I was up on stage. So, throughout that whole thing, that was the part of my life that was working out.

See, all those factors came together. It was June of '71 when we all quit our jobs and went into the band full-time. If I hadn't left Boston Gear, I'm sure they were within a week of firing me. But it didn't matter because the next day I started on something that was going to lead me to where I was supposed to be.

And a really important factor in all of this is that we had no plans to have children, so there were no innocent victims. Morag had her teaching certificate by then; she was quite self-sufficient. So there really didn't seem to be a downside to taking a shot at doing the band full-time. What better time than when you're somewhat young, and without dependents? If you fall on your face, so what? Big deal. It's awfully tough to do that at forty, when you've got all these strings.

I remember sitting there when Morag and I were thinking of quitting our jobs. We figured out that if we could make eighty-five dollars a week, we'd be

When Steve decided that their folk-based group should switch from acoustic instruments to electric, the band morphed into the rock act, Jason. *Above Left:* Steve as Elvis—"hairier than Elvis, yet more athletic," praised a local music critic. *Above Middle:* Slob's Grease Gang, the band's salute to the music of the Fifties. *Above Right:* Morag belting out a Fifties hit during one of Jason's crowd-winning retro sets.

okay. If we made a hundred and fifteen dollars a week, we'd be doing as well as we had done while teaching.

Well, we never came close to making as *little* as we had made teaching. And this was like, "Huh? That can't be right!" We gave up the money to do something we enjoyed, and here we were getting *both*.

And that has happened over and over and over again.

WANTING IT ALL

MAG: *At that stage of your life, what was your biggest fear?*

STEVE: I think it was failure. I don't think there was anything special about that. I never wanted to excel at anything, but I sure didn't want to fail. I just wanted to be in that comfort zone. One of my favourite shapes was the bell curve, especially right in the middle of it. I just thought that was a neat thing.

You know, life has turned out to be my Grade Eleven class. I can look around and there are a couple of achievers, and there are a couple of people who are probably going to go to jail. But most of us will probably just survive okay and probably have a happy life. And that's good enough for me.

For the rarefied air of being the big hit, there's a huge price to pay and I was never sure I wanted to pay that price—just the sacrifices you have to make to get to be at the top of any field. As an athlete or an executive…the choices that you make every day, you have to put aside something that you might enjoy doing, or something that might reward you in some other way to stay focused.

You know, you see these Olympic athletes who are practising sixteen hours

Below Left: Jason, the band. *Below Right:* Bandleader Steve at the keyboard during set-up for a Jason gig in 1973.

Unlike other musical artists of the Seventies, Steve rejected the emaciated, naked-chested rock star look in favour of a floor-length fringe.

a day and are on this specific food regimen. They're not with their families, they can't practise whatever it is they do where they live. So all of a sudden they're living in Arizona or some place where they can do their event all year.

I just felt that the success wasn't going to give me enough to justify not spending time with my friends. That was a price I wouldn't pay.

MAG: *Was there a price you would pay?*

STEVE: You know, when we had our band, we had a P.A. system—Traynor equipment, built by Pete Traynor. And I was talking to him one time and he was saying that if you wanted to raise the power on your P.A. system—let's say it was a hundred decibels—and if it took five thousand watts of power to make a hundred decibels, then to have a hundred and three decibels took ten thousand additional watts—you had to double the wattage every three decibels. And I thought, "Well, life's a lot like that. Why don't we just live with a hundred?"

Because to double my input into that particular thing to go a *little* bit higher, I'd rather use that energy to have more balance. I'd rather play golf or have friends, have a wider life. I'm not that driven. I *am* driven, but not to that extent.

I *do* want it all. It's one of the reasons I stayed in Canada. I do want the whole thing. I want to be a father and I want to be a neighbour and a friend. I don't want to just be a guy who makes millions of dollars, who's absolutely totally one hundred percent pure driven.

SCRAPING BY

MAG: *So the band took off and you were making good money. What ended it?*

STEVE: The band started off well, but by December of '74 Morag and I decided to leave the band because we wanted to do our own material and the rest of the band wasn't interested in trying to do original stuff. So it was just easier to go

Left: In 1976 Steve and Morag pursued their career as a duo and left behind the band, the fringed vests and most of their income. They were vindicated in 1977 when they became an instant and long-lasting hit with television audiences.
Right: Morag dressed as Steve, and Steve dressed as a friendly woman without many romantic prospects.

out on our own. Our act was called *Smith and Smith* and we were hardly working. We were so wrong for the places that we were playing because there was nowhere for us to play with the mixture of satire and music that we were doing, other than being on television.

And then we got fired off a job in Vancouver. We were just the wrong thing. That was a huge life moment for me because it suddenly occurred to me that maybe I wasn't as important as I thought I was. I wasn't really the centre of the universe. Maybe I should back off a little bit.

We were broke. We were fired. We had no work. I was selling our equipment to pay the rent.

And I said to Morag, "You know what our problem is? We're scraping by. We're not doing well, but we're scraping by. That's no good. That's a living death. Either we need to fail totally or we need to succeed. 'Getting by' is not going to cut it. I think we need some debt motivation."

Now, previously, back when the band had been doing really well, we'd owned a house. But after Morag and I went out on our own, we'd sold it because I didn't want the worry of it. I didn't want to be compromised. I didn't want to buckle for some stupid thing like I had a mortgage payment. Maybe we could have made it, but it wasn't worth compromising the decision that we'd made, which was, "Let's give this every possible chance to work, because it might be two years without income." That's why we hadn't kept our first house.

I said to Morag, "Your dad was really upset when I sold the house, so I think he'd lend us some money to buy another house."

So I went to her dad and I borrowed five thousand bucks. We bought a house in Hamilton for five thousand down. And then I went to the bank and said, "I want to start my own company. I want to call it S&S Productions, and I want to borrow five thousand dollars."

And the woman said, "Well, do you have any equity?" And I said, "Yes, as a matter of fact, I do. I've just put down five thousand dollars on a home." I didn't tell her it wasn't *my* five thousand dollars. So I got that loan.

Now I'm ten thousand dollars in debt, no income, no nothing going on. I come home to the apartment to tell Morag the good news. She's not there.

Where the hell is she?

She finally comes home and that's when I find out we're going to have a baby.

DAD TO THE BONE

MAG: *Had you and Morag made a conscious decision to have a family?*

STEVE: I wasn't going to have any kids. Before I married Morag, I said, "Look, I don't want to have any kids." And we were married ten years before we did have kids, so I wasn't *kidding*.

And it wasn't that we decided to have kids, but we decided not to do anything *not* to have kids, and just see what happens.

When we found out that Morag was pregnant, we were ecstatic. I think back to that now—there was not a twinge of doubt. It was fabulous. And I think, "If that was our instinctive reaction, even in the face of being broke and out of work, why would I ever worry about anything again?"

That's how we got Max, and then seventeen months after him, Davy came along.

I remember coming home from the hospital after Max was born, and I was so shaken. Morag and Max were still back at the hospital, and I was coming home alone to the house. I was just shaking because I had planned to be the kid. And now suddenly, my wife and I both needed a husband.

I remember sitting in the car in the driveway and saying to myself, "I can't be the kid anymore. That job's taken."

And Max didn't ask to be thrown into this. He didn't apply to be my assistant. So, I thought I'd better figure this one out pretty fast.

The double whammy for me was that I wasn't sure what Morag was going to do. We'd always been a double income family. I didn't know what was going to happen in the long term. In the short term, I knew for sure she wasn't going to be working. It wasn't just an emotional shift; it was a financial one too. That was pretty big.

MAG: *How did you get through that?*

STEVE: I took a job working for a friend of mine. He had been our manager for the band in the early Seventies. This was now '76. My job was that I would rehearse with various bands. I was pretty good at arranging vocals and stuff. I didn't know the specifics of the music, but I could hear it, I knew what was right.

So, I worked with them and most of the bands got better and became more successful. It made a big difference.

Then at the end of that, I had to come to a decision. What do I do now? By that point, Davy's on the way. And you know, I do this sometimes—I kind of set the terms and then I let the outside world decide, like, "You make the call."

I figured out what I needed financially to get by. And then I gave my friend first shot at it. I tried to be clear that this was how I was prepared to go ahead. But he came back with a counter-offer.

And you know, I just…I wasn't negotiating. I wasn't trying to twist his arm. It was obvious that I needed what I needed to meet my expenses, and through no fault of his, I'd put myself in a situation where I needed a certain amount of salary. It wasn't a whole lot of money.

But I wasn't bluffing. I've never bluffed. I do ask for outrageous things sometimes, but I'm not bluffing. Because if I don't get 'em, I'm not going back. I convince myself that what I'm asking for is right, is fair.

Anyway, that didn't work out.

So I went to the television station and that *did* work out. Morag and I did a pilot and then they offered us a series—thirteen episodes

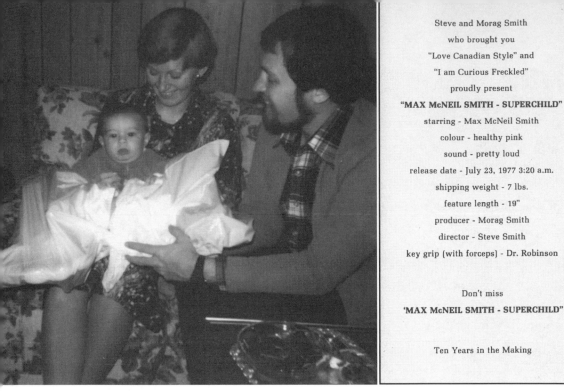

Considering they had never planned to have children, Steve and Morag took to parenting with remarkable ease—Morag, Max and Steve, 1978.

at five hundred dollars an episode. And we had to do everything—writing and performing—so that was a ton of work.

So we were okay. This was now '77, '78.

NO GOING BACK

MAG: *Did you ever wish that you had stayed in the music business rather than moving into TV?*

STEVE: No. For five years, I was in a band and I had absolutely no right to be in a band. I didn't have the talent to be in the music business, and I knew it. But the band was just something that ended up as a stepping stone to something else. And for that, it had value.

Looking back at it now, I would never take on something like that again. Maybe I'm too old for a stepping stone. I felt that if you're going to go into something and you're expecting success, then you better be pretty realistic about what you're bringing to it, because nothing outside you is going to bring success.

For example, I was in the music business, number one, because I like music. Well, who doesn't? And, number two, I had actually factored luck into my business plan!

Which is fine until, at thirty, suddenly we have a baby. And he's not that impressed with luck. He's the one with the luck. I now have to get a job.

Anyway, it was certainly a learning experience. And people say, "Oh, your band was really good." We were probably better than the average bar band and we all made money. It was a very successful time for us all, but for me it was, "You're doing the wrong thing and you better find something you *can* do because this is going to get old in a hurry."

MAG: *But if you hadn't done the band, you wouldn't have had your stepping stone.*

STEVE: That's true. And also, if I wasn't in the band, I *would* have had a job.

Whether I'd stayed in teaching or whether I'd stayed with Boston Gear…as every year went by with my having a job…you know how you start to fall in love with your captor? I would've started to think that I really needed that job, and I'd be more and more afraid of going out and trying something. So the band really freed that up.

There were times I would've taken a job in a flash, but I just know I'm such a useless employee. I'm pretty good on the phone. I can kid around with somebody. If somebody calls to place an order, I'm very nice to them. Complaints, I'm not that keen on. "You whiner. Fix it yourself and shut up."

Actually, between the band and our getting the TV show…that was the hugest, shakiest time because all of a sudden I was twenty-nine or thirty. This is getting serious now. And then Max comes into play. That was a time of thinking, "Gee, I wonder if that was such a smart move because there's no going back."

"My most emotional moments have been with the kids"—Steve with son Davy, 1979.

CHAPTER THREE

THE EARLY TV YEARS

FROM STAGE TO SCREEN

THE EARLY TV YEARS

FROM STAGE TO SCREEN

SMITH AND SMITH

MAG: *Earlier you said you came home to tell Morag that you'd taken out a bank loan to start a production company. That's the same day you found out she was going to have a baby.*

STEVE: That was September '76. She was *just* pregnant because Max was born in July '77. We had left the band to work as a duo and we were in tough financial straits.

MAG: *So how did it unfold that you and Morag ended up with your own TV show?*

Opposite: Smith and Smith picked up steady traction with TV audiences who enjoyed the couple's affectionate banter, goofy skits and wide-ranging musical repertoire.

MAY 3-9
401 INN
KINGSTON

MAY 10-30
STRAND-ATLANTIC
ST. JOHN'S

JUNE 7-20
CARLTON TOWERS
OTTAWA

JUNE 21 - JULY 4
OXFORD HOTEL
WOODSTOCK, ONT.

RANDY LEFT TO DO A DUO WITH ALTHEA AND WE
WENT BACK TO BEING SMITH & SMITH
WE PLAYED JULY 6 - 18 AT THE NEW WINDSOR

WE THEN DECIDED TO GIVE UP ON OUR CARRERS. WE BOOKED
A 6-WEEK HOLIDAY IN EUROPE AS OUR FAREWELL TO SHOWBIZ
A COUPLE OF WEEKS BEFORE WE WERE TO LEAVE, WE WERE
OFFERED 6 CONCERTS AS OPENING ACT FOR AL MARTINO.

WE CANCELLED OUR HOLIDAY AND DECIDED TO GIVE
OURSELVES ANOTHER CHANCE.

SEPT 7 - HAMILTON PLACE
HAMILTON

SEPT 10 - SASKATOON
SEPT 11 - REGINA
SEPT 18 - CALGARY
SEPT 21 - WINNIPEG
SEPT 28 - OTTAWA

WHEN WE RETURNED, WE PUT TOGETHER A PRESS
KIT AND APPROACHED CHCH-TV ABOUT GETTING OUR OWN
SHOW. THE VICE-PRESIDENT HAD SEEN US AT HAMILTON PLACE
AND LIKED US AND AGREED TO LET US DO A PILOT. WE
DID THE PILOT MAR 31/77 AND 2 WEEKS LATER THEY
BOUGHT 13 SHOWS TO BE AIRED EARLY IN 1978

STEVE: We had one job coming up. We were opening for Al Martino at Hamilton Place. Frank DeNardis, the VP and General Manager of CHCH, was in the audience. The performance went well for us so we were able to get a meeting with him.

So in December, we got the go-ahead from Frank to do a pilot episode. Morag wasn't really showing yet. We shot the pilot for *Smith and Smith* in March, and by that point she was starting to show. The bosses at CHCH came back to us in June and said they wanted to go ahead with a series, but let's wait until Morag has the baby.

CHCH, Hamilton's local television station, began transmitting to the public on June 7, 1954, as a privately owned affiliate of the CBC Network. After changing ownership several times in its 44-year history, CHCH is now owned by CanWest Global.

She had the baby in July and two months later we started shooting thirteen episodes. By the time *Smith and Smith* went on the air in February of the next year, Morag was pregnant again and it was pretty obvious. So, they called me and said, "Look, we're prepared to go ahead with a second season, but you've got to stay away from her!" I was just so excited about things going well that I couldn't hold myself back.

We ended up doing a hundred and ninety-five half-hour episodes over the next seven years. It wasn't a big budget, maybe $20,000 an episode. And that amount had to cover studio rental, cameras, lights, writing, performing and editing. The standard budget for a big network variety show would have been more like $100,000 to $150,000, but our show was just low-level Canadian content to satisfy the conditions of the station's license.

But the advertisers bought our show. It sold out every year. There'd be no commercial spots left available on *Smith and Smith*. CHCH had never had that happen before. They couldn't figure out what was going on. So that's what kept us going for seven and a half years. The first season they paid us $500 an episode, and that was for both of us, including the writing.

Opposite: In a scrapbook, Steve chronicled the couple's decision to give up on their show business careers in 1976, but a shift in fortune interrupted their plans.

Above Left: Morag and Steve performing in the *Smith and Smith* pilot, March 1977.
Above Right: Steve and Morag share a jive during the first season of *Smith and Smith.*
Opposite: The Smiths sharing a billboard with Jack Lord, Ricardo Montalban and Hervé Villechaize, circa 1978.

MAG: *Did your budget go up each year?*

STEVE: Well, it took a big jump the second year. I said, "I really want to be a producer, so although you'll be paying me more to write and perform the show, I'm also going to take on a lot more responsibility." So, they could justify the budget increase.

And I was willing to work. For example, at that time there was a television technique where they could squeeze the picture and then another picture would come on over the top of it. I mean, it's nothing now, but at the time it was a big thing.

I wanted to go from one scene to another doing that squeeze thing. And they said, "Well, that's a million dollar switcher that you'd need, and we don't have that."

I said, "Okay. What *do* you have?"

They said, "We can do chromakey."

Chromakey is a technique where you shoot people doing a scene in front of a blue or green screen and then you can electronically substitute any picture for that colour. So, I'm looking at this squeeze thing. The picture doesn't go across linearly; it kind of compresses as it leaves the screen. And I'm thinking, it's almost like the picture is on a drum as it rolls by. That's the effect of it.

So what I did was, I made a drum out of a cookie tin. Then I had the CHCH art department do a title graphic that took up a third of the circumference of the cookie tin. And that would be the title of our next segment. The rest of the tin was painted chromakey blue.

And then I'd put the cookie tin on a record player at sixteen rpm. So, the camera would start on the blue part of the cookie tin, which would be replaced with the video of the scene we're in. This is all live to tape. Then the graphic would wipe across and it was slightly bigger than the picture...so while the graphic is on, the guy has to quickly switch over to the next scene on the blue screen. As the title wipes through, we're now into the next scene. I couldn't have a million bucks, but I could get that effect—just mechanically.

And they're all going, "You idiot."

But it worked, you know? I'd be down in the basement building that thing and I'd go in there and try it. The guys in the studio would have some downtime between shooting and I'd say, "Could you just try something for a sec?" And then when it worked, they'd say, "That's kind of neat."

There were a lot of examples like that where we knew we didn't have the money, so we didn't even bother. You had to think of other things. I really enjoyed that, and I learned a lot.

MAG: *While you were doing* Smith and Smith, *you were pretty busy with the creative work of writing, acting and producing. What about the business end of things?*

Above Left: Steve's brilliant chromakey substitute for a million dollar switcher—depicted here in a not especially brilliant drawing. *Above Right:* Steve in Shakespearean garb with then producer of *Smith and Smith*, Larry Schnurr, 1980.

STEVE: When we did *Smith and Smith* at CHCH, each year when it came renewal time, Frank DeNardis would call me and I'd go in there and tell him what I wanted and we'd shake hands. And that was it.

Then sometime in the next month I would write up a letter, just one piece of paper, saying that this is what we agreed to. Then they had something to put in their filing cabinet, and that was it. For eight years, that was it. I knew that Frank wouldn't renege, and he knew there was no way that if I ran into a problem I'd come to him and say, "I need another $100,000 'cause something went weird."

ME AND MAX

MAG: *Why didn't you continue with more seasons of* Smith and Smith?

STEVE: We were bumping our heads against some things. Variety was dying and we were kind of like a *Sonny and Cher* thing, and all that stuff had gone by the board. Sitcom was really strong, so there was a lot of pressure to do sitcom.

MAG: *Is that when you came up with the sitcom* Me and Max, *which starred you and Morag and both of your sons?*

STEVE: Yes, and we experimented with doing multiple characters using the blue screen technique, so we had some scenes that had eight people, but it was really only Morag and me playing four roles apiece.

We did *Me and Max* for a year, and it was just too hard on the kids. They were great about it, but we just said, "You know what? That's not right. These are not their choices and let's just drop it."

When we finished *Me and Max*, Frank called me up to his office. The show had already run on the station. Everything was done. And CHCH wanted to run the show again.

Now, I didn't have a lot of money. I never had a lot of money. So Frank called his programming people for a number and then said, "We'll pay four thousand an episode for another two plays of this show." And it was twenty-six episodes, so that was $104,000. That was a huge windfall for me.

Now, in my original agreement with CHCH, we had always been equal partners if the show got any sales. So I said, "Tell you what—let's split the money. If this sale came from another station outside, we'd split it. Just because you're the buyer, I don't see why the rules should change. I don't see why you should be penalized."

And that's just the way it was. That's just fair. I have very clear ideas of what I think "fair" is in all of these dealings. And if something ends up unfair, I'm not happy, and it's not going to work out well. Even if I

A production shot from the family sitcom, *Me and Max*. "It was just too hard on the kids."

pretend that it's okay, it's not going to be okay. In a couple of days I'm going to phone somebody and say, "You know, I just don't feel like doing this." And then I'll just go and do something else.

COMEDY MILL

MAG: *I know a bit about what you did next because I was involved. It was the most fun I'd ever had in any television job.*

STEVE: Yes, that's when I came up with the *Comedy Mill* idea. We cast the show and wrote the first season in 1986, and started shooting in '87 with a budget of around $50,000 per episode. And within the first week after we started shooting *Comedy Mill*, the bosses at CHCH were let go and I had a new President to deal with.

MAG: *Really? When we started shooting the* Comedy Mill? *That must have been difficult for you.*

The cast of *Smith and Smith's Comedy Mill*—Linda Kash, Morag and Steve, Peter Keleghan, Mag Ruffman.

STEVE: Oh yeah. The switch was done at the Board level. Somebody came in and made a big offer for the shares and they all said okay, so the ownership flipped and the old management was gone and a new guy came in and it was a problem.

MAG: *And this was all going on in the first week of shooting?*

STEVE: Well, you were there.

MAG: *Yes, but I had no idea you were operating under that kind of stress.*

STEVE: Yes, there was a lot of stuff going on. A lot of problems.

MAG: *You covered it up pretty well—I had no idea at the time. I do remember you being upset when your father died that year; it was around Christmas. I remember you talking about that. It hit you pretty hard.*

In the *Comedy Mill* premise, Steve and Morag headed up a team of would-be comedy writers (played by Linda Kash, Peter Keleghan and Mag Ruffman). The team was headquartered in a restored mill where they brainstormed and churned out sketches, skits and music videos. The series was shot at CHCH.

The cast was totally unaware of the pressures Steve was under during the first season of the *Comedy Mill*. Especially Peter.

STEVE: I think the date on the death certificate was January 2nd, 1987. He'd probably died at the end of December '86 but wasn't discovered for a few days. Morag and I were on a Christmas holiday down south with the boys when we got the phone call.

I was inconsolable for at least three days. I mean weeping uncontrollably. Pretty much sat alone in the bedroom for a few days.

MAG: *Did the boys understand why you were so upset?*

STEVE: Yes. I think I made it clear to them. They had never seen me that upset in their lives and it threw them a little. Me too.

MAG: *I remember you decided not to go home for the funeral. Is that because you knew you couldn't fix your relationship with your dad now, so there was no point going to the funeral?*

Looking back at it now, I had never given up on my dad.

STEVE: There was less than no point. The physical funeral had no meaning for me. The death that I was mourning was the chance for closure, not just the passing of a loved one. And at the time of my father's death, the rest of my family had given up on him. They'd lost touch with him. I was the only one who still talked to him. So the funeral would have put me in the midst of people who didn't share my grief, which would have made the grief even more difficult to bear.

Looking back at it now, I had never given up on my dad. I probably never would have. When he died, I had to deal with that on a very private, personal level because I knew it would affect almost everything that was yet to happen to me. The reason I was so upset about my father's death is that I realized that my relationship with him would never be right, would never be what I wanted it to be. I was shocked to realize how much I wanted it to be right.

What came out of that was a new resolve to identify important relationships in my life and do what I could, while I could, to make them right.

It took about three months for me to get back to not thinking about my

A rare photo of Steve, Davy, Max and Steve's dad, Howard, circa 1983.

dad's death all the time, and a full two years before I had put it behind me.

ROCKY ROAD

MAG: *Yet you still managed to get through the first season of* Comedy Mill.

STEVE: Yes, and then we got picked up by the new President for a second season. And then suddenly he was gone and then there was nobody there. That was the late Eighties.

So I went back to CHCH and said that I wanted to repackage *Comedy Mill* because the first year had been disappointing and never really did anything. I felt that I could repackage it and give it another life by adding segments to replace things that didn't work so well.

And also I wanted to do *Red Green*. I had come up with the character of Red Green during *Smith and Smith*, and I wanted to expand it into a series. I was in survival mode again. I felt that the *Red Green* thing would probably get some traction and I also wanted to give *Comedy Mill* a chance to carry on. So, we did a deal where all CHCH gave me for *Comedy Mill* was the use of the facilities; there was no money.

And with *Red Green* I was back to the *Smith and Smith* type budget—around $28,000 an episode. And I remember in our original deal, I was supposed to be able to go into the studio for eight days, then go out and do the field shooting, and then come back in the fall for another twelve days to finish the studio stuff. But two weeks before we were going to start in the studio, I was told, "You just get

We had to do twenty-four episodes worth of shows—the studio portions—in eight days.

the eight days. That's it. You can't come back in the fall. We're not changing the deal, but that's all the studio time you get."

MAG: *How did that affect the show?*

STEVE: We had to do twenty-four episodes worth of shows—the studio portions—in eight days. And the show was heavily studio-based. There was no live audience, thank God. It was Patrick McKenna and me. That was it. For the

first season of the show there were no studio guests, no nothing. I would set up the Handyman Corner and I would do twelve of them in a day. Then the next day I'd do another twelve. And then we'd change over the set and do a whole bunch of other stuff.

I remember one day McKenna and I did eighty-five pages of script. The whole crew was like, "Holy Cow." No cue cards, no prompter. Nothing.

After I did the eight-day thing, I got a call from the General Manager at CHCH. The station wasn't going to air the show that fall. They didn't need the Canadian content. They didn't need to air the show for another year, till September of 1990.

And I said, "What am I going to do? Even if you like the show, you're not going to need new episodes for two years. So, you're kind of screwing me."

He said, "Sorry."

I remember that one. It had been kind of a rocky road for a few years and that one was tough. I got off the phone and went and threw up. And I'm thinking, "Oh God, what are we going to do now?"

Steve and Patrick McKenna during first season of *Red Green*, 1990.

Meanwhile, I had just bought a new house but still hadn't sold my old house. If you ever think you're not aging fast enough, I highly recommend owning way more real estate than you can afford. So, I put both houses on the market. The one in Burlington had been for sale for eight months without any action. I now put our house in Hamilton on the market too, and the first person to look at it was the new President of CHCH.

That wasn't a happy moment.

YOU'RE KILLING ME HERE

MAG: *Did things get better after that?*

STEVE: Yes and no. In the following few weeks, I had some meetings with the new President and he was quite affable. You could talk to him. He wasn't just a goof. I explained the situation to him. I presented the show to him. He didn't even know what we'd been doing, so I showed him stuff that we'd shot. He thought it was great.

So I said, "Here's the problem. By not putting the show on until next September, you're killing me."

Suddenly they decide to put the show on the air in March. I thought, "Well, okay. This is better than September." So I went and got some press and geared up and everything, and they started running the show. And the show did great. But after five or six weeks, they took it off the air.

And I'm going, "Uhhhh…I don't get it."

They told me, "Oh, it's doing too *well*. We don't want to blow it now. Nobody's buying advertising now. We want to save it for the fall."

Well, how do I win, you know? I said, "Okay, look, I need a renewal. I need it right now. Because if this thing's a hit, by the time you decide to renew it, I'm going to be gone. I'll be out of business. There'll be no set. We'd have to start again. I've got everything stored. I can't afford to start over. Either we keep going, or we'll never, never start again."

So, the President gave me a renewal for Year Two after five episodes had aired. I thought, "Okay, I've got some breathing room." It was a stay of execution

Patrick McKenna plays Red's nephew, Harold, the fictional producer and director of *The Red Green Show*. Harold has a pronounced overbite, a falsetto laugh and a sensitive, intelligent grasp of the world. In 1989, when Steve was looking for a second banana he could play off in his first season of *Red Green*, he saw Patrick perform in *The Second City* comedy troupe in Toronto. In one skit, Patrick played an adolescent boy, and Steve instantly knew he'd found his sidekick.

really, because of what was to come later. But at least that bought me some time.

And then CHCH proceeded to almost end the show by getting creatively involved. This new President wanted his bosses to put money into the show and he could only get the money if he changed it, made it more expensive. He had all these ideas about how he was going to increase the production values and add a whole bunch of people.

I'm working on that basis and then at the eleventh hour, he said, "I couldn't get it. Couldn't get the money. You'll just have to go ahead and make the changes,

Sales information for the first season of *The Red Green Show.*

S & S Productions Inc.

The Red Green Show

A Comedy Series featuring the hobbies, pastimes and idiosyncracies of manly men in the Great Outdoors.

A show for people who don't think men should be taken seriously.

The funny si
hunting, fis
woodwork
appliance re
inventing, ou
adventure, m
ter truck fixat
hermitism,
refitting,
generation
the male ego
other inflatabl

The Last
Men on the P

Vintage photo of Undercliffe, Steve and Morag's home in Hamilton, Ontario.

but at the old budget level."

Well, now what? Here I am trying to do a sitcom on $28,000 an episode when a sitcom budget normally starts at $200,000. And at the end of that season is when I got the hook.

MAG: *Wow, you had a couple of bad years.*

STEVE: I had a bad spell in there. Of course that was when the economy was going south. And I had the two houses up for sale. After I'd put the Hamilton house on the market, I think within forty-eight hours we had an offer, while in nine months we hadn't had a single offer on the old house in Burlington.

Now a normal person would say, "Well, sell the house in Hamilton." Not me. That's the one I've got to keep! So, I phoned the real estate agent in Burlington and said, "I'm sitting here looking at an offer on my house in Hamilton. I've got twenty-four hours. I don't want to sell this house. You need to make something happen."

The next day he came in with an offer. It wasn't great, but it got me to sell the right house.

So, yes, there was a rough spot. You know, I would honestly say that from the time we ended *Smith and Smith* to the time when *Red Green* got picked up by CBC—I would say that whole period was a struggle. And that was from '84 to '96. Twelve years. I mean we survived and everything, but it was a scramble.

GETTING THE BOOT

MAG: *CHCH cancelled* The Red Green Show *in 1993, which ultimately led to freedom and success for you, but I'm sure it didn't feel that way at the time.*

STEVE: It was probably the angriest I've ever been in my life. I was so, so stinking angry. I didn't know what I was going to do. It was just a blind rage.

I was at home. I got a phone call at home and it was the President of the station, and he had with him the Vice President, the Chief Financial Officer and the Program Director. So there were four of them, on speakerphone, firing me.

They were telling me that they weren't going to honour the contract to do the show, even though I was in the middle of production.

The station was having financial difficulties. They'd looked at the numbers. They were just not going to honour the contract. That's what the President said—"We're not going to honour the contract, and we know you'll understand and you won't even think about legal action. For future ramifications, we suggest that you just make the best of this."

A tough weekend at the television trade show after CHCH cancelled the show. "Patrick and I went to NATPE and stood there and the whole world went by. Nobody picked up the show." *Opposite:* Production halted in 1993 when CHCH cancelled the show in the middle of shooting.

I was so mad. I was so mad on so many levels. Number one—I live six blocks from CHCH. I'd been with the station about fifteen years. I'll come over. You can humiliate me, but at least do it to my face.

Number two—I don't need these other people listening in. This is between the President and me. Why are these other three people in the room on speakerphone? To make me squirm? That was just him doing his rooster thing.

I said, "We need to do this face to face. I'll be in tomorrow at three o'clock. And I want everybody who's there now to be at that meeting." I didn't sleep that night. I was just so friggin' angry.

See, here's the thing. Whenever I have a setback—this is something I always do—I am absolutely focused on turning it into a step forward. If I can't turn a setback into a step forward, I'm just beyond the beyond. So, I absolutely have to do that.

And if it gets as pathetic as me convincing myself that whatever I'm doing is a step forward, that's good enough. But it *has* to feel like a step forward. It's not enough to take the punch. There has to be some kind of counterpunch, or the realization that maybe it pushed me in a direction that I needed to go. I absolutely have to get a positive out of it.

So, as angry as I was, I wanted to go and meet with them. I didn't know what I was going to do, but I knew I was going to do something. And I was going to have to come out of that meeting with a feeling of satisfaction. So I went to the meeting.

MAG: *As you were on your way to the meeting, did you work out what you were going to say?*

STEVE: No, because all I knew was that they were not going to honour the contract. And I was not going to let them off the hook. I was going to take legal action or I was going to do something. My rationale was not just my anger, because who cares about how angry I was? I have contracts with all of my entertainers, and the union is not going to be as forgiving to Steve Smith, and they don't care about "future ramifications." So I was going to be on the hook for paying all of those people.

> *The audience is the boss, and everybody else is middle management.*

Then the other thing I thought of was that the station had always been my partner. We would produce shows together, and they would own fifty percent. This had been going on since the early days. For nine years, we did it on a handshake alone, and now suddenly a contract wasn't enough.

But, I thought, I have to believe in myself and what I'm doing, and that what I'm doing has value, and that there may be an opportunity here for me to own myself outright. And that would be a worthwhile step forward to help me deal with this setback.

TURNING IT AROUND

MAG: *What happened at the meeting?*

STEVE: They were all there. I started with the thing about not letting them off the hook and I was going to take legal action unless we could find some other acceptable solution. So I said, "I need you to tell me the core motivation behind your not honouring my contract."

So the President said, "I'll tell you. It's real simple. We've invested money in this show, and we haven't seen a return. I cannot continue to invest. CHCH is basically bankrupt. We can't continue to put money into something that's not showing any return."

So I said, "What kind of return would it take for you to be okay, for you to be even, for you to get your money out of it?"

He said, "We need $145,000."

I said, "Okay, here's what's going to happen. I'm not going to sue you. I'm going to let you out of the contract. And I'm going to write you a cheque for $145,000 so that I'm not a black mark in your books. But I'm going to own everything that I've ever done here.

"And the only other consideration I want," I said, "is that I have to be the one who releases this to the media. I don't want you making this announcement. You've already put me out of business. I've got to word the announcement in such a way that I don't *stay* out of business."

He agreed. I shook his hand and that was the deal done, and he openly laughed at me, like, "You *idiot*."

As I was leaving his office, I couldn't turn around and look at him because I couldn't stop smiling. I didn't want him to see my smile because I thought he would reconsider. It was probably the only time in my life where both of us thought at that moment that we had won. Maybe we both had.

The next day, I was over there picking up tapes and throwing them in the back of the possum van. I had no income. I had no job. I was about $50,000 overdrawn at the bank because I was in production, and the reality is that you've got to front it. It wasn't like I *could* write the guy a cheque.

He had called me on a Thursday, Friday we had our meeting and Saturday I cleaned out the tapes.

On Monday morning, I picked up the paper and it said, "CHCH AXES FAMED WOODSMAN."

MAG: *You hadn't called the media?*

STEVE: I hadn't called anybody! I was trying to figure out how to couch this. What I wanted to do was to get another deal and then announce that I was moving. But that went out the window. It makes it really hard to find another customer when the old one has announced they don't want you anymore.

So I phoned this bonehead and said, "This was part of our agreement. You've already voided it on the first day." And he said, "It wasn't me. We had an internal memo."

"There's no such thing as an 'internal' memo," I said. "You just had to keep your mouth shut." He said, "No, I had to let my employees know."

I said, "Well, what's going to happen now is, I get until your year-end to pay." I knew that as long as my cheque showed up before his next fiscal report, he was alright. And he said, "Oh, that's fine."

MAG: *How much time did that give you?*

STEVE: This was March. His year end was August 31st. So I had this plan that I wasn't going to present the cheque unless it was to the President of the whole network. I was going to write him a letter and tell him, "I've got a cheque for you to be delivered by me, in Hamilton, at CHCH, at your convenience. When you want the cheque, give me a call."

I'm motivating myself.

I started putting some things together, and soon I had about $20,000. So I thought, "I don't need the big boss to come. As long as those same four people are in the room, that'll be enough."

Now we're getting into June, July and finally it came to August 31st and I get a call at home from the CFO, who was one of the four. He said, "Weren't you supposed to bring a cheque in today?"

And I said, "I dropped it off at security two days ago." It was so inconsequential for me. By then *Red Green* had been picked up by a lot of PBS—Public Broadcasting Service—stations in the States. The $145,000 was just a drop in the bucket.

What they had done was just absolutely stupid, but it was better for them and it was definitely better for me.

And within a year, every one of those four people was gone, including the President.

So, you just don't know. I think that as more things like that happen in your life, it makes you not be so quick. You don't *know* everything. Five minutes of humility can make a big difference.

MAG: *That's a* long *time to be humble.*

STEVE: I know. I used to try it for ten minutes, but I realized it was hopeless. I finally thought, "That's for *lesser* people!"

Anyway, things started to come around.

Maclean's, a Canadian news magazine, picked up the story of *Red Green's* cancellation and subsequent resurrection.

Red all over

It is a return from the wilderness. In March, Hamilton's CHCH TV cancelled its comedy series *The Red Green Show*, which made fun of male machismo from the fictional fishing retreat of Possum Lodge. But loyal viewers of the cult hit promptly fought back. "Letters came in on lunch bags, sandpaper, birch bark, whatever was handy," said **Steve Smith**, who plays host Red Green. The tactic paid off, and on May 24 the show will run on 20 Baton Broadcasting stations in Ontario and Saskatchewan and nationally on the youth cable network YTV. Said Smith: "The show caters to the eight-year-old in every man. Like we say at the lodge, 'If you can't stay young, you can at least stay immature.'"

Smith as Green: back at the lodge

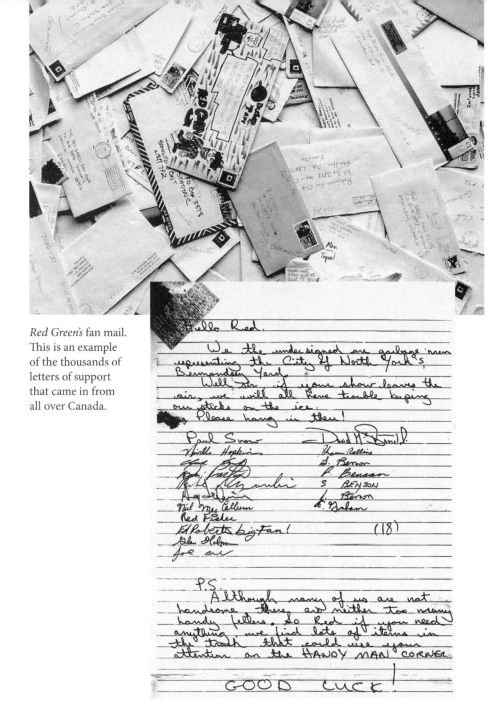

Red Green's fan mail.
This is an example
of the thousands of
letters of support
that came in from
all over Canada.

Hello Red,

We the undersigned are garbage men representing the City of North York's Bermondsey Yard.

Well sir, if your show leaves the air, we will all have trouble keeping our sticks on the ice.

Please hang in there!

Paul Snow   David McDonald
Nicolle Hopkins   Sham Collins
                   S. Bernon
                   P. Benson
                   S BENSON
                   Bernon
Neil MacCallum   K. Graham
Red Fisher
Ed Roberts big Fan!   (18)
Glen Holm
Joe an

P.S.
Although many of us are not handsome there are neither too many handy fellers. So Red if you need anything, we find lots of items in the trash that could use your attention on the HANDY MAN CORNER!

GOOD LUCK!

THE LAST HURRAH

MAG: *You often talk about learning and moving forward. What did you learn from being cancelled?*

STEVE: When *Red Green* was cancelled and then there was all that business where they leaked it to the paper—that was the first and only time in my life where an external force came in that I was completely not expecting, and it saved the day. That external force was the letters that I was getting. They were unbelievable. Unbelievable. So supportive. We were getting a thousand letters a day. I don't know how many letters there were all together, but there were tons.

And that was when I went, "Wow. I *forgot.* I forgot that it's the audience. It's not the guy in the front office or the guy in the funding agency. It's the people sitting in their living rooms." So I said, "I'm never going to forget that again."

That's when we went to having a live audience and I got into that whole theory that the audience is the boss, and everybody else is middle management. And the day that I decided that, that's when things started to go better for me.

It was a very educational time. It's like there's another thread going on that you're not aware of—like a subplot—which was that the show was connecting with people for some reason that I don't understand and never will.

Before we got cancelled, I felt I needed to deal with the people who make the decisions. Yet the audience was the part of the equation that ended up saving the day initially, and then ended up creating everything. And the audience was what I had almost completely ignored.

If the show hadn't been cancelled, it probably would have run its course in five years. But because it was cancelled, it ran strong for fifteen. When I would go down on sales calls to PBS, I would take that big hockey bag of mail. And I remember one or two guys—they would just reach into the bag, randomly pull out a letter and read it. Just to see.

I never flinched. "Take out as many as you want. See? They're even in different handwriting."

MAG: *Was the giant mail bag the secret behind your convincing PBS stations to pick up the show?*

STEVE: It took a little more than that. The way it happened was that in January of '92, this same guy who was trying to turn the show into a sitcom—the CHCH President Version 4.0—went as a buyer to NATPE. That's a huge television trade show in the States sponsored by the National Association of Television Production Executives. So this guy took *The Red Green Show* with him to try to sell it. I didn't ask him to do that. He just wanted to do it because he was doing what he could to make it work.

He was not successful at selling the show, but he took the show to Hearst Entertainment at NATPE. They were interested in distributing the show. So the following year, in January of 1993, Pat McKenna and I went down to the trade show in San Francisco and stood in the booth dressed as Red and Harold, and the whole world went by. We didn't get picked up, nothing happened.

So Hearst washed their hands of it and CHCH cancelled the show. That was the last hurrah.

Public broadcasting in the U.S. gets around $400 million annually from the U.S. government, which covers about 15 percent of local station budgets. Most shows are funded primarily by producers, viewer donations, private foundations and corporations. Televised pledge drives are annoying to many viewers, but successfully raise enormous capital contributions that ensure continued programming.

MOVING FORWARD

STEVE: Meanwhile, one guy who worked for Hearst Entertainment, Steve Weiser—his territory was the Midwest—he had a feeling that this show could work for PBS in the Midwest. So around March of '93, he called on one guy, Gerry Trainor, who was Manager of WTVS, the PBS station in Detroit.

Gerry was kind of seen as a leader amongst the PBS folks, particularly in the Midwest. Gerry looked at the show and said, "I think this could be a franchise for us." So he took it on. By September of '93, we had been picked up by Detroit, and then by Mt. Pleasant and Marquette in Michigan, and by South Bend, Indiana, and Toledo, Ohio. And that started it off. Then there were ten

Above Left: Steve has signed upwards of 5000 rolls of duct tape during PBS appearances (He can autograph 200 rolls an hour). *Above Right:* The first *Red Green* fundraiser was broadcast live to PBS stations across America via satellite uplink from CHCH in Hamilton, 1995.

stations. And then twenty. Then thirty. And I think we're at about a hundred now.

MAG: *What did Gerry Trainor mean when he said the show could be a franchise?*

STEVE: He meant that the show could work as a pledge vehicle that would encourage the public to donate funds to PBS stations. Gerry had the advantage that WTVS is carried in a lot of Canadian markets. And Canadians—I mean they had responded well to the show on Canadian TV anyway. But for a Canadian who sees the show and he knows it's kind of odd and he likes it—here's a show that represents *him*. And, Holy Moly, Martha, now it's on an *American* station. Huh? Who's the dummy now? I'm going to pledge a hundred bucks!

So, I went down to Detroit in March of '94 and did the pledge show and I didn't know what the hell I was doing, but it went pretty well. And then I did about sixty pledge drives over the next few years. I'd go down and do ten stations in a whack and I got really good at it. "If you like the show, send in a little bit of money so they can keep it on the air. If you don't like the show, send in a lot of money so they can afford to buy something better."

Just disarm them. That was fun. It was fun for me. And the phones would just light up.

By that December, we had about forty stations or more, and I could only physically do about ten in the annual two-week pledge period. So, I'd do ten and then the other thirty stations would be insulted. "Why didn't you come here?"

That's what led me to the idea of doing a live fundraiser. We did our first one in March of '95, live to satellite. We were broadcasting via uplink from CHCH in Hamilton. The cameramen were shaking because in thirty seconds we're going to be live in sixty-five U.S. markets. It was exciting.

During the show we always kept the bottom quarter of the screen clear so that each individual PBS station could key in its own phone number for viewer pledges. And the phones started ringing all over the United States.

The station manager in Iowa, Dan Miller, had seventy-five phone lines in the studio and twenty in a spare area. He had bought the show the year before but didn't put it on the air right away, so it just sat in their library for a year. And then something didn't come through, so he decided to put *Red Green* on the air. He'd only been running the show for about three months, and then we did this live pledge drive. He was up in his office doing some work while the pledge show was airing. And his phone rang and it was a viewer phoning in a pledge.

MAG: *It had rolled to his line?*

STEVE: And he thought, "This has got to be a mistake." But all ninety-five lines were full. They made about two hundred thousand dollars in an hour. They were freaking out. That was fun.

Then after the first live thing, I set each station a target. I would make up the target based on the market size, so it was a level playing field. We had this huge graph made out of duct tape, where each station was listed. The percentage that you exceeded your target was the determining factor. And the incentive was that I would come to visit the top ten stations. So, that's what I did.

We did that for a few years, and those fundraisers were very successful.

Our show became the top fundraising series for PBS, and we held that position for five years.

MAG: *How did you ever get PBS to okay the live satellite feed in the first place?*

STEVE: We went to PBS headquarters in Washington, D.C., and met with them. I said, "You know, you have a problem. You're asking people to pay for something they can get for free. That's an emotional decision. Yet you have intellectual programming. So, you're trying to get an emotional reaction to intellectual programming. That's why you have to airlift these *Eagles* specials and *Peter, Paul and Mary* concerts into your pledge periods—because your programs don't elicit emotional reactions.

But I have a program on your channel that *does* get emotional reaction and will raise money for you. And when the people pledge for *Red Green*, they tune in next week and they say, "My God, the show's still on! It's part of the schedule!" But when they tune in next week to see the *Eagles*—where the hell are they? So they say, "Where's that special? Where's that concert I pledged for?"

That meeting took ten minutes.

MAG: *Where do you come up with this stuff about intellectual versus emotional reactions?*

STEVE: It's just logic. It's the way I think about everything. "What is the basis, the core of the PBS problem?"

And emotion wins every time.

THE SUBVERSIVE COMIC

MAG: *I'm struck by the fact that although you've always had a quick mind, you never used humour in a malicious way, even as a kid. Why is that?*

STEVE: Remember, I really value people who keep their word. A very close second is that I like to see people laughing. I just think people are absolutely at their best when they're laughing. They're immortal, they're open, and they're disarmed.

I think you learn more when you're laughing than you ever do at any other time. You're just wide open. There's no resistance—that's important to me.

Obviously it affected a lot of my career choices. I've been lucky enough to have a gift where I can make people laugh. I even make myself laugh. I say things I don't think I even thought of. I'm hearing it with everybody else, and finding it funny.

So I want to live in a place where people laugh a lot. And I want people to keep their word. That's Utopia for me.

Production Manager Sandi Richardson shares a laugh with Steve and the crew, 1995. "Sandi is very valuable to me. She does a great job. She's incredibly reliable and she always makes the best of things. If we've got a problem, BANG, she goes right to the heart of it. And she's fearless."—Steve

If I'm mean to people, I'm moving away from that. Being mean to a person is, in a way, not keeping your word. There you are with them in a social environment, so you've implied some sort of acceptance of them. And then you nail them. And, more importantly, they're not going to laugh.

I was never drawn to comedy as a weapon. I was drawn to comedy as a uniting force, not a dividing one. I grew up with Jack Benny, Burns and Allen, *Our Miss Brooks*, and then Sid Caesar, Red Skelton and Jackie Gleason. They weren't using their comedy as a political weapon or as a tool for anarchy. They were trying to get people to forget about their problems for an hour and have a few laughs, have a short interlude of visiting and friendship and social interaction.

I like that. There are enough things to get people riled up about. Let's not take one of the forces for good and turn it to the dark side. That's just never appealed to me. I used to say that comedy is the courier, not the package. Sure, you can take some pretty awful things and use comedy to disguise them. People laugh, but then there's that, "Eww…," that aftertaste.

And then there are people like Victor Borge. To me, it just doesn't get any better than that. When I was twelve, I saw him perform at the Canadian National Exhibition. He said, "The Steinway Company has asked me to announce that this piano is a Baldwin."

People say to me, "What make is the possum van?" I say, "Well, I get $10,000 a year from Ford to tell everybody it's a Dodge." Like, I'm doing Victor Borge's line from 1958, and it's *still* funny.

MAG: *How do you categorize your style of comedy?*

STEVE: It's just fun, that's all. There's no agenda. The message is very simple— "Lighten up." That's all it is. "Lighten up." We're not trying to get you to vote this way or that way, or like these people and not like these other people. It's just, "Put it down for a minute, and have a laugh."

MAG: *That's quite subversive.*

STEVE: That's an odd response.

MAG: *No, it isn't.*

STEVE: Well, what do you think is subversive about that?

MAG: *Everything.*

STEVE: It *is* totally subversive.

MAG: *So now you agree? Then why did you say my response was odd?*

STEVE: Well, I just… Just…nobody's ever said that before. It *is* totally subversive.

To me, it addresses the things about all of us that are alike. Whereas a lot of people live and die on their ability to address the things about us that are different.

ON MY OWN TERMS

MAG: *You said that when you were young, you enjoyed singing and you'd often put on shows for your family. Have you ever been self-conscious about performing as an adult?*

STEVE: I used to be nervous getting up and performing in front of people, or even just getting up and speaking. That started when we did our live act—*Smith and Smith*. We had left the band, where I was used to being onstage with five people and tons of equipment and a huge P.A. system. Now suddenly it's just the two of us and I've got a little wee amplifier and a drum machine. Oh man, it was so rinky-dink. And I had to try to make this look like a reasonable decision.

I think that's when the nervousness started. It was really funny—I'd be pretty calm before the show, and Morag would be a basket case. As soon as we got onstage—*boom*—nothing fazes her. And I'd be freaking out.

And then, you know, even when I was doing *Red Green*, when I was doing the show in front of a live audience, I was just so comfortable because that audience wanted to be there. I wasn't nervous doing the show, but the first time I went out to do a speech I was nervous. Because you go out there and if you're doing comedy, it's an absolute shock how long half-an-hour is, when you're asking for a laugh every ten seconds. So that was kind of a jarring thing for me.

And then finally, what changed it was that I started thinking about the *audience* instead of worrying about myself. I thought, "I have to have value for those people. They have absolutely no use for me nervous. If I'm going to be nervous, they may as well get their Uncle Fred to come up on stage. He can probably do nervous better than I can."

The only purpose the audience has for me is if I come out there *not* nervous, and do what I do.

As an entertainer, I don't know if people are going to appreciate my sense of humour. But I have to believe that a large percentage of them will. Because if I don't believe that, why am I an entertainer? You can't be an entertainer for twenty-five years and then, suddenly, when you've got to perform, start thinking, "What if they don't find me funny?" You can't afford to start thinking now that you have no value, because you will then conclude that you've spent the past twenty-five years ripping everybody off.

Not that I haven't bombed. I can remember doing a *Red Green* thing at a resort up north. It was just awful. It was very early in the life of the show. It was one of these things where a bunch of marina operators were having a convention and somebody thought *Red Green* would be the perfect speaker.

The P.A. didn't work and there was no lighting. I'm in a room full of five hundred guys and I'm standing in a corner and nobody could hear me, or see me. It was just brutal. I was probably supposed to do half an hour and I did about three minutes and got the hell out of there. So, yes, I've had my share.

MAG: *Are you actually a good judge of when you do bomb?*

STEVE: I think so, but I usually find a way to rationalize it. I think things like, "That's just the wrong venue for me. I wasn't wrong—the audience was in the wrong place." It's one of those things I have to believe. Because I've got to do it again tomorrow, so not believing that is not an option.

But I've never liked being the centre of attention. The comedy that I enjoy, or the way I like to be, is where I'm the guy making comments on the side when there's something going on. I'm reacting. I always prefer that. I hate, "And now Steve will get up and say a few words." Because the expectations are so high.

I'm most comfortable with a limited amount of scrutiny. It's a very narrow gap. I want you to be paying attention, but just barely. I don't want one hundred percent of anybody's attention because I find it creepy and I'm not worthy...

and although I know I'm not worthy, I really didn't want to share that fact with you.

Whereas if you're focused over there and then I say something funny…you know…I've had huge laughs from being that guy, the bridesmaid. Give me the bridesmaid every time.

MAG: *It's an unusual combination though, because you don't like to be the centre of attention, but you* do *want people to care that you're there. And you don't want to fail but you don't want to* work *very, very hard. Or at least you say you never want to work very hard, which I'm not sure I totally believe.*

STEVE: I think there's a possibility that my saying, "I didn't want to be the centre of attention," was really based on not having very much confidence.

I wanted to build my confidence through people noticing what I was doing. I'm not ready to be *there* yet, but if I do okay over *here* on the sidelines, eventually I'll get to the point where I don't mind being the centre of attention.

It took me a long time to be comfortable. Took me a long time to get the confidence. It doesn't seem sensible that I didn't want to be the centre of attention—I've chosen the wrong career not to be the centre of attention.

MAG: *To me, this is like when you were a kid. You didn't want to be forced to sing in the Red Cross show, but you liked being able to speak out in class. It's part of that subversion. It's on* your *terms.*

STEVE: Exactly. On *my* terms. That's the scariest part of me. It bugs me and I hate it in myself. It always has to be on my terms, and if it isn't, I go like a rag doll and you can't do anything with me. It must be very frustrating for other people.

As I'm getting older I'm actually forcing myself to say, "You know what? This is just you having a bit of a tantrum here." That's a hard one. It's one that I have to fight. I don't win all those battles.

And Morag will say, "That's not my thing, that's your terms. If you want to do something on your terms, you do it. Don't expect me to do something on your terms." And yet I do expect her to do things on my terms. Nice work if you can get it.

"When I was doing the show in front of a live audience, I was just so comfortable because that audience wanted to be there."—Steve talking to the CBC audience during Season Thirteen of *The Red Green Show*.

A FEW WORDS FROM MAX SMITH...

It was a great childhood. I can't complain about anything.

Dad worked a lot. You know how the business is. You go crazy and then there's a point when you're home a lot and probably not working much for maybe two weeks or a month. He always did things to try to be at home more. He set up an edit studio in the basement and worked on his home computer. We were together a lot when he was writing. We'd go to the cottage and he'd write there.

Friends—Max and his father in 1981.

My brother and I worked on *Red Green* pretty much every summer from when we were quite young—going through fan mail, responding to email or working on set building. So we got to hang out with Dad pretty much every day—that was cool. He put in a lot of hours of work, but I think he tried to intertwine the two—work and us.

I remember my dad's father; he was kind of quiet. We went to his place, but we didn't really spend time with him. My brother and I would get put in the basement, so we'd root around and try to find something fun to do. It was just social calls—maybe only four or five times ever.

We were in Jamaica when my grandfather died. I didn't really know him…it was a big shock. A fortune teller had just told my dad two or three things that had happened or were about to happen. One of them was that something was wrong with his father. Right after that we got the phone call. Dad was freaked out about the whole thing. To us, he just put it in simple terms—his dad had never told him that he loved him, ever.

Dad's a really happy person. The times when he was really unhappy would pretty much come down to his dad dying, my mom getting sick, and the time after the show got cancelled when he was rethinking everything and thought he needed to go into another career. My mom's thing was longer. But even then he was still cracking jokes.

The stuff Dad did with us when we were kids was awesome. He had a snowmobile, and he built a trailer unit that my mom painted red and black, with a white racing stripe. It was on skis, hitched behind the snowmobile. My dad would drive on a trail, and my brother and I would ride along inside the trailer. It had a little door and a bench seat. It was the coolest thing ever. Dad jury-rigged a doorbell with a wire that ran up to a light on his console. So if we had any problems, or if we needed to pee or needed a cookie, we'd just hit the doorbell. His light would come on, and he would stop.

A couple of years after that he bought this Scout. It was a four-by-four, a beater with no windshield, no doors, no cab. It had the really cool six-point harness seatbelts. It became the firewood-gathering automobile. We would get in that Scout and strap down. There was no road. Dad would just drive right through the middle of the forest, knocking over trees, and then we'd go back and pick them up. Awesome. I mean, you avoid the big trees.

I've never had anything that I would drive headfirst into a forest. I've been basically spending the rest of my life trying to replace that coolness. One day.

On my fifteenth birthday, I went outside and there was a flatbed truck in the driveway. This amazing, crazy fibreglass car was on the back of it. It had been in an accident. The front fender was smashed in. It didn't really run, but I didn't care—I loved it. It lived in our garage for a year, and we got it working pretty good, except for the gas gauge.

The first day of school, I'm driving with my brother. I'm thinking, "I'm just the coolest kid." But we run out of gas, so the big entrance is Davy pushing. And me trying to salvage the cool, but I don't think so.

POSSUM PEARLS

It doesn't take long for men
to make a decision.
It's making a decision look
smart that takes the time.

You may have to grow old,
but you don't have to mature.

Keep your stick on the ice

I'm pulling for ya.
We're all in this together.

If the women don't find you hand
they should at least find you hand

The Red Green Show is kind of like the flu; not everybody gets it.

If it ain't broke, you're not trying.

Motto:
Quando omni flunkus moritati
(When all else fails, play dead)

CHAPTER FOUR

RUNNING THE SHOW

THE RELUCTANT LEADER

RUNNING THE SHOW

THE RELUCTANT LEADER

BIG FISH IN MY OWN POND

MAG: *Even when you were pretty young, you were running the band. You just took on the management role. Then you moved into TV. You had to develop some really strong leadership skills to produce TV shows and manage people. How did you learn to be a leader?*

STEVE: There's no more reluctant leader than me. I don't want to be a leader. I just want things to go my way. I think the whole leadership thing was based on me wanting to control my own life growing up as a kid.

The truth is, I could never see a place for myself in the world. Ever. Even today. So I had to create my own world. And then I knew that I'd find a place in that, because I'd made it.

I think that, even as a kid, if I had been able to assimilate better into society and be more normal, everything would have been different, because I would have been very comfortable with that.

But I was so uncomfortable in that world that I went the other way, and made my own. I've convinced myself that that choice has been very rewarding and was the best choice for me. So, I'm not motivated to go back on it.

So when I say, "Okay, I'll be the leader in my world," I will then accept the responsibility of making all the decisions. The other route of trying to fit in to someone else's world would be so uncomfortable for me. I just couldn't be what I consider to be a normal person.

I always let them decide how it's going to happen. But I decide what is going to happen.

I wanted to lead my *own* life. That was very key to me. So you know that thing about being a big fish in a small pond? Well, the fish was me and the pond was my life. I wanted to be the big fish in my own life. And then I did whatever I felt was required to maintain that. The decisions were always based on the fear of losing my own self. Losing the control over my own life.

MAG: *Hasn't the success of* Red Green *turned your life into a pretty big pond?*

STEVE: Until my brother came on board at S&S Productions—that was in 1995—our office was the size of a small room. We had a warehouse to store the set and I had an office there. The company was never based on a drive to form a business or anything. My brother grew the company into a business and now suddenly we've got all these people and we've got all this equipment and we've got all this investment—all those just came along with it.

Not everybody wants my life because there's uncertainty about not having a regular job, which would drive some people crazy—yet, here I am, facing retirement, and I haven't had a regular job since 1971. And I consider that everything I've done is available to everybody—I don't know why they don't do it. I probably have some special ability in the comedy field, so, okay, that's one difference. But everything else is just average or below average. But a job, in certain circumstances, can be the absolute worst thing that can happen to a person. I think if everybody had a regular job, we would be so far back in our evolution.

Still, it's been a real struggle for me to keep the control in my life as all that stuff has been happening around me. A lot of things came in under me. It's kind of like I got pushed up rather than me pulling things up.

MAG: *But it was your idea to include Dave in the company.*

STEVE: Oh, completely. But I didn't ask him to build a huge company. I hired him to help *him*. And then he ended up helping me way more than I helped him. He's been letting me down like that for fifty years.

MAG: *You may not see yourself as a leader, but I don't think you can ignore the evidence.*

STEVE: I think people respond positively to what I've accomplished and they'd like to figure out how to do that. They'd like to connect to some of that or at least know how it works. And out of that I've become a leader.

But that's not really a leader. Like, if you look at all the people who work at S&S Productions…they wouldn't even be working there if it wasn't for Dave. He's been able to create the stability and figure out the finances and all of that.

I think I'm just kind of a renegade. I haven't been very successful. I've been successful *enough*. But it's the way that I've done it—by not really doing it the proper way, not going by any of the rules. My whole life has been an end run. I did an end run around university. I did an end run around the whole corporate world. I tried to go around the music business, but I got clipped by a free safety.

End runs are fun. For one thing, you're out there on your own. And you're moving pretty good.

> In North American football, the free safety is a defensive position. He stays 10–20 yards behind the line of scrimmage. If an opposing player gets past the linesmen and linebackers, the free safety's job is to make sure they don't get past him on their way to the goalpost.

MAG: *Yes, but you don't know if you're going to get hit or not. There's still a strong element of risk.*

STEVE: Well, you have to deal with that before you take the ball. You've already made that commitment. There's no turning back.

MAG: *When you do have a setback, or something isn't going your way, or there is some chaos that you weren't expecting—how much of your feelings are you masking? How do you deal with your emotions given the fact that you have to be the lead guy?*

STEVE: First of all, I have a huge temper, and when something like that happens I'm instantly angry. I want to know who did it, and how fast I can punish them. That's what's happening *inside*. But I don't express that. I bury that and it goes into a deep dive mode. There's just a glaze happening in my eyes.

And then I'll start responding with very sensible stuff. "Okay, let's just step back and take a look at the overall thing. What are we going to do, blah, blah, blah."

Because, you know, that first thing—the anger—is really the wrong tool for the job at that point. It's an emotional response. It goes somewhere and it has to come out eventually. And it does come out when I go home. The way I tell the story to Morag is quite different than what everybody else saw around the writers' table. So it does come out.

Steve rehearsing a scene with Laurie Elliott and Patrick McKenna, 2003.

But I don't *act* on it. I don't act on the anger. And I'm not upset with myself for being angry because I have a certain amount of fire. If I didn't have that, nothing would happen.

But, you know, the weird thing is that when somebody comes to you with a big problem, it is very, very rarely a big problem. It's very rarely even a medium-sized problem. It's usually a small problem.

When they either don't come to you at all, or they come to you with some casual kind of problem, look out for *those* ones.

The martyr approach is based on poor self-image, a sense that you're worthless. If you have a basic sense of the value of humanity, and you're human, then you should be one of the ones on the list.

Usually if they think it's a "big problem," it's something that makes them look bad, it's some mistake that they made, but in the overall scheme of things, a mistake that they made in something they do at their level is not going to bring the whole company to its knees.

So actually that helps balance me because when somebody says, "We've got a big problem here," I immediately relax.

THE GUY IN CHARGE

MAG: *I'd call your leadership style "firm but relaxed." When I've had the chance to watch* Red Green *rehearsals at CBC, I've noticed that both the cast and crew seem to take their behavioural cues from you. You are clearly setting the tone. Are you conscious of doing that?*

STEVE: Yes. That's what I always wanted. I don't actually like being the guy who has to make a thousand decisions an hour, but if you want to be the guy in charge, then the decisions come with that. In my mature moments, and I do have some now, I think, "This is what you wanted, and this is what comes with it."

MAG: *Do you ever have problems with actors in the show, and if so, how do you handle it?*

STEVE: We tape the same show twice a night in the studio, and we always have a meeting between the shows. Bruce Pirrie does the talent directing, so he usually starts the meeting. He's very good. He goes through the script page by page with lines that he has suggestions for.

Well, we sat down the other night and I said, "Before you get started, that was all garbage. I can't use anything out of the first show. So, you guys either get your act together or I need to be doing something else." That was the whole meeting. I just said that, and left.

I've never done that in fourteen years. And they all stepped it up. The second show was great.

MAG: *Were you mad during the first show when you saw that they weren't getting there for it?*

STEVE: Yes, because I'm always editing the scene while I'm doing it. So, some guy taking five minutes to do a ten-second bit is like—what am I going to do with this? And he's moving all over the place, I can't even cut easily. You're killing me here.

And they usually pull it together for the second show, but this particular night I really wasn't open to whether or not they were going to pull it together. I was going to let them know that this was not an acceptable level of performance. Because I really didn't want to look at another twelve taping days of this.

It hasn't been a problem since.

MAG: *You recalibrated their quality indexes?*

STEVE: Yeah. "Faster; funnier." You know? There's no magic to that. And Pat McKenna is *so* good. He can sense it. He can feel the audience. He knows when to go and when to move on. I'm good at it too. And you just expect everybody to do it because they've been there a lot of times. Like, can't you sense the audience?

But all in all, when I get to the editing room, it's like, "These guys are so good. I'm so lucky to be working with such solid, solid guys." I never finish editing and think, "That guy's got to go."

And they all came and apologized to me. Separately. Which I thought was really great. They didn't feel like I was wrong, either in content or delivery.

MAG: *When people around you make these sorts of mistakes, are you generally a forgiving person?*

Steve supervises during the second season as the crew works with an extremely sticky giant roll of duct tape, 1991.

STEVE: You know, I do think I *can* forgive people. But usually I have to be asked in a very special way—non-verbally. Words are way too easy. Things people say rarely go very deep. I've said everything in my life. I've said horrible things that five minutes later I knew I didn't mean. We've all done that. But when you take action, when you do something, that's a little different. That's a much more premeditated, thought-out, deeper statement.

And so, if you're truly sorry for something you've done, then it's going to take that kind of statement to reverse it. So let's see some *actions* that imply an apology.

I think I'd be forgiving for that. I can't remember a situation where I've just said, "Nahh." But I have said, "That's not good enough," when somebody apologized to me verbally after doing some ridiculous thing. They weren't genuinely sorry.

So what I do is, I say, "Okay, thank you." But nothing changes for me until I watch their actions for six months or a year. I wouldn't necessarily shut them out, but I'm looking for more proof than that.

GOING FORWARD SEPARATELY

MAG: *You've told me that friction between people really bothers you, but doesn't putting together a show and dealing with networks automatically involve some degree of conflict? How do you deal with conflict in business?*

STEVE: If I'm in a confrontational environment, I'm very uncomfortable. Like contract negotiations. I don't bluff in business. I never bluff. I figure out exactly

Above Left: Script discussion, 2003. *Above Right:* Production manager Sandi Richardson surrounded by "her boys" backstage at a CBC taping—from left to right: Wayne Robson, Jeff Lumby, Sandi, Bob Bainborough, Patrick McKenna. *Opposite:* Patrick McKenna and Steve in the first season. The chemistry was irresistible from the start.

what I think is absolutely fair. That's the offer I go in with and I'm prepared for them to say no.

It's really important that now there's a guy like my brother, Dave, who can buffer that. Dave is very good at putting it all together. You can say "no" to my brother without upsetting him, and people know that. They like that. I think the broadcasters end up being a lot more honest with him. They don't have to worry about a reaction.

Because if I go in asking for more than what I think is fair, I think less of myself, and if they come back with less than that, I think less of them. So, it's really a terrible "my way or the highway" way of doing it, and it's not the sign of a good businessman. It's probably been a limiting thing for me.

I don't like confrontation. It's a conflict of goals. If my goal is in conflict with the other person's goal, I find that very disturbing. If we can find a goal that we can agree on, then we just argue about how to *get* there. I have no problem with that, and I'm very convincible. But, you know, if our *goals* are in conflict, we're never going to get along well.

MAG: *When you have people working for you, you are inevitably going to have conflicts. Have you ever had to fire someone?*

STEVE: Oh yeah. I've had to fire people. Morag says that I'm the only person she knows who can fire somebody, and they'll come round and thank me. There's no ill will or anything. I've been able to get along with people and also get through situations that other people might have found difficult—like, when it was over you'd never be talking to them again. And I've been able to get through those situations without that happening.

So it's better to have me managing situations with people than to have somebody else managing them—because maybe I can find some middle ground and work the thing through—and it ends up moving forward rather than blowing up.

MAG: *So you're actually good at conflict resolution—which is what firing somebody really is. What is it that enables you to do that so well?*

STEVE: I don't know. I try to give the person some hints early on. I don't let things go. I'll sit them down and say, "This is not okay and I don't like the way this is going." And I try to be very specific. I put time into explaining why it's not working for me and what I think is wrong. If they have any suggestions, I'd love to hear them—let them have their side, see what they have to say.

If you're right about something, then it's an eternal truth. It can wait two weeks.

And I'm hoping they've thought of something, hoping that they've got something that they're going to tell me, and then I'm going to feel better. Because I don't really want to fire anybody.

But when it comes down to it, the goal is that I want this person to move forward in their life and I want to move forward in my life. We're just not going to do it together.

So then I figure out what's the best way to accomplish that goal. I start with a presentation to them of why this is not going forward. And then they determine where we go from there. If they throw something back to me about,

Rehearsing the Possum Lodge word game with Jeff Lumby and Bob Bainborough, 2003.

you know, "This is unfair. I didn't do this. I didn't do that," then we go to the next level. I always let them decide *how* it's going to happen. But I decide *what* is going to happen.

I don't find that they're ever surprised. I was trying to think of a situation where somebody was surprised or shocked, or fought me. And I can't think of one. They're hearing the truth; that's the sense that I get back. I've never found out later that that was the beginning of the end of their lives, the beginning of a downward spiral for them. Every one of them has moved on to other things.

I don't take any pleasure in demeaning somebody. Getting rid of somebody, having somebody who's been a problem not involved in your life anymore— that's enough of a reward. I don't also have to stomp them into the ground.

I make a decision as to how much people can give. When I see them giving that, I'm okay with it. And some people have more to give than others.

A TWO MILLION DOLLAR LESSON

MAG: *What kind of management style do you use with the people who work for you?*

STEVE: I decided a long time ago that you're better off to support the people that you've entrusted with some authority. If they have an area that they're responsible for, then that's their area. I'm not going to micromanage and say, "That person did such and such and needs to go." I want to support whatever decisions they make.

And if they make a mistake, I believe that they'll correct the mistake. They don't need me to step in and correct their errors. That's the kind of company I want. So I've got to start assuming that's the company I have and then let them prove me wrong. If I assume that I don't have that kind of company, I have to get in there to make sure everyone is absolutely perfect at what they do so that I'll eventually have the kind of company I want—I'll never live that long. Also, I'd be doing it all on my own. This way I get them to help.

A friend of mine in Florida, a guy I golf with, made a huge mistake, cost his company two million dollars. He'd been with this pharmaceutical company a long time. And he was just shattered. So he resigned.

So the President of the company calls him in and says to him, "What the hell's this?"

He says, "It's my resignation."

"Yeah, but I don't know why it's here. What happened?"

My friend says, "Well, uh, that deal I just made was a big mistake."

"What did it cost us?"

He says, "Two million bucks."

"Wow… Did you learn anything?"

He says, "Yes, sir, I sure did."

And the President says, "Well, why would I let you resign when I just spent two million training you?"

It's fabulous. Now that guy is ten times the employee he was before that. To me, that's a great example. That's the way I'd like to be. Support the people and let them figure it out. I'm the last resort, not the first one.

And I'm not doing it that way because it's just better for them. It's better for me too. I like to be fair, but I'm on the list too. Whatever decision I make, I want to make sure that it's fair to me too. I don't respect the selfless approach. I don't respect the "I'll be a martyr, I'll do anything for you" kind of approach. If I did respect it, I'd do it.

To me, at some level, the martyr approach is based on poor self-image, a sense that you're worthless. If you have a basic sense of the value of humanity, and you're human, then you should be one of the ones on the list.

DECISION MAKING 101

MAG: *Listening to you talk, you seem like an extremely decisive person. What's your process for making decisions?*

STEVE: Whenever I have to make a big decision in life, I always make it pretty quickly. But then I don't act on it for a while. It's like with writing. You've got the first draft, then the second draft, and then somewhere along the way you think you've got it. Then it comes to the actual day of shooting that script, and suddenly you're looking at it with twenty-twenty vision and the utmost scrutiny. And that's when it makes its biggest change and you find out what's really right.

That's what it's like with decisions. I'll make the decision right away, and then I'll just try it on, see how it feels and maybe adjust it a little bit. When it comes down to the moment of the decision, I actually abandon all logic. I have the sense that this just feels right to me. Or, this just feels wrong.

MAG: *How do you know when something feels "right"?*

STEVE: I think hard and deep. And I need to be alone—I'll *be* alone anyway, even if I'm not. People around me might be upset with my non-responsiveness, but that's just the way it goes. So I do the thinking—that's Step One.

The mental and physical effort of trying to achieve something generates other opportunities that I haven't even considered.

Then I come up with a theory and look at it from different sides. If it passes that test—and it might take a few days—then I find myself saying the theory aloud, as if it's true. I just present it straight out to people…that this is a good thing to do, or this is a fact. Partially, I'm looking for their response, but mainly, I'm listening for my own response. I want to know how my theory sounds coming out of my mouth. So that's Step Two.

I put *some* credence in their response, but I put a lot more in my own. A negative response would never overpower my feeling, but if I feel *somewhat* their way…okay.

And then Step Three is—I wait as long as I possibly can before acting on it. I try to wait a week or two to see if it holds true. Because some things that I believe are "fixed" truths or values—are not. They change, and then suddenly the whole formula is out of whack. And what was true today is not true two weeks from now. So I'm better off to wait.

Because if you're right about something, then it's an eternal truth. It can wait two weeks.

IF YOU'RE SURE YOU'RE RIGHT

MAG: *If someone challenges you on your decision—where does that hit you? Or does it?*

STEVE: Oh, I really like that. There's absolutely nothing bad that can come out of someone challenging me. If I'm right, their questioning is going to absolutely galvanize me because I'll be able to prove to myself that I'm right in my response to them. And if I'm wrong, I'm going to find out that I'm wrong, and then I can have a better theory.

Being challenged is exciting. It's like something breaking—I can go and see why it broke, and not only fix it, but maybe fix it in a way that it won't break as often.

Sometimes when somebody disagrees with me, I immediately react negatively. Often I'm under a time constraint and I don't want the hassle of dealing with an objection. But the truth is, in the big picture, it's often a good thing. Because when someone disagrees with me, I can test my reasoning and see if anyone can poke holes in it. If I'm going to base the rest of my life on that reasoning, I'd like it to be right.

Steve at the helm.

But again, the key thing is that when I try to talk somebody into my way of thinking, I'm really trying to talk *myself* into it. I'm exposing them to my thinking. If they reject it, fine. But it's how *I* feel about my decision that's important to me.

It's back to Davy Crockett—"If you're sure you're right, then go ahead." That felt right to me when I was a kid. That still feels right to me.

MAG: *Davy Crocket has been your role model for a long time.*

STEVE: Yeah. It was 1955 and I was nine years old. When I first saw that show, it was like, "*Phew!* Way to go, Davy."

Talk about handing you the reins to your own life. "If you're sure you're right, then go ahead." Well, okay! All I've got to do is be sure I'm right. I don't have to ask anybody for permission. I can get advice, but I don't need permission.

MAG: *When you've made a decision but you're not yet* sure *you're right, that's a vulnerable place?*

STEVE: Oh, absolutely. And even if you were *sure* you were right, and then you went ahead and it was wrong—well, what's the lesson? The lesson is to spend a little more time making sure you're right.

GIT 'ER DONE

MAG: *There's something I'd like to clarify. Sometimes you get to a point where the action you're taking now feels bad. You're just muscling through it. And even though it doesn't feel right anymore, you just keep going because you said you'd do it.*

STEVE: Yes.

MAG: *Well, for me, when something stops feeling right but I just keep going with it anyway, my energy drops. I feel drained. But you don't check in again once you've made the decision; you're going to get it done no matter what.*

STEVE: Yes. I think that's the vulnerability of that approach. Over a period of time, things that weren't immediately obvious may have changed, or maybe I didn't notice them, and so the decision wasn't as good as I had hoped.

And rather than me being able to stop and say, "You know, I'm going to make another decision now," I just tend to just keep going on the same path.

The other day, Max and Morag and I were talking about this. Max is very much like me. Once we've made that decision...

MAG: *Git 'er done.*

> *If you have a gift, you've got to do the thing."*
> *—Ruth Purdy*

STEVE: Yeah, git 'er done. Whereas Morag's thing is, "If you're trying to do something and it's not going well and you're meeting with obstacles that are very difficult, those are signs you're doing the wrong thing." When she said that, Max and I almost spoke together, saying, "You'd never get anything done!"

Because there are always going to be obstacles. If every time you met one, you just said, "Oh well, obviously I'm doing the wrong thing; I'll go start something else," you'd start a thousand journeys of a hundred yards each, rather than ever going ten miles.

I don't know what the answer is. But I guess you look for signals that the balance has shifted, and that you're actually hurting yourself. I think you need a way of factoring it back to the big intent of what you're trying to accomplish, which is to bring peace and harmony to yourself and others—that really is the big goal, rather than just finishing that specific task.

For me, that's hard to remember. Once I've made a decision to do something and I start on it, it's not going to bring me any peace and harmony to stop going forward. That'll just…that'll kill me to stop—in the early stages. Maybe at some point when I've gone past that early stage it would be good to stop. But I think I have a fault of not realizing when I'm in the area where to stop forward movement—or at least veer off on an angle—would actually bring me more peace and harmony.

Figure out what your aces are, and play them.

A MAN OF ACTION

MAG: *Even though you don't necessarily check in to see how the action is making you feel right now, the sensory apparatus is still functioning—because you are aware when it feels like an uphill journey. But you're going to do it anyway.*

STEVE: Yes. Well, I think the negative responses are physical, and the positive ones are emotional or mental. My mind will stay as strong and as committed and as convinced that this is the way to go. But on a physical level, I'll start feeling bad. I'll start getting headaches or I'll be exhausted, and my mind will be unable to block out those things that my body is trying to tell me. So eventually it gets my attention.

MAG: *Why do you want to block out that much evidence?*

STEVE: I think it's just a belief that if you falter, you won't get there. The funny thing is, I've never gotten to whatever goal it was that I had put all that planning and effort into. But while I was pushing forward, something *else* always happened. And I've always thought that those things that happened would never have occurred if I hadn't had that focus and just kept moving ahead.

So I feel that the mental and physical effort of trying to achieve something generates other opportunities that I haven't even considered. And that means that I end up over *here*, which is good…it's actually as good or better than where I thought I was going. I never consider that a failure because if I hadn't tried to go there, I never would have gotten here. I would still be back where I started. I don't think if I'd just sat there and waited, that this opportunity would have come along.

I don't know, but I'd rather believe that it wouldn't.

MAG: *I understand—you're a man of action. You believe that if you're working toward something, you get something. If you sit back and wait for stuff to come to you, you'll get nothing.*

STEVE: Exactly! To me there are some vulnerabilities to that approach, but I think that the good stuff far outweighs the bad.

MAG: *Can you give me an example of a time when you persevered through a really difficult situation and something better came along?*

STEVE: I remember when I was really in trouble financially—like 1992, somewhere in there. My relationship with CHCH, which had been my income source for fifteen years, was over. I had a net worth of negative $700,000. I needed a miracle and I needed it immediately. Despite all logic and science to the contrary, both of those things ultimately happened.

I had a huge emotional response to the financial crisis. There were a lot of tears. I was in free fall. I could not find a safe landing area from which I could create a plan.

Now, some people would feel that when they have so much negative information, they can't find any way to feel good. But that doesn't cross my mind.

I got over it by pushing the immediate reality off to the side for a few days while I took a look at the bigger picture of what historically had been my marketable assets. I believed that my strengths in the past would have the most chance of solving the problems I had in the present. I could then re-examine the current problem and come up with a plan that used those strengths from the past to forge a future.

That was a tough one, to find some way to feel good out of that mess.

BREAKING IT DOWN

MAG: *How did you do it? What did you find to reach for that felt better?*

You never want to make a decision based on weakness...you're always going to make a bad decision from weakness.

STEVE: Instead of just worrying generally about a financial disaster, I actually found it helpful to quantify it very specifically, and absolutely find out what it was. And then, okay, now something has to be done about it. We can't ignore this. This has to be dealt with.

That brought me to the next phase of dealing with the problem, which was—what would have to be done here in order to make that problem manageable? And then it was, okay, now we have an overall plan. And now we break that down into little steps. What would be the first step in executing that plan?

And that brings me to a commitment. I'm going to work really hard at executing this plan. If I fail, I won't be worse off than I was before I started. I will *never* be further back than when I started. So I think, "Okay. That means I must be moving forward!" Now I start to feel good. And then Step One goes well. And then Step Two goes well. Now I'm starting to get some momentum. Now I'm feeling good.

And then two years later, it's like, "Oh yeah, I remember—there was a problem, wasn't there?"

I think the biggest thing, though—the most important starting point—was sitting down and absolutely being brutally honest about identifying the extent of the problem. In a way, this implied that I felt capable of conquering it if I just knew what it was. It's a tough step because if you think you *can't* handle it, then you don't want to know about it. You want to ignore it.

MAG: *You deal with hundreds of details every day to write and produce your show, and it seems like you really pack your days full. When you wake up in the morning, what's the first thing you think about?*

STEVE: I always think about what's happening in my world. I don't mean the outside world, like CNN. I just mean, how has my world changed since I went to sleep? So I like to check my email. I like to check my phone. I'll look at the weather.

MAG: *The moment you wake up? You don't lie there and think about your dreams or anything?*

Do unto others as you'd have them do unto you, because you are doing it unto you.

STEVE: No. I just really enjoy being productive. I like getting a lot done. I mean, a while ago I was at the office. A meeting didn't go as long as it was supposed to, so I ended up with an hour and a half on my hands. There were lots of things to do at the office. I could sit there or I could go and schmooze with everybody.

Instead of that, I went home, I brought in all the summer lawn furniture, stored it all away, took the screens off the windows, put the storm windows up, turned off the outside water and drained all the pipes. And then I went back to the office and did whatever I had to do. But it was just like, man, that's packing a pretty good day.

And the next morning we were having a creative meeting and everybody was supposed to come with ideas. And I had five times as many things written out as anybody else. And I am by far the busiest.

I like that. That's why when I wake up it's like—Bang! Okay, game on! I'm not going to lie there and think about things. I just get 'er going. I think about things while I'm doing *other* things. And it's really important for me, I find, to have a lot of things going on. I thrive on that.

SPONTANEOUS COMPULSION

MAG: *I've noticed that you seem to feel time very keenly. Do you feel like there's a certain amount that you need to get done in your lifetime? Do you always have another goal that you want to accomplish?*

STEVE: Yes. It probably goes back to that vision of myself as lazy and not getting anything done, so I need to get things done. I need to accomplish things. I *enjoy* accomplishing things, too. I'm not just doing it for the sake of getting it done.

There's probably some fear at the root of that. I'm afraid of being punished for not accomplishing. Or I'm afraid there's something coming, some catastrophe coming that I don't even know of, and my only defence is to be so far ahead in other areas that I can survive it. I think there's a lot of that.

My dad used to say there are only two motivators in life—hope for gain, and fear of loss. And of the two, fear of loss wins every time. I think that's true. I think that I'm afraid of losing everything, so I put extra effort into getting things done to the best of my ability as quickly as possible. And then getting on with the next, getting more and more things done, to somehow make me less vulnerable to that loss that I feel is coming.

Sometimes I feel so lucky, like my success is a complete fluke. And the only way that I can show my gratitude is by going as far as I can, not backing off. So I feel like I've got to do this, because I *can*. Because people who don't have the opportunity would hunt me down like a dog. My teacher, Ruth Purdy, would come back and say, "You've got to go do it. If you have a gift, you've got to do the thing."

MAG: *An American poet named Robert Bly claims that everybody has five inspirational, emotionally-charged words that stick with them throughout their lives. I think if I picked one for you, it would be "spontaneity."*

STEVE: Absolutely dead on. Spontaneity is huge in my life. Everything I do, at its beginning, is absolutely spontaneous.

So whether I'm trying to write a script, or something occurs to me in the moment of a conversation, or I'm trying to think about what I should do with a career problem or family problem or *any* problem, what I always go back to is the spontaneous generation of all kinds of ideas.

And it's just so exciting for me because in thirty seconds I'll have ten choices of what to do about the problem. The thing to be careful of is that you're so impressed with your ability to come up with a solution, you think you then have to *do* it. But it may not be the right solution.

I think if it wasn't for that spontaneous generation of ideas, nothing good would have happened in my life. Being able to evaluate a problem is one skill. But without the ability to generate solutions that can work, what does it matter? If there was one thing that I would never want to give up, it would be that spontaneous thing.

And when I'm writing a script, a lot of times I just start writing. It's just something spontaneous, and it comes out as a thirty-page script, but it's really five hundred spontaneous thoughts that have somehow linked together.

I need to be me for a million reasons – there's no other reason for me to exist. If I'm going to simply be a version of somebody else, why not just let them do it?

So, spontaneity is huge. I love spontaneity. But for me, it has to then survive the process so that it comes out the other end as something that fits in with all of the other factors that I think are important.

MAG: *Like being able to control your environment?*

STEVE: Yes, and that's why Canada is absolutely the perfect place for me to be. Especially with my personality. I want to control everything and here I am in an environment where nobody cares. How great is that? As opposed to going into an environment where everybody cares and I'm not allowed to control anything, but they'll pay me a lot of money to shut up.

MAG: *Wanting control seems like the opposite of being spontaneous. What's the relationship between control and spontaneity for you?*

STEVE: I think at some point I decided that the part of me that's spontaneous is the part of me that has real value. I think it's special. I think it's something that not a lot of people have, so I try to put it into a protected environment where it will live long and prosper.

I've found through experience that when I put that element of myself into a situation where the environment is under someone else's control, it doesn't work well. If that part of me is being directed to do something where it feels like it's just being used—where it's not being treated as a gift but as an expected service—then that element tends to shut down. I think I know that part of me better than anybody. So I always try to control things to make sure I can be the best that I can be.

I figured out early on in my career that you've really got to play your aces. This idea that you can sit down and lead with the two of hearts, and you're going to come back later and trump it with a jack—well, there's nobody at the table by the time you get to your next card. So figure out what your aces are, and play them. And if you've only got one, play it.

But, you know, I decided that the element of me that's spontaneous and fun is really my ace, and that, for some reason, I can't seem to play it in absolutely every situation. Maybe somebody like Jim Carrey can be that way everywhere he is. I'm not that way. I need to feel comfortable with where I am and what I'm doing, and then that thing kicks in.

MAG: *What happens when you're in a situation where it just seems impossible to do what you want to do?*

STEVE: Things that are unattainable are not that exciting for me. I'd just rather not know. I'm not saying don't make something unattainable. Just don't tell me. Don't tell me it's impossible because that will force me to shut down in so many areas that have nothing to do with that specific goal.

MAG: *Do you really shut down or do you just shut down temporarily and then start figuring out how to achieve the impossible?*

STEVE: I stop going that way. Honestly, if I'm convinced that something's unattainable, I stop going that way.

For example, back in the early Seventies I pursued the idea of doing a sitcom for American television. I talked to some agents and so on. I don't remember the specifics, but I thought about going to Los Angeles to write and star in my own sitcom.

Nobody was excited about my talent, that's for sure. And I was too old starting. I was already almost thirty and the guys who were writing sitcoms were twenty-two. And I didn't graduate from UCLA with a writing degree. I wasn't even an American. And I didn't do drugs. Occasionally a Tylenol, but that's not what they were talking about. So I decided that was unattainable.

So I shut down. I didn't try to prove them wrong. I just said, "Okay, that's out. So instead, I'm going to try and find something that *is* attainable, something that I respect.

IN THE FACE OF FAILURE

MAG: *What would you say is the thing you've resisted most in your career?*

STEVE: I avoid at all costs putting myself into a situation where I believe I will fail. I wouldn't do that. So it probably makes me a little more cautious because it's not whether somebody else thinks I'll fail, it's whether I think I'll fail.

If I think I'll fail or if I have a pretty good chance of failing, I feel that the damage would be so drastic to me that it makes the risk not worth taking. Because the reward's not that great.

Like, for me to take an acting job or a writing job or any kind of responsibility that I didn't think I could handle—I wouldn't do that. No amount of money would make up for my discomfort.

That's why I always try—before I take something on—I try to really go deep into myself. I ask myself, "Are you going to feel comfortable? Do you honestly think you can do this?"

Because all the people who say you can do it, they're wishing you well and they *want* you to be able to do it. But when you don't pull it off, *they* go on, while *I'm* in a deep cavern for six months.

MAG: *What does it feel like when you shut down?*

STEVE: You know, I resent the time. That's the biggest negative emotion I have. Periods of my life when I have felt low—and they are very, very few—but when they happen, I resent the time that I've put into the thing that's now causing me the grief. I feel like I shouldn't be going through this now, and I shouldn't have spent the last hour going through it, or the last week, or the last year, or the last ten years.

If I can do something that I enjoy and that satisfies my needs in terms of putting a roof over my head, that's all I need.

So resentment is a huge emotion for me. It propels me forward. I think that's one of the reasons I left teaching. I knew then that it was not for me, and it wasn't going to get better. I was able to face that and move on.

I've talked about the sense of accomplishment that my dad told me about— I've really found that to be true. When I shut down, I feel I haven't accomplished anything here in this situation. So, what am I doing here?

Then I try to learn something from that, and mainly what I've learned is, "Watch out for those situations and don't get into them, because you don't do well."

DO UNTO OTHERS

MAG: *Can you tell me the story of how your brother, Dave, ended up working with you?*

STEVE: That came about because of something that's happened to me a lot in my life. When I see somebody who I think could use a little bit of help in some

Steve's brother, Dave, backstage before a taping in 2000.

way or another—and it's almost never financial— if I decide they could use a little bit of help, I make a real effort to help them. And it always helps me more than it helps them.

My brother is a perfect example of this. He was the President of a big company for twenty-five years and then that company was bought by a huge conglomerate. They moved Dave to Florida to take over another company that had lost eight million dollars the previous year. My brother turned the company around in one year, and they rewarded him by letting him go and putting the company up for sale.

He came back to Canada a different guy. He decided he wanted to start his own business. He didn't want to work for anybody anymore. And who could blame him?

I went over to see him after he got back, and I'd never seen him like that. He seemed like a broken guy. And he was talking about getting a printing business or something like that.

So I said, "Well, you know, why don't you take a look at my business? That might interest you. Maybe we can do something together." He looked at it. We had a meeting that brothers should never have. We talked about money and how much he'd need.

Anyway, I got home and Morag said, "What are you doing?" And I said, "I can't ever see my brother like that. I've got to do something. I don't know what I'm going to do, but I've got to do something." I was far more upset about his situation than he was. He would have turned things around. My job offer didn't come out of his need for help, but rather my need to help him.

So, I ended up saying to him, "I'll guarantee you six months." And I wasn't Mr. High Roller or anything. The company was bankrupt, basically. But I said,

"I'll give you six months." Just to give him time to think over what he wanted to do next.

It's like I always say to my kids, "You never want to make a decision based on weakness. You at least have to convince yourself that you have options so you *feel* you're making a decision from strength. Because you're always going to make a bad decision from weakness."

I can honestly say I made that decision one hundred percent out of my need to help my brother. No doubt about it. And man, if I said the company is ten times the size that it ever would have been, I'd be low.

And now I can go to Florida for the winter because he's here. But all that time, I thought *I* was helping *him*.

Did I ever tell you my addition to the Golden Rule?

MAG: *No.*

STEVE: The Golden Rule is, "Do unto others as you would have them do unto you." Well, I changed it to, "Do unto others as you'd have them do unto you, because you *are* doing it unto you."

If there's anything that I would say to people, it's that if it's clear to you that somebody could use help and you've got the help that they need, just do it. Do it for yourself.

HELP IS A FOUR-LETTER WORD

MAG: *You've just talked about helping other people. What about you? What's easier for you—asking someone to do something for you, or thanking someone for doing something for you?*

STEVE: It's much easier for me to thank somebody for doing something. Absolutely. And I do that…I thank more than I ever ask anybody. I try everything before I'll ask anybody to do something.

But to ask a friend or a neighbour or a relative, you know, "Would you mind doing this?" That's something I don't do. I'll ask the boys to do something, but I even hesitate to do that. I mean, to be honest with you, it's just not something that I do. I really value my sense of self-sufficiency and asking for help erodes it. Something's wrong if I have to ask somebody to do something.

If there's an emergency, then there's some leeway there. But if it's not an emergency, then either I'm incapable, or I made a bad plan. Either way, it comes down to the fact that I screwed up.

MAG: *Is it easier to ask for help from people who work for you?*

STEVE: If it's an employer-employee situation, that's different. They have something to do, and I'll just lay out what their responsibilities are for that day as per our employment contract.

But, you know—even with employees I don't ask for help much. I don't

Steve asks his son Max to be a human tow for a barbecue unit that needed to be transported to a party several miles away. Steve swears this is not illegal in his Florida neighbourhood.

think I'm very demanding in the area of, "I need you to do this, I need you to do that." I'm demanding in levels of performance and ways of doing things. But the actual picking of the things to do? No.

I mean, look at the way I shoot my television show. I drive that truck and trailer to the job; I'm one of the first people there. And then when I come home I dump out the holding tank and fill the thing up with water. I don't want to ask somebody else to do that. I don't want to ask somebody to drive my trailer out to the job when I'm perfectly capable of doing it.

MAG: *Do you* want *to do it?*

STEVE: I do. I think it helps my relationship with everybody, including myself, that I'm not above them. They're driving cube vans, which is way easier than driving that tractor-trailer of mine.

MAG: *So you don't want them to think that* you *think you're above them. But they do know you're the person in control?*

STEVE: Well, I think we're all aware that I am, but I don't need to grind it into their face. I don't need to arrive in a limo after everything's set up and no one is allowed to make eye contact with me and all that kind of stuff.

It's not how I see myself and it's not how I see them. There's just no respect in that. I don't think that when you show people respect it means that you're on the same level, either up or down. It's just the right way to do it.

APPROVAL RATINGS

MAG: *We've talked about how hard it is for you to ask for help. Is there anyone you seek approval from?*

STEVE: Well, approval means a lot to me. I pretend that it doesn't, but it does.

And *disapproval* means even more to me than approval.

I'm surrounded daily with positive feedback, and yet there'll be one negative thing that might happen once every three months—that's the one that sticks with me. That's just a vulnerability issue. And it doesn't bother me nearly as much as it used to because I'm feeling less vulnerable than ever before.

But I'm not one of these people who doesn't care about the public. I can read a bad review of something I've done, but the truth is, I wish it were a good review. It's not neutral to me. I don't just say, "Well, that's just one man's opinion."

I say, "No, you know what? That hurt."

But it didn't hurt enough—it doesn't change me. When something happens where it's really somebody saying, "Why can't you be more like me?"—well, I can't do anything about that.

Although for a brief instant I feel sorry that I'm *not* more like them, I need to be me for a million reasons—there's no other reason for me to exist. If I'm going to simply be a version of somebody else, why not just let them do it?

So if something negative happens, if I have disapproval, I'll go down for a while. But I come back. And what I'm finding with the *Red Green* experience is that I've had so much approval, and I get so much approval still, that I was almost feeling like I've got to keep doing the show because it would be ungrateful for me not to keep doing it. But I'm past that too.

Because really, what they're approving of, is that they like what we're doing. If what we're doing changes for the worse they won't like it anymore. So I'm going to save them that, I'm going to stop doing it before it gets worse.

MAG: *So, ultimately, it's the audience's approval that means more to you than the approval of friends or family.*

STEVE: Yes. You know, bias is never a good thing, even when it's positive. It just throws off all of your instruments. I want to know what somebody who *doesn't* know me thinks of me. That is a way better indicator of the temperature than the thermometer that's sitting right next to the stove.

And how many people get the kind of feedback that I get? There's nobody I know who gets more positive feedback than I do.

MINING STORIES

MAG: *I was thinking of asking you how you've been helped in your life and who has helped you the most. But now I know how much you dislike asking for help. So I think you* have *helped yourself, just by being aware and alert. For example, a lot of us would hear people's stories and forget them, but you don't. You have a great memory for stories and you tend to get the meat off the bone. You look for the meaning.*

STEVE: I mine those stories. They're huge. I just have a fantastic interest in people's stories.

For example, the guy across the street from me is about eighty-five. His father had a nothing job and died when the guy was only twenty. His brother was twenty-two. The mother never worked.

We're going back sixty years. So what the heck are they going to do? Well, the first thing he does is drop out of school. His brother was already out of school, working in a factory, and they've only got the one income.

So he goes down to the basement. His father had been a part-time inventor, so he's going through about three hundred inventions in the basement, all over the place, half-done—flotsam and jetsam.

Anyway, he finds this little two-burner hotplate that plugs into the wall. This is 1930 or so. This twenty-year-old kid says, "Okay, *this* is what we're going to do."

He takes this invention and goes around to stores trying to get them to pick it up. Simpsons picks it up. The first order is, like, a hundred units. So now he's got to make them.

His brother, who is the factory worker, knows how an assembly line works. So his brother puts the manufacturing together while he does the sales, and away they go. Bing, bang! Next thing you know, they're making stoves and he's a multi-millionaire. He goes back to school, gets a degree and ends up starting York University.

And it's just like, man, that wasn't a setback to him. That was, "Okay, let's take a look, just stand back."

MAG: *But you* are *editing out all the doubt he felt.*

STEVE: Exactly. You have to. That's what I'm telling you; I'm looking at the other end.

MAG: *But achieving the end goal isn't people's whole experience of life. What do you say to the people who might find themselves wondering how to move forward…I mean, the guy had to feel some doubt.*

STEVE: Oh, for sure he did.

MAG: *What makes him capable of going past his doubt?*

STEVE: I don't know what it was in his particular case. But his initial response was to see what he could do that would be at a higher level than just getting a job beside his brother on the assembly line. His reaction was, "That's not going to do it. I know that's an option, but that's not going to do it."

Instead, you start with, "Is it attainable?" With no regard for the difficulty, the obstacles, the time frame, just—"Is it attainable?" If you decide it is, then you go to the next phase—"I can't fail."

As soon as I *don't* at least try something, I fail. So, I try it. And if that doesn't work, I try something else. But the thing is, if I don't *try*, I've failed before I begin.

What are we worried about? Stop worrying, and take some chances. What are we so afraid of?

MAG: *You said it yourself—"failure."*

STEVE: Yes—but you've got to define success first.

DEFINING SUCCESS

MAG: *How do you define it?*

STEVE: Success is a very personal thing. You can define it and you can create it, but you have to be really honest with yourself about what it is that you consider success. If it's all the trappings, all the things that cost money, then you've got to face that. And you've got to go find a way to make all kinds of money.

But if you're lucky, like I am—where it's all happening in your own mind— then if you have people around you who you care about and vice versa….well, it ain't bad. And if you've got some shelter and the basics, that doesn't feel like failure to me. I can't get upset about that or consider that to be a wasted life.

You know, it doesn't take a lot to make me happy. If I can do something that I enjoy and that satisfies my needs in terms of putting a roof over my head, that's all I need. I don't need to be driving around in fancy cars and living in fancy houses.

MAG: *You don't need to be, but you are.*

STEVE: I absolutely am. And proud of it. Damn proud of it. And the more I can do to convince somebody who's nineteen right now, somebody who has a lot more talent—and, believe me, there are lots of them—that they can do what I did, they can do it this way and have a great life, the better.

People might get mad that I drive a nice car and live in a nice house and they think that's really showing off. But I'm proud of that achievement. And I think it's a great example. I never saw anybody in the Canadian entertainment business when I was growing up who had been successful monetarily, and stayed here, in Canada. They all go to the States—that's the normal option—but why does it have to be the only option?

The final cast shot of past and present lodge members at the taping of the 300th episode, November 5, 2005.

CHAPTER FIVE

PUTTING THE SHOW TOGETHER

FROM IDEA TO SCRIPT

PUTTING THE SHOW TOGETHER

FROM IDEA TO SCRIPT

READY, AIM, FOCUS

MAG: *Back in the* Comedy Mill *days, I used to admire your ability to focus. You could be surrounded by total chaos and you would seem unaware of it as you worked on writing a script or memorizing lines. What is the secret of your ability to concentrate?*

STEVE: You know, it may be something that you're born with—that you're looking through a microscope rather than binoculars. You have that ability to just absolutely convince yourself that something is just so important that whatever else is happening in your life, it comes *after* that. It's through some doorway. You can't get through that door unless you get this thing done.

Opposite: Steve wracks his brains to remember the last time he was lazy.

I think it's my nature to absolutely focus on something. I've got to do that thing because I'm going to pick up the secret key while I'm doing that, and that's going to open the door into the next thing. So, I think I start with that as my nature, and then I've been tremendously rewarded for having that attitude.

I get a lot of work done. I don't know any writer, honestly, who's as prolific as I am. I focus and—bang!—I can just do it. Just focus in, and get it done. Then you get it done and it's not bad and you build a career on it and you're thinking, "That's pretty positive feedback from that particular approach." So it encourages you to do it the next time.

Writing is a part of me that I can't control, and that's frustrating.

I do think there's some connection between keeping your word and focusing. Like if I said I would do something and I didn't do it, it just haunts me. I can't sleep at night. I have to phone someone or do something. Mainly, the key is to just do it. I do the thing to avoid the pain that I know I'll feel if I don't do it. If I let someone down, I let myself down. Ask Max and Davy about that, how I feel about keeping your word.

MAG: *When you're working and you can feel a new idea percolating in your mind, can you check on it and track it?*

STEVE: Oh, definitely. My head has different zones. The forehead is just the reception area. But all the decisions—the real stuff—are happening in the back room. Nobody gets to the back room. That's where it's all going on.

And I know when something's going on because I always get this sense that I can't use all of my brain to do things. It's downloading something or other. It's working on something.

THE WRITER

MAG: *With writing, what is it like for you to get into the right mood? Or are you always in that mood?*

At the cottage in 1985, Steve writes on his first computer—the "transportable" Panasonic Senior Partner—a 35-pound behemoth that came with its own handtruck.

STEVE: Writing is a part of me that I can't control, and that's frustrating. So it's like having a little kid who's a child star, and the family derives its income and defines itself around this uncontrollable thing. When you want it to do something, it doesn't necessarily feel like it. It's not that it's trying to be obstinate; it just doesn't feel like it at that moment. That part of me is oblivious to the needs of the rest of me. So I work on *fooling* that part of me.

I don't say this to people, but—when somebody gives me a writing job or I've taken on a writing job—the big fear is that I'm making a commitment for that part of me that wasn't at the meeting and did not make the agreement, and may not take kindly to it. That scares me a lot, that I take on work hoping that this part of me will come around.

So I tease it. That's why I write on a boat. Or I surround myself with things that would make a very nice life. I'm trying to shame that part of me into feeling some sort of gratitude or indebtedness. "You're being rewarded, this is a pretty good deal, so come on, you keep your end of the bargain."

I never get up in the morning and say, "Oh boy, I can't wait to write." But I'll say, "I'm looking forward to going down to the boat." So I'll go down to the boat. I'll take my computer. And I'll turn the computer on. Maybe I'll play a game or maybe I'll check my email. And before you know it, I'll get that part of me. It comes.

You know, there are some times when that part of me is just exploding. It just wants to go. It's got a whole bunch of ideas. And that's just fun. I'm just sitting there taking dictation, basically.

But writing for television is very hard on that part of me because of the quantity of it. You're not just going to sit down and even write a book. We

Steve focuses on memorizing a monologue for the "mid-life" segment of the show, 2003.

do seven hundred pages a year. That's probably four books. Then—boom!—it's gone. And then the next year you do another four. Holy Mackerel, that's a lot of stuff.

I don't think I'm that good a writer. I think I'm good, but I don't think I'm that good. I think I'm actually right where I should be, writing for TV. I can handle the quantity. It's not painless, but I can handle it. And I think I'm good enough that people find it amusing, but they're not going to be sitting there reading my scripts in public school twenty-five years from now.

Steve's writing haven on his houseboat, Queen B. This is where Mag conducted all of her interviews with Steve. The cool thing about the coffee table between the couches is that it's mounted on an old barber's chair pedestal, so it can be pumped up to regular table height for dining.

MAG: *You say that sometimes the writer part of you is just burgeoning, full of ideas. Does it have to do with feeling rested, or being under pressure or some other condition? How do you get into that state?*

STEVE: I'm the opposite of most people. I usually get into the mood to write when I don't feel pressure. When I'm not close to a deadline.

I also have another part of me—a second string—that considers itself a writer and fills in when the first string is on the bench or didn't show up for the game. So I can fill in the pages. I can cover that. The second string is usually the part of me that kicks in when I get under pressure.

> *When it comes to keeping your word, my dad is a raging zealot capable of unspeakable acts of human suffering. But he has a point.*
> *—Max Smith*

Right now, for example, by the time I go to bed on Saturday night, I have to have a whole bunch of work done, and I'm behind. It bothers me. I hate being like that because I pride myself on planning that I won't be behind. I keep a regular schedule so I don't get behind, and yet, here I am. And I somehow get behind every year, no matter how much I try to stay on top of it. I know how I get here—that little brat doesn't want to work some days.

MAG: *Are there any rituals, like having coffee or something, that you do before you start to write?*

STEVE: In Canada, I have coffee and a raisin tea biscuit every morning. I go to Tim Horton's coffee shop. And I eat the whole tea biscuit and then I drink the coffee. I don't want to just put coffee into my stomach, you know? So I get the tea biscuit—the shock absorber—in there first. Then I throw the coffee at it. And I really, really like that.

On a shoot day, I pick up the coffee and tea biscuit in the car as I'm driving to the marina to get the trailer, but I won't have it until I'm on the highway.

MAG: *What about when you're in Florida? You've been spending winters there since '96, so you've done a lot of your writing in that environment.*

STEVE: In Florida, I don't go out. I just make the coffee. It's a whole different thing in Florida. Our house is just...open. We have a door at the back that's probably sixteen feet wide, one of those sliders that folds into itself. So I get up in the morning and I just open that up and it's just like, "Oh man, this is pretty neat." I don't need to go anywhere. It's very welcoming. The weather isn't daring me to go outside, so I don't feel the need to get myself jump-started. I'm already going just seeing that.

LAZY DOES IT

MAG: *You said you have a second string guy who takes over the writing when necessary. Do you ever find that he doesn't have anything to say? What do you do then?*

STEVE: I have a momentary sense of despondency, and then I just leave it. I go do something else. I've written a lot of stuff in a short amount of time before—when a fire is burning, it will consume things quickly. When it's not burning, there's not too much you can do to use up the firewood. You might as well wait till the fire's going. But when it goes, it really goes.

I have a certain level of annual output, but I don't do it evenly. On a day when I don't write anything, I know that tomorrow I'm going to write two days' worth. Or that someday soon, it will all even out. So I don't get too bugged about it.

But I do consider myself to have a lazy streak. So I'm very sensitive to the signs. If I got into the pattern of, "Well, I'll give it half an hour," then, if it's not happening, it'd be, "Oh, it's not happening today." I can't do that. I just could *not* enjoy that day, because I'd be wondering which of those revelations came first—the one that I'm having trouble, or the one that today's not the day.

MAG: *Give me an example of a time when you were lazy.*

STEVE: I haven't been lazy in a long time. I just think I have that natural tendency.

MAG: *Well, what's a lazy moment for you? Or a lazy day?*

STEVE: You know, if I was supposed to cut the lawn and, instead, I went to the movies— I'd put that into the lazy category. And, like a dog, not caring about what's going to happen later. I mean, I think we all know something's going to happen later. But, honestly, I haven't been lazy in a long time.

MAG: *You can't remember a single example of being lazy?*

STEVE: Oh! I'll give you lazy!

Back when I was delivering mail, I would sometimes just dump the contents of the mailbag back into the mailbox and go home. All of the letters would go back through the system again and I'd get them again the next day.

MAG: *Okay, that's a bit lazy.*

STEVE: Yeah.

MAG: *But that was thirty-five years ago.*

STEVE: And then when I worked for that gear company, I was supposed to do cold calls on factories to sell them gears. I would drive up and down the streets and just write down the names of the companies and make up a name of a guy,

Steve prefers an immaculate environment, while Red (*Opposite*) feels that an unholy mess is evidence of sincere effort.

or I might go in and ask for a name. I'd never *see* the guy. And I'd fill out those reports.

I had that job for about a year. That was one of those jobs I quit about a minute and a half prior to when they were going to fire me.

BULLDOZING THROUGH

MAG: *Nowadays, you seem extremely diligent and organized with writing deadlines and scheduling your time. And you're pretty fastidious too. You like your environment really tidy, and things have got to be in the place they're supposed to be.*

STEVE: I freak out if somebody's taken the phone book and hasn't put it back where they got it. I sure don't mind them using it, but this is a community here.

Either we each have our own phone book, which seems a little excessive to me, or we put the phone book back where it was.

Now the thing is, I'm not perfect. I might sometimes take the phone book and not put it back where it's supposed to be. But I feel *bad* about it! With other people it's just like, "Good Lord, it's a phone book!" No, this is nothing to do with it being a phone book. It's a system of *order*.

There's a time to delegate and there's a time when you just have to put your head down and bulldoze right through.

I think that started for me when I left my last job and we went into the band. There was no safety net. You know, when you're teaching, you can phone in sick. In a band, although it seems like a pretty sketchy, frivolous occupation, you're actually on the line all the time. You've got bills to pay and any missed detail can scupper you—having the vehicles running, getting the equipment to the job and working properly, having everybody be on time and with all their stuff together.

MAG: *When was that?*

STEVE: It would have been 1971. I think that's when it started because I was the leader of Jason, our band, and I kind of felt more like a parent. I was three or four years older than anybody else in the band. One guy was in Grade Eleven or something, and I just felt really bad for him. I didn't want him to go down the tubes. So it started with that.

And then when I got into TV, I really found that if I wanted to get where I wanted to go, I had to be able to handle a lot of information. I had to be so focused on seeing things through, making sure to take things all the way to the end, not just get them started.

I know people who talk about how they can delegate. Well, there's a time to delegate and there's a time when you just have to put your head down and bulldoze right through. If you're surrounded by people who care far less than you do, then it's extremely dangerous to delegate. I always felt that I was the one who cared the most, so I figured I should be running the show.

The same thing goes for parenting. Morag and I would talk about parenting and, you know, somebody's going to discipline your children. If you don't do it, the teachers will do it. If the teachers don't do it, the kids' friends will do it. If their friends and teachers don't do it, the neighbours, the relatives will do it… then the police will do it. And eventually society does it. It's not like your kids are going to get away with it.

So, if you accept that they're going to be disciplined, shouldn't they be disciplined by the people who care about them the most? Isn't that the better way to do it?

MAG: *Right. I've often heard you say, "Whoever cares the most should be in charge."*

STEVE: Yes.

MAG: *And you care a great deal about writing, so you don't delegate that. As head writer on* Red Green, *how much of your time do you give to writing? Do you work every day, or how do you pace it?*

STEVE: I work every day. And I resent it and appreciate it both at the same time. I resent it going in, and then when I've done it I always feel better, so there's a reward at the other end. If I go for two to three days without writing anything, I'm cranky.

I need to do that exercise and have that outlet. And it has to be something worthwhile. If I didn't have a use for the writing, if I didn't have a contract or some worthwhile purpose for it, it wouldn't be the same. I need to satisfy myself that it's worth the effort, that I'm not just treading water.

There are times when I write something and I think, "Oh, what a great feeling." That's just a great feeling, regardless of what happens from here forward. But in Florida I find myself much more prolific than I am here. I only work half a day in Florida. I get up about seven, I'm usually writing by seven-thirty, and by noon I'm done. And that's it for the day.

I get so much more done because in the afternoon I'll go play golf or whatever I want to do. And here, I mean, I'll work eighteen hours a day and not get that output. It's bizarre.

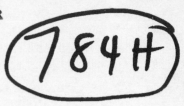

SHOOTING SCRIPT # 784H
FINAL DRAFT

RED STANDS IN HIS WORKSHOP.

> RED
> This week on the Handyman Corner
> since I'm on the water diet, we're
> going to build a water purification
> system. The human body is about 70
> percent water so that's important. ,
> The rest is cholesterol and fat and
> additives. Okay for starters you're
> going to need a big container of
> some kind..

SWINGS A BIG PLASTIC GARBAGE CAN UP ON TO THE BENCH AND
STARTS WIPING OUT WITH AN OILY RAG

> Clean it out real good but that's
> not enough.

PICKS UP PROPANE TORCH AND LIGHTS IT

> You have to sterilize it, which is a
> scary concept to most men. But all's
> you need to is burn the crap out of
> it. There are germs and bacteria
> that can survive soap and water but
> die in a good sized propane flame.

WAVES IT AROUND THE INSIDE OF THE CONTAINER.

> If you can't take the heat, get out
> of the water purifier.

RED TOUCHES OFF FLASH PAPER HIDDEN UNDER RIM

> There's a bad bit. Glad I didn't
> drink that.

PUTS TORCH DOWN BEHIND BENCH.

> Okay, now we need water purification
> tablets, halizone tablets, but I got
> these from Old Man Sedgewick...

HOLDS UP TWO JARS OF PILLS

> which means they're halitosis
> tablets, which is pretty much the
> same as halizone I believe. And
> these are his nitro pills which
> we'll throw in because we can.

STARTS POURING PILLS INTO THE TUB.

> Okay, now we need something to
> filter the water. Now fish tanks
> have charcoal filters, and fish
> don't just drink water, they do
> everything in it. So the charcoal
> must work good.

PULLS OUT BAG OF CHARCOAL BRIQUETS AND POURS IT IN THE TUB.

> Just lay your charcoal in there. And
> remember, we're trying to remove
> germs and particles and chemicals

THE FIRST STRINGER

MAG: *You said that if you're not writing well, you drop it. What do you do then?*

STEVE: I generally really like doing things with my hands. Like, I'll do a jigsaw puzzle; I'm almost always doing jigsaw puzzles. I have a slot machine here on the boat. I have a pool table at home.

I love it when something breaks, when something's not working, because I know how to fix it. If the motor's not working on the boat or something, I just love that.

I'm trying to impress myself one way or another. I like to make myself laugh.

Then at the end of the day I know I've accomplished *something.* Whereas just sitting there in front of the computer could be a huge waste of time. So if you're doing something *while* you're thinking, even if you're cutting the lawn while you're writing in your mind, you know one thing—by the end of the day the lawn's going to be cut.

And I find that tends to free things up, too; takes the pressure off. I'm not very good under pressure, I can tell you that for sure. I'm absolutely not very good under pressure.

MAG: *With writing?*

STEVE: With anything. If I walk into a group of people and feel an expectation, I just recoil. If I sense it'll be there before I go, I won't go. I'll do anything I can not to be in a situation where I sense expectation.

MAG: *You've talked about your first stringer, that part of you that brings the value to your writing. How do you protect it?*

Opposite: A single page of script, one of seven hundred produced by Steve and his writing team each season.

STEVE: Well, I think if you had a friend who you cared about, you would respect that friend. You'd be sensitive to that friend's wishes and you'd try to help make their life better.

So, if you consider that part of your mind as a friend, not a tool or a slave, then it's something that you are sensitive to, that you respect and want to take care of. You base a lot of your decisions on wanting to protect that part of you.

If I could recommend any version of success, I'd recommend mine.

If you know that putting that entity into a certain environment is going to be very difficult for it and will have repercussions that may last weeks, you just don't do it. In my case, because that's all I've got that's in any way special, I'm not going to be messing it up.

MAG: *When you're writing, what's your aim? Is it to make yourself laugh?*

STEVE: Yes. Absolutely. I'm trying to impress myself one way or another. I like to make myself laugh. The thing is, I get really fed up with other people who write for me if they start to write like my *second* string. I don't need that. I can do that. And over the years, I tend to weed them out, but once in a while I'll get something from somebody and I'll think, "Oh, this is fantastic. Oh, thank God."

MAG: *Which part of you—the first or second string—edits your own work or someone else's?*

STEVE: The first string—the part of me that's so hard to deal with, the part of me that doesn't necessarily want to write. It's the first one there when it comes to editing. It's going, "Who do you think you are?"

How weird is that?

MAG: *I can see that. If the guy who's your second string sits down to write a script, it just makes the first string guy want to come out and do it right.*

STEVE: I'll say to the first stringer, "If you stay over there, *I'm* going to write this!"

MAG: *You're trying to coax the first stringer to come online by taunting him with the possibility of inferior second-string work.*

STEVE: Right.

MAG: *So in a way, you're two people.*

STEVE: I'm sure everybody is two people, but I don't know everybody, I just know myself. It's almost like there's the person and there's the valet. And the two of them kind of come together and you never know which one you're talking to. I definitely have the two. And I think each of them knows what his role is.

BEGINNING AT THE END

MAG: *You seem to have a high value of your own opinion.*

STEVE: Yes. Is that bad?

MAG: *I don't know. How has it affected your life?*

STEVE: Well, I'm convinced that I can make people laugh. I can't make everybody laugh, but I can make a lot of people laugh. I can make *enough* people laugh. And when I'm making them laugh, I'm doing what I think is funny. I don't have to worry about adjusting it for what the market is like. "Right now everybody likes jokes about blondes." "Okay, well, I'll write jokes about blondes." I don't even think about that. I just do what I think is funny right now.

I've had experiences before where I'd be hired to write an episode of a sitcom or something like that. *They* tell you the script, they tell you the *jokes*. I guess that's just the format. And it's just like, "Ugh."

So what happened out of that was, "This is crap. Okay, I'm writing crap."

And you get paid well for it. Then they produce it, it's crap. It goes on TV, it's crap. Everybody thinks it's crap. I learn *nothing*.

But if I do something that I think is funny and it's crap, I learn something. And if I do something that I think is funny and it catches, I learn way more. I've been encouraged. Probably the worst thing that could have happened to me is if I'd been a writer on a bad sitcom and it clicked.

Steve and Patrick McKenna rehearse a sizzling scene in the show's second season, 1992.

I knew enough people like that who had had tremendous financial success and were so disappointed by it that it enabled me to rationalize mediocre success.

If I could recommend any version of success, I'd recommend mine. It is absolutely the best. I've got just enough money. I can't afford to buy something that would really kill me. I can only buy things that would hurt me a little bit.

And I'm famous enough that enough people say, "Hey!" But I don't need an entourage. I can go anywhere. The worst that's going to happen is the chef's going to come out and get his picture taken with me. I mean, who would I envy? So I recommend that.

MAG: *You've talked about how you like to envision the end goal so you know what you're working toward. When it comes to writing—can you feel the end of a script before you start to write it?*

STEVE: Oh yeah, absolutely. With every script, I have the end in mind first before I can write anything. I've got to know where I'm going.

I start with the ending. I've got the ending of the scene or the ending of the script in mind. And then I try to go backwards in the most interesting way, so that I end up with a starting point way over there.

A writer is someone with a new point of view.

Like, what would be the most bizarre way to get to Hamilton? You could get to Hamilton through the Cape of Good Hope. No one would ever expect that. Not unbelievable, just surprising.

MAG: *Do you actually track all of the events backwards, or is it more of an intuitive sense?*

STEVE: It's intuitive. The way I work with the writers on my show is that I don't let them write scripts. "Send me your ideas. What's your idea for a script?" I don't want them invested in some script that I don't like. Even a three-page thing. Don't write three pages. Write me a little idea. Because I might have done it before—that's what I say to them as an excuse, but really what I'm saying is, "Where's the ending?"

I want to see the ending. I don't want to wait three pages to see it.

A NEW POINT OF VIEW

MAG: *How do you define a writer?*

STEVE: A writer has to have two things. Number one, an ability to look at the world differently than other people. And, number two, a positive reaction from people who see that viewpoint and go, "That's interesting. I've never looked at it that way before." If you don't have those two things, as far as I'm concerned, you're not a writer. You don't have anything to say.

A writer is someone with a new point of view. When you see Jerry Seinfeld and he just fires out a thousand new points of view—man, that's just such a gift.

If your point of view is the same as everybody else's…I guess there's some value in just *articulating* it better, but that's more of a secretary than a writer.

I don't think you can fix something through add-ons and re-jigs and re-fits. You can put a spoiler and Michelin tires on a Lada—but it's still a Lada.

I think that is the key, whether it's television or whatever it is. You might get tied up in the technology and the appearance and the mood—all the accessories—but if that basic thing is not there, I don't think it works. I don't think it'll get an audience.

Even these reality shows. The core of those is someone who had a new point of view, a new way of looking at relationships or drama or whatever. And everybody goes, "Wow, that's kind of interesting." I mean, *Survivor* is not just throwing a bunch of people on an island and seeing what happens. It's totally produced and managed. It is a script.

Is reality television here to stay? No. Nothing is here to stay. Somebody will come along with another new thing. But the big changes are always that fresh new way of looking at things.

MAG: *When you hire writers, are you looking for their point of view in a conversation before you hire them? How do you know that they have a new point of view?*

STEVE: Usually people submit scripts. I don't go and talk to people about writing. I just judge it by the script. And if I see something interesting in the script, something where I go, "Wow, that was kind of neat," that's good enough for me.

MAG: *As you're writing, do you find that you're surprised by what comes out of your own brain?*

STEVE: All the time. And I don't have to be writing—I'm surprised in conversations. My mind, for better or for worse, is extremely fast. It makes associations and I'm saying the words before I've even *thought* of them. I've always had that. My mind makes very quick associations and sometimes they're very odd. I like that.

RED GREEN III STORY IDEAS

1. PARKING PROBLEMS

TO RELIEVE THE PARKING CONGESTION, THEY DECIDE TO DIG
THEIR OWN UNDERGROUND PARKING LOT WITH A HOMEMADE
TICKET MACHINE AND A MEMBER TO TAKE THE MONEY. THEY
DON'T DIG DEEP ENOUGH AND THE VAN JAMS IN THERE AND
THEN IT FLOODS AND FREEZES AND EVERYBODY'S CAR IS
EMBEDDED IN ICE.

2. FISHING CONTEST

THE VARIOUS WAYS THE GUYS CHEAT IN THE VARIOUS
CATEGORIES. LONGEST FISH, HEAVIEST FISH, THICKEST FISH,
MOST UNUSUAL FISH, OLDEST FISH, SMARTEST FISH.

3. WIFE DAY

MAKESHIFT ALTERATIONS AND CLEAN UP OF THE LODGE TO MAKE
IT ACCEPTABLE TO THE WIVES AND GIRLFRIENDS COMING UP ON
WIFE DAY.

4. CROSS THE LAKE RACE

THE VARIOUS TECHNIQUES USED BY THE MEMBERS TO WIN THE
ANNUAL RACE ACROSS POSSUM LAKE.

5. LODGE GARAGE SALE

WHAT CAN BE SOLD AND FOR HOW MUCH. BETWEEN THE
GUYS BRINGING ALL THEIR CRAP FROM HOME AND THE
RELUCTANCE OF THE LODGE TO PART WITH ANYTHING,
BY THE END VERY LITTLE IS PUT UP FOR SALE AND
NONE OF IT SELLS AND THEY END UP WITH MORE JUNK
THAN THEY STARTED WITH.

6. WILDERNESS SKILLS DEMONSTRATION

CHAINSAW CARVING, CROSS BOW TELECOMMUNICATIONS, SHOTGUN
SIGN MAKING

7. CARPENTER ANTS AT POSSUM LODGE

THE PROBLEMS AND SOLUTIONS OF ELIMINATING THE
CARPENTER ANTS AND THEIR DAMAGE.

8. FUEL CONVERSION

THE MEMBERS ARE CONVERTING ALL OF THEIR
VEHICLES TO RUN ON FIREWOOD.

9. POSSUM LODGE PROMO

So, yes, I get surprised all the time. I love it when it's just rolling because I know, when it's rolling, I can't get my fingers down on the keyboard fast enough.

MAG: *Do you have a theory of what humour is?*

STEVE: I have a million theories of what humour is. Mainly, I think it's just a gift. It's a way of processing information that's unusual and surprising. And rare. I'll say something and I'll think, "Man, that was *funny*." I never saw it coming. I'm hearing it along with everybody else.

I even have dreams and somebody will say something in the dream, and I'll think, "That is so funny! Why can't I think of things like that?" And it's *my* dream!

MAG: *I always think that the guy who makes the joke is the one with the broadest perspective on the situation—he's coming from a place where nothing is a problem.*

STEVE: That's right. He's so much in control that he can make fun of whatever's going on. If you can say what everybody else is thinking in a funny way, you're gold.

CREATING THE SCRIPT

MAG: *How much do you rework your material after you write it?*

STEVE: Well, I'm an odd writer in that I don't do very many drafts. I'll do them if I have to. The first one takes forever, but it's so close to what we end up doing.

Overleaf: A page of script ideas for Season Three from long-time staff writer, Rick Green (Page 1 of 13).

I'm always writing. The ideas are always churning around. Like, I'm writing right now in my mind. I'm working on a movie spoof now for *Steve Smith Playhouse*. This episode is called "Terror in the Rented House." The whole movie's in my head. My mind is reworking scenes and changing the dialogue of the characters. That's all happening right now while we're having this conversation. I won't even get to that till Thursday night, but by the time I get to it, I've already done four drafts in my mind.

Steve Smith Playhouse is a series in which Steve takes B-movies, cuts them down to half an hour and uses his voice to replace that of the lead character while all the other characters' performances remain untouched, often changing the plot and tone of the original movie.

So the first draft is not really a first draft.

I have a writer who will send me twenty scripts, and maybe two of them have got something in them. In the same time he wrote twenty, I've only written three, but all three of mine are useable. It's just a different approach. I think more people are like him than like me in terms of churning out the quantity, rather than limiting themselves and letting it go through the process.

Whereas I don't think you can fix something through add-ons and re-jigs and re-fits. You can put a spoiler and Michelin tires on a Lada—but it's still a Lada. So if I see a script that I don't like, I don't want to waste the effort.

For me, one of the frustrating things about getting scripts is if somebody's late on a script for me. I'm going freaky, I'm emailing them everyday, "What's going on? Have you got a problem?" I finally get the script, I open it up, it sucks! Brutal.

MAG: *When you start reading a script, how soon can you tell that it's a tanker?*

STEVE: Usually in the first half-page, it's like, "Uh, oh." Then I'm looking for some glimmer of hope, and I get to the end and it's, "Ooops."

So then I just start over. I start with a blank page. But I'm really *mad* because if I'm going to start from a blank page, I could've done that a week ago. That gets me fried.

And they know. This is another thing that happens. Writers know when they just don't quite have it, and there's nothing that can be done by anybody, including them. Chastising people over their writing isn't going to do any good. You're not telling them anything they don't know. They just, for whatever reason, didn't get a good fit.

I mean, Mickey Mantle strikes out. He walks back to the dugout. What are you going to say to him? Nothing. There's no point in saying anything. He's a great hitter who happened to strike out, you know? So you just kind of let it ride. But I convince myself that the writer has the potential of helping me, and that they work hard. That's all.

Steve as host of *Steve Smith Playhouse* on SPACE.

WHEN SCRIPTS GO BAD

MAG: *How do you deal with bad scripts?*

STEVE: When I get a bad script from somebody, it's not really that I'm angry that the script is bad. It's that it's really hard for me to convince myself that this writer is going to be able to help me on the next script. So I'm like, "Uh oh. I'm more alone than I thought I was."

And the reverse of that is, when I get a good script, it's, "Oh, thank God. I'm not alone. Next week when I have to do another forty pages, I'm going to have help. This guy's going to come through again."

I think if you were building something, doing carpentry work, it's much more reliable. The guy knows how to use a hammer and a saw, and he's probably going to do that same amount of work everyday when he shows up for work. You can kind of rely on that.

Writing just is not that way. You don't know what you're going to get. But I can't go to a broadcaster and say, "You know, we just didn't have it. We tried, but nothing happened that day."

I would love to write and not be paid for it. I would love to just be paid on whether they buy it after the fact, rather than be paid to do the writing. When somebody gives me a contract to write something, I consider that a huge negative. I'd like to say, "No, no, no, no. Let me write something that I *want* to write, and then if you want to buy it, I'll sell it to you."

But that's tough to do because you need to be able to risk spending all that time and not getting any reward for it.

MAG: *Does it cause weirdness between you and the writers if they're giving you bad scripts?*

STEVE: Uh-huh.

MAG: *So by the end of every season you find yourself distanced?*

STEVE: Yeah, I usually let a couple of writers go after a season.

MAG: *Only one season?*

STEVE: I don't usually carry the same team year in, year out. I find that some guys can write for a certain amount of time. If we were doing five episodes, they'd be great. But then they're burnt. They just can't do it. They've used it all up.

When writers start with me, they're Contributing Writers. So I assign them a script and they write it. If I like it, I assign them another one. I might assign them two or three or whatever. And they can get comfortable with that.

But all the time they want to be a Show Writer. And once they get to be a Show Writer, they're so delighted because they get an eighteen-episode contract and it's a lot better money than being a Contributing Writer. But what comes with that is the expectation. I expect them to generate their share and rewrite everybody else's. And that bogs them down.

MAG: *Consistently? They all bog down?*

STEVE: I have a couple of keepers.

MAG: *How do you schedule writing the scripts and then shooting the shows?*

STEVE: I always stay six weeks ahead of the shoot, and it's not negotiable. Like with the writers, if they haven't written their thing, I'm not delaying it by twenty-four hours. If they haven't got it, I write it. And then you better not see me for a while.

But it's not a surprise. I tell them that New Year's Day. My deadlines are locked. That's how I work. It really helps everybody. I don't think you get better writing by waiting, and it also gives the production crew a chance to actually prepare the props and special effects in the scripts.

For me, it's the "finite-ness" that on September 30th I will finish writing the whole season. I still have six weeks of taping, but those are the six weeks I really enjoy. I'm just doing the show—I'm not having to write it. So that's the bonus.

If we were just a week ahead, I'd be writing right up to the last week, sweating that out, and then you get a week of shooting and then goodbye. There wouldn't be enough fun in that.

MAG: *How long is a script?*

STEVE: I publish forty-two pages of script a week. That means we have to generate forty-two pages of script a week. If I get twelve pages from all three of the other writers combined, then I generate thirty. But I'm not happy about it.

MAG: *How many pages do* you *want to be generating?*

STEVE: I want to be generating my share—ten or eleven pages—because I also rewrite everybody's work, and my rewrites of their stuff are often pretty severe. When I see a script that's not going to work, I've always got three options. One is to send it back to them and say, "Try a little harder." But I'm not dealing with guys who are shifty. They've already given it their best.

The second option is that I rewrite it heavily to turn it into what I want. And the third option—I've actually thought of this—is that I just go ahead and produce it the way they wrote it. I've always insisted that the writers come to the shows when they're being taped to see how their stuff works. So, they'd have to stand there and watch it die and see us die with it.

But I've never actually convinced myself to go with that option.

MAG: *Maybe the writers just have more faith than you do that your performance will make it funny.*

STEVE: It's the other way around—it should be funny just reading it. You shouldn't have to perform it.

Having your writing performed in front of a live audience and seeing what pushes the buttons—you can't ignore that. So all of that helps to keep your instruments calibrated.

Another thing—I really like tight writing. One of the writers sent me a script the other day—twenty-one pages long. It's three scenes. It should have been ten or eleven pages. It wasn't a bad script, I can hack it down, but—"What are you doing? Why do that?"

I feel like everybody wants content. Even in conversation. If you can

Before a live taping, Steve's son Davy runs the audience through the Possum Lodge motto: Quando Omni Flunkus Moritati ("When all else fails, play dead.")

say something in fifteen seconds, don't take ten minutes. Don't be using our friendship to grab that other nine and three-quarters minutes out of it. Because that's not fair.

Anyway, what it comes down to for me is that comedy, or anything creative, is very subjective. Ultimately, what we're saying is, somebody's got to make the call, and I've put myself in the position where I'm going to be the one to do that. And it doesn't matter whether what they wrote was funny or not. All that matters is that the audience agrees with my call.

So rather than beat the writers up because they see things differently from me, the truth is, I shouldn't be mad at all. Because I've got the power.

If I was the one who had the right answer and didn't have any power, that would be bad. Or if I was the one who had all the power and didn't have the right answer, that would also be bad.

FOUR STEPS TO A GOOD SCRIPT

MAG: *You clearly have high standards for your writers. Your son Davy is writing for you now. Do you have different standards for him? What happens if he disappoints you?*

STEVE: I tell him.

Both Max and Davy are very open to direction from me, or criticism. I don't always say it nicely. They're just fantastic. They're unbelievable.

When Davy started writing for me, I told him, "This is what I like. These are the four steps I want to see in a script."

Steve's son Davy joined S&S Productions in 2001 and began working as a Contributing Writer for *The Red Green Show* in 2003. In the final two seasons of the show, he was a Show Writer and also worked at every studio taping as the warm-up man for the audience.

MAG: *What are the four steps?*

STEVE: There's the Explanation, which is what you're trying to do. The Complication, which is what goes wrong. The Revelation, which is what you discover out of trying to fix the thing that went wrong. And then, the Twist.

Just a twist ending. A little extra bonus, a cherry on the whipped cream.

What I had Davy do was, when he'd send me ideas, he'd list the Explanation, the Complication, all of the steps. For maybe two or three months he had to do that. Just so I knew he was thinking that way. And now he just writes that way and his scripts are good. With him, I could break it down into those four simple steps. I wouldn't say that to one of my other writers.

> *You can't start solving a problem until you've identified it. That, to me, is something to take your time on.*

MAG: *Why not?*

STEVE: Well, they're just too fragile. They would consider that to be like telling them the letters of the alphabet. Whereas with Davy, I just say it. I don't care if I'm totally simplifying it. Because he knows I really like him.

So if something came across as harsh, Davy would blame it on something else. He'd think I must be mad at something else. But he would not fight the message; he just wouldn't take any offence in the delivery. He's really good. Max is the same way.

MAG: *So you can be frank with your sons, but with writers who have fragile egos, you find yourself holding back?*

STEVE: Oh, yeah.

MAG: *Are the writers aware of it?*

STEVE: I don't know. But I don't think it's a bad thing that I hold back. I think it's good for everyone. Because when I get a bad script, I don't want to see that person again—just for about five minutes. Then I'm okay.

But I'm thinking, "At what level was this good enough to send me? You've wasted electronic energy sending this through the air. You polluted our atmosphere with that script. How can you read all the stuff that we've done this season—we've done eighty-seven location scripts and we've done two hundred and eighty-five pages of studio script—that's a lot of stuff. That's what we're looking for. How could you send me yours and think it measures up against those other things?"

MAG: *You don't actually say that?*

STEVE: No. That's what's going through my mind. But what do I want out of it? Do I want to just vent my spleen and then somehow I'll feel better? No. That's not enough. I want these guys to write better. Would me venting make them write better? No. I think it'd just intimidate them.

So what I do is, I rewrite the script and send it back to them. When they see that only two words of theirs got used out of the whole script, that's my way of saying, "Take it up a notch."

At the end of the season, I go through all of the scripts and see who originated them. If a writer is taking twenty-five percent of the budget and generating eleven percent of the scripts, they have a problem. They know that. I tell them that going in. I do that every year.

MAG: *How do you know how much each writer has contributed in a season?*

STEVE: All of the scripts have the writers' names across the top. The first name is always the person who initiated the script, but I know how much I've changed it. It doesn't take a lot to figure it out because the bad writers don't get much produced, and I only look at the produced scripts when I'm adding up the totals. If a guy is consistently having his stuff heavily rewritten, chances are most of his scripts didn't even get produced. So he doesn't end up with much of a tally on the produced script total.

It's like having a mulligan in golf. It wasn't bad luck, it was a bad *swing*. And if you do it again, you'll have another bad result. So, it doesn't really change much. But at least I feel like, in doing it this way, it gives me my best chance of reaching my ultimate goal, which is for them to write

In golf, a mulligan is a shot retaken after a bad swing. Mulligans are strictly prohibited in the official rules of the game, but are commonplace in social golf.

better scripts. I feel it's much more educational than just yelling at them for not doing the right thing.

I assume they want to do good work because they're good guys. I'm assuming best efforts, and when they see how the script got changed—whether they think it's better or worse—they'll at least see, "This is the kind of thing he likes."

I'm not afraid of confrontation with them, but I don't want to be alone the next day having to write the rest of the season all by myself.

HIRE BEWARE

MAG: *Have you ever gotten into a real head-butting situation with a writer you've hired?*

STEVE: Never happened. I can't even think of a writer who didn't thank me for the experience. I mean, at the very least, they've got that on their résumé.

Although I don't yell at them or anything, I think they can sense when they're really not quite delivering. And part of the deal with me is that you have to come to the studio for the tapings so you see how the script works. Because, in addition to performing the studio scenes, we also play back all the stuff we shot on location, so the audience gets to react to it.

So, as a writer, it's not just that you're seeing the studio scenes you wrote, you're also seeing the location stuff you wrote. And if you're seeing consistently that other people's writing is getting the big laughs and your stuff is never getting anything—or not enough—and there's not very much of your writing being used either, well, it can't be a big shock to you when I say I'm going to go another way next year.

And I always do that really early. I let writers go long before there's even a hint of renewal. So it's not like they read in *Playback Magazine* that the show's been renewed and then they're waiting for the call. Plus, it makes it easier for me to say, "Whether we get picked up or not, I'm going to make changes."

Cracking up in rehearsal, 2003.

MAG: *Has anyone ever come to you and said, "I don't know what I'm doing wrong. I think I'm doing good work, but you just keep sending it back revised." Has anyone said, "Help me"?*

STEVE: Help me—no. Whining—yes. I've had that happen once. A writer who said to me, "Don't you like my writing? Because none of my scripts are getting approved. Do you not like my writing?"

That was a long time ago, and what I was thinking was, "Well, I think that's obvious." But what I said was, "Well, no, no, that's not it. It's just, you know, what I do is, I always have—" and this is true "—I always have about a dozen scripts I'm working on and I always work on the ones I like best. It doesn't mean I don't like yours, it just means I have others that I like better."

What I really should have said was, "Well, obviously I don't like your scripts. I'm not looking to have to do extra work. If I'm not doing them, I don't like them."

But I didn't do that. I would do that now. I resented being asked because it really wasn't a question. That person knew the answer. That was just his way of saying he didn't really appreciate my actions. I mean, what kind of question is that?

MAG: *Has it ever happened that you've submitted something and somebody just doesn't get it or see it?*

STEVE: Oh God, yeah. It's happened a bunch of times.

Like, early on in my career, I did a show called *Laughing Matters*. The director and I just didn't get along. We had a totally different sense of what was funny. And I was the head writer.

I was two or three weeks into a thirteen-week contract, and it was pretty good money. And I just said, "I'm done. Cancel the contract. Don't pay me. You've got a bunch of writers. Re-hire. I'll let you off, let me go away, I don't need the frustration and you can hire somebody you *want* way cheaper than what you're paying me."

They wouldn't let me go. The producer stepped in and said, "No way."

It was a very painful experience for me because, you know, the director was making the creative call. I was talking earlier about how I'm making the call now. But then, *he* was making the call.

Those experiences go into, "Okay, what's my reaction to that?" Well, my reaction is, from now on, *I'm* going to make the call. I would rather make the call on a low-budget show than have to live with somebody else's call on a high-budget show that sucks.

FAIR FACTOR

MAG: *Your eldest son, Max, has been working with your company for the last few years, and he's taken on a lot of responsibility. How much do you help him handle difficult situations or problems with networks?*

STEVE: I pay a lot more attention to how Max feels about the problem than to the problem itself. He doesn't get upset. He takes it all in stride. The main thing I could do to help Max, I'd already done by the time he was seven years old.

MAG: *What was that?*

STEVE: Help him to be the kind of person who can handle stuff like that. Give him a fairly strong sense of self and a belief that he'll be able to handle any setback. And hopefully, a way of dealing with people that doesn't totally alienate them.

But Max, with all the problems, absolutely loves his job and he's at it twenty-four hours a day. He just beams. One thing about Max is that he comes across as a pretty cool customer. But he's got friends all around the world, some that he's had for twenty years, and he's still got them. And they'll say to me, "Boy, I've never seen Max happier. He loves what he's doing."

Max produced *Sons of Butcher*, an animated series that ran for two seasons (2005-2006) and 26 episodes on the Teletoon Network in Canada. Due to its bizarre storylines, unique mixed video/animation style and original music, the show and its subsequent music video garnered a strong underground fan base and worldwide attention.

MAG: *In the course of writing, acting, producing shows and running a business, you must do a lot of problem solving. Would you say you're good at identifying problems?*

STEVE: I think I am. I think I'm way better at that than solving them. I think it's the same thing we talked about earlier—begin with the end in mind. It's like writing scripts backwards.

If you don't identify the problem first, nothing else matters. It's much more important than the solution. You can't start solving a problem until you've identified it. That, to me, is something to take your time on.

If somebody comes to me and they're upset or there's some upheaval of some kind and they're in tears telling me the story or whatever—I listen. But I probably don't come across as being very sympathetic because I'm *not* being sympathetic.

As I listen to what they're saying, I'm trying to figure out what really is the core problem of the thing. I find that if I can do that and then say it to them, then all of a sudden they're not in free fall anymore. And then I can say, "Okay, now you need a plan for how you can solve that."

MAG: *What's your method of figuring out where a problem is? Do you talk it out or write it out?*

Max and Steve take a golf break while attending the Banff World Television Festival, 2000.

STEVE: It's a mental process. I don't ever write it out. It might be something like when you go into the Emergency Ward and they ask you a few questions. The doctor's got an idea of what it is, but he asks you a few questions about what kind of pain you're having.

So I'll ask the person a few questions, get a little more information, but it's just a mental process of sifting through all the possibilities. I can do it pretty quickly.

And the longer I've known a person, the easier it is for me, because I may have seen something like this with them before. People tend to be more like they *were* than like they're about to be.

I really like doing that. I'd rather help the person identify the problem and let *them* solve it.

MAG: *Well, it'll help them more if they think of the solution themselves. And they need to make those decisions. Nobody else can.*

STEVE: Right. And I don't want them coming back next week saying, "What now?"

MAG: *You've talked about fairness a lot. How important is it to you?*

STEVE: I have a huge bond with fairness. I just feel that fair play and what's right are really important—it's really important that they prosper.

If you come to me and say, "What you're doing is not fair"—boy, you have one hundred percent of my attention. Rather than, "What you're doing really makes me mad." Then you get maybe sixty-one percent of my attention.

I like to stand up for what I think is fair and right. If we don't stand up for what we think is fair and just and right, then we're going to end up with a chaotic society where we can't trust anybody. And I don't want that.

I base everything on a sense of fair play—in my marriage and in my family and in my career and how I deal with my friends. It's completely based on an absolute core belief in fairness and fair play. So, if I see that core belief threatened or questioned or maybe it's even suggested that that's not the case, that maybe life is based on something entirely different than fair play—it just *can't* be. It's very upsetting for me. I wouldn't know how to deal with anybody then.

If we don't stand up for what we think is fair and just and right, then we're going to end up with a chaotic society where we can't trust anybody.

My experience is that successful businesses have great integrity. I've never had a business situation...well, I can't say "never." But ninety-nine percent of the time in business, if I'm being fair with some person, they really appreciate it and they don't try to take advantage of that.

That's a pretty good record.

A FEW MORE WORDS FROM MAX...

Dad's great. We're very close. I choose to live five blocks away from his house. I mean, he's obviously full of advice and he's got his own ideas on things, but he doesn't try to ram it down my throat. He knows that I'm pretty stubborn, and I'll go ahead and make the mistake he warned me about.

He's really persistent—it's one thing to decide that this is a good idea and he's going to pursue it for a while, but it's another thing to keep at it when *all* signs point to "No." It's funny because basically he spent his entire life not really listening to other people telling him that he shouldn't do this or he can't do that. So when he comes to me and says, "You shouldn't do this," or, "You can't do that," I'm like, "That's exactly the advice that you'd ignore. Do I take what you're telling me now, or do I take *you* as an example to me?"

Usually I ignore his advice and do it. Sometimes it's wrong, sometimes it's right.

We don't have the sort of relationship where there are things I don't say to him. I don't feel like he doubts how I feel about him. I hope he doesn't. He'd better not.

Happiness has been pervasive with my dad. I don't think of him as an emotional person. He was always the parent that didn't get mad quickly. When he got mad, it was *bad*. Normally it was mostly my mom getting mad, and then my dad making fun of her for being mad.

So if my mom was mad and my dad was there, you were probably okay. If my mom was mad by herself, it was dicey. But if my dad was mad, you had no allies—to her credit, my mom did sometimes make fun of him for being mad, but it didn't work as well.

My dad always made it very clear that you make choices all the time and if you make bad ones, he'd be disappointed. It was always in my mind anyway, that to do this thing or not do it...if my dad found out, he'd be angry or disappointed. It was never worth getting in trouble because his disappointment could be really...intense. You wouldn't want to see that. I'd seen it in small cases, and it's just like, "Oh man, I really shouldn't cause that again."

We're not talking about big stuff because I never got in any real trouble—but if I broke curfew or something, he'd generally be let down. So I tried to be good about that stuff.

He's like a really good mix of supportive and give-you-a-kick-in-the-ass. With *Sons of Butcher*, he sat me down and basically said, "Okay, you said you were going to go into production." So far I had done a bunch of corporate films and some stuff for Raptors TV that didn't pay very well, but it was a good experience and I learned how to edit. Anyway, he said, "You need to get out and do something. You need to make something bigger happen because you're basically just leaching off the company." Fair enough, because I wasn't doing much.

I told him, "Well, I got this show thing going with these guys," and we were going to make it for the Web. After that conversation with my dad, I met with those guys and I was like, "Let's pitch it." Within a month we had pitched it to Teletoon and we had a development deal. But I probably would have just hung out for another year or so, except that it got to a point where my dad was like, "All right, go do something bigger." He's been very supportive.

Morag and Max, Tournament Winners at Hamilton Golf and Country Club, 2000.

Another thing I admire about him—to have that much success and not have screwed anyone along the way, you know? He didn't make any enemies. That's probably unique.

NEWSLETTER AND OUTFITTER'S CATALOGUE

Nov. '94 – Vol. 2 Issue

RED GREEN ANNOUNCEMENT

Welcome to all new members of Possum Lodge. We may be odd but there's over twenty thousand of us, and many of us are allowed to vote.

We are pleased and somewhat amazed to announce that the RED GREEN FAN CLUB has grown to the point that we have had to bring in professional help. STARTING IMMEDIATELY the Fan Club and all associated merchandise will be available exclusively through:

**Possum Lodge
P.O. Box 4433
Markham Industrial Park Post Office
Markham Ontario L3R 6G9
1-800-Y-POSSUM**

Fan Club Members will be pleased to learn that there will now be at least three Newsletters a year coming from Possum Lodge. However the Fan Club (which now stands at about 21,000 members) will no longer be free. There will now be a one time entrance fee of $3.00 to help defray the cost of membership cards and Newsletter mail-outs.

Keep an eye out for the Red Green Merchandise coming soon from Mowat Trading, and watch for THE RED GREEN BOOK from Macmillan Publishing coming for March of 1995.

Ice Fishing Hints

STEP 1. Do this activity in the Winter. No kidding.

STEP 2. Learn how to hot-wire a snowmobile.

STEP 3. Hot-wire a snowmobile and send the least popular guy out on the lake. Chances are he will sink through the ice and drop like a stone to the bottom. DO NOT ATTEMPT TO FISH IN THE RESULTANT HOLE. THAT'S IMPORTANT. Instead, go to a different lake before the cops arrive and you waste the whole day explaining how it happened.

STEP 4. Hot-wire another, nicer snowmobile and go out onto a safer lake. Hold up a three foot length of 4 inch pipe and stick the bottom end into the ice. Fill the pipe with gasoline and light it. In no time at all, you will have a four inch hole in the ice. If you park your snowmobile too close to the burning pipe, you will end up with an even bigger hole and an interesting story to tell all the nurses at the burn unit.

STEP 5. Bait your hook and drop it into the hole. Try not to think about your feet until they are completely numb. If you have a chainsaw, you can cut a trough in the ice and troll. Otherwise you're pretty well limited to jerking the lure up and down and letting your mind wander. DO NOT FIGHT THE BOREDOM. IT IS AN INTRINSIC COMPONENT OF THE SPORT.

STEP 6. If you catch anything other than pneumonia, you may need help reeling it in. Especially if it's thicker than four inches. Many of today's sophisticated fishing reels are not meant to be operated with frozen fingers so thaw your fingers out by putting them in your mouth, unless you really don't like the taste of bait. Once you've landed the fish, stick them face down in the snow until frozen. This will eliminate the need for a stringer as you can mount the fish on popsicle sticks and throw them into your cooler.

STEP 7. Once you're back to the cabin, cover the fish in a light coating of bread crumbs and butter and then fry them up in a quart and a half of scotch. Take them out of the pan and feed them to the cat while you drink the broth. This will remove all memory of the outing and will allow you to go ice fishing on another occasion.

INSIDE THIS ISSUE
On Your First Job
Official T-Shirts
Poet's Corner
And not a whole heck of alot more...

CHAPTER SIX

ONE DOOR CLOSES

A WHOLE WORLD OPENS

ONE DOOR CLOSES

A WHOLE WORLD OPENS

AN ELEMENT OF VULNERABILITY

MAG: *If there were a chink in your armour, what would it be—what is your biggest vulnerability?*

STEVE: Confidence. I can crash down. I'll say to myself, "It's all useless and I don't know what I'm doing and I've just been pretending all this time. I've fooled a couple of people, but now I can't fool anybody and therefore I can't even fool myself." That's my biggest vulnerability.

People are asking me why I'm not going to do the show anymore. Well, I've run out of patience for the vulnerability. I've felt vulnerable for too long and I just don't want to do that anymore.

Opposite: Steve and Morag at the wrap party after the 300th taping—looking forward to a reduced stress level.

The vulnerability can be with the weather because we're trying to shoot outside, or there are airplanes going over making noise, all the millions of things. Or one of the special effects doesn't work. Or it's not funny.

Or the broadcaster says, "We *kind* of like the show but I don't know whether we're going to pick it up next year or not."

Shut up! You should be begging me—"Please, please, have you thought about it? Will you do the show again? Have you thought about it?"

I call it a "coincidence" because I just happened to be at the right place at the right time, doing the right thing. If any one of those factors is missing, the moment is gone.

"I don't know. I'll get back to you."

In my mind, that's the way it should be. Because I just give everything I've got to it. So for them to treat it as, "Maybe I'll have veal, maybe I'll have chicken," just seems way too casual. They don't have the right to treat it at that level when I'm treating it at a whole other level.

Anyway, that's the whole vulnerability thing.

I'll say things about broadcasters and whatever, but the truth is, I care. I want them to approve of what I'm doing. I want them to see me as somebody who's helping them in some way. Either being a big addition to what the station is doing, or a part of people's lives that they look forward to. I don't think you ever get over that one.

THE POWER OF COINCIDENCE

MAG: *You've told me how you like to be in control, but can you talk to me a little bit about how coincidence has had an impact on your life and your career? You got together with Morag because you just happened to need to rent space for the band and she just happened to get off the phone with her boyfriend.*

STEVE: Coincidence is huge. And the thing is, I don't know if the cycle would have come around again with Morag, or if it would have been gone forever.

MAG: *The cycle would've come around again. Coincidence was already giving* *you a second chance with Morag, since you'd decided at seventeen that the timing wasn't right.*

STEVE: Okay. I like that. I've had a few moments where I've known that whatever just happened was going to have a big effect on my life. For example, when we were performing at Hamilton Place and the Vice President/General Manager of the station was in the audience, and that's how we got our pilot—how coincidental is that?

There've been four or five times in my life when I just knew something was going to happen. I call it a "coincidence" because I just happened to be at the right place at the right time, doing the right thing. If any one of those factors is missing, the moment is gone.

With Morag—I started in Toronto, she started in Scotland. We both ended up in Streetsville. And if the programmer hadn't changed at CBC, there's no way *Red Green* would ever have been on there.

But what you can't know is the other things that were going to happen. You

Steve in 2005 with Frank DeNardis, the CHCH President who gave Steve his start in television in 1977.

only know what did happen, and everything that happened subsequently was somehow connected to that. There may have been five other paths that were all completely acceptable. You don't know. You can't have two lives at once.

MAG: *Can you look at your life and see a plot line?*

STEVE: I do, because I do it internally. Because it's nothing to do with those external decisions or coincidences.

It's like my life is me as the only pupil at this school. Almost every day I get another lesson. Some days I get a really big lesson. Sometimes I get an exam. But it's all part of that process. And of all the advantages that I've had, the biggest one is that I've been allowed to see a lot of things and meet great people and hear stories.

It's like my life is me as the only pupil at this school. Almost every day I get another lesson. Some days I get a really big lesson. Sometimes I get an exam.

People I've met, and even daily emails, give me access to points of view and people that I would never normally see. Most people have maybe twenty people they interact with— the people at work, the people at home, and that's it. I get thousands of people a week. That's a great opportunity. So you get to see patterns of behaviour, you get to see results. Someone takes this action and you get to see the result of it; somebody takes another action and you see the result of that. I think it all helps you. You get so much different information.

But the coincidence part scares me, to be honest with you. Because I think it's true, and it's like, a fluke. It feels like a fluke. Do you know what I mean?

MAG: *Why is it scary?*

STEVE: Well, I just feel undeserving. Like I'm a lottery winner. I think there is an element of coincidence. I can't deny that.

You know how sometimes you just miss an accident, or if you'd turned a certain way, you wouldn't be here anymore? And then you think, "Well, maybe there was some fate, there was a hand in there that stopped that from happening because it wasn't supposed to happen."

Maybe everything that happens is supposed to happen, so it really isn't a coincidence. It just *seems* like a coincidence to us because it doesn't seem to be predictable that those events would happen.

So I'd probably prefer to think that it was supposed to happen, but it just *seemed* real fluky to me. I will take credit, though, for putting myself into a position where I could take advantage of a coincidental opportunity.

A LONG RUN

MAG: *You've had a longer run with* Red Green *than almost any other comedy in the history of television. What is it about the show that appeals so strongly to people?*

The Red Green Show ran 15 years, surpassed only by *The Simpsons*, which, in 2008, had been on the air for 19 seasons.

STEVE: You know, I get interviewed a lot about trying to identify the appeal of *Red Green*. Lately I've been saying, "I think there's something that's appealing, generally, about a person who is comfortable with himself." Like, this guy's okay. I don't think I come across as being needy, and I think people like that. I don't think Donald Trump comes across as being needy either, but if you can be self-sufficient without arrogance, I think there's something about that that people like.

Who doesn't like a cowboy or a farmer—somebody who can just take it and do it and shut up? I mean, we've had Don Harron—Charlie Farquharson—on the show and we did the word game with him.

Don Harron first portrayed rural farmer Charlie Farquharson in 1952 on the CBC series *The Big Revue*. The character reappeared as part of the cast of the American country music television hit, *Hee Haw*, in the Seventies. Dressed in a moth-eaten wool sweater, Charlie delivers satire heightened by double entendre and mistakenly used words.

This is a game where the contestant is given a description of something and can only give one-word answers. I love the word game because it's the essence of why we can never have a meeting of the minds. At least one of the minds is not even there.

So I told the guys I wanted to do the word "entrepreneur" because entrepreneur is like—"Oh, that's high tech, that's Bay

Above Left: A 5x7 photo from an early *Smith and Smith* supporter—"Me in front of Toronto Chapter—*Smith and Smith* Fan Club—faithfully, Gordon Pinsent." *Above Centre:* Steve cracks up while rehearsing a scene with Gordon Pinsent, 2003. *Above Right:* Don Harron as Charlie Farquharson in a 2003 episode of *The Red Green Show.*

Street." Baloney! Farmers have been entrepreneurs for ten thousand years. So in the word game, every time we try to set up "entrepreneur," Charlie's referring to farming.

MAG: *I know how tough the final season was for you when just about everything that could go wrong did go wrong. Some of the cast members were ill. CBC Television, your long-time broadcast partner, was crippled by an extended strike that forced you to hire an independent crew and studio space to complete your shooting schedule. And you still managed to finish the season.*

STEVE: I always knew I was going to make it, but I actually made it with quite a bit of myself left. And I don't think I alienated a lot of people. That was my biggest fear. I could picture thirty years of goodwill going out the window in the last six weeks.

Finishing the writing was huge. And I finished a week ahead—September 23rd. And then just doing the shows at night...the audience was laughing.

Above Left: Mike Hamar (Wayne Robson) being a public nuisance to Morag and Steve's mother, Mary Muncey, at the taping of the 300th episode of the show. *Above Right:* Steve introduces cast members at the start of a live taping. "I haven't had one second of regret over my decision to end the series."

The show was still funny. I wasn't worried. I knew it was going to be okay. And my feeling was, I'm not ending the show, I'm completing it.

It's like you see these houses where they did one too many additions—I've had that house—or if the guy had taken another year on the Mona Lisa he would have ended up with a couple more clouds and a happy face on there, and a caption, "Have a nice day."

I haven't had one second of regret over my decision to end the series, so that reinforces that I did the right thing. I had some people not happy about stopping the show, but it didn't in any way dissuade me.

And the people in the audience—I told them first thing every night. And their biggest concern was that some external force was stopping the show. Once they knew that *I* was stopping the show, they were good, they were fine. It wasn't a problem.

Wayne Robson is an extremely versatile actor with well over a hundred television and film credits, starting with *McCabe and Mrs. Miller* in 1971. Wayne plays Mike Hamar on *The Red Green Show*, an ex-con on probation who is trying desperately to break his criminal habits.

MAG: *You were so worried that it wasn't going to be a happy completion. What was that feeling of apprehension based on?*

STEVE: Well, when Morag and I left the band in December of '74, the rest of the band was crying and saying that they'd never have anything so good again. Morag and I were shocked because we felt that the best times were still ahead of us.

So, with *Red Green*, I was a little worried that somebody was going to say to me that they would never match this again, that this had been the best experience of their lives, and they were just devastated that from here on out it was going to be some pale impersonation of what they'd been enjoying over the last five or ten years. I had a lot of people in the cast and crew who were enjoying what they were doing with our show more than the other things they do. I felt that in some ways, I was taking away the thing that had been the most fun for them.

So I was worried. But it never became an issue, and I think it would have come out if it was going to come out.

MAG: *You don't strike me as a worrier.*

STEVE: I *am* a worrier. I am, but not to the extent of letting it affect my decisions. I'm concerned that I may be doing something that will negatively impact other people, but it doesn't make me not do it if I think it's the right thing to do. I'd just rather sort of do it by email.

Gordon Pinsent is a renowned Canadian actor, director and writer who plays the beloved Hap Shaughnessy on *The Red Green Show*.

I remember Gordon Pinsent telling me that he was doing a series, and he said he just got tired of it. I think he did two seasons and then he just didn't want to do it anymore. And he said he's really so sorry that he quit. Many times subsequent to that, he thought, "What the heck was I thinking? I should have let that go as long as it could."

I think he made the decision to quit based on incorrect information. He thought that, somehow, for him to do that show was limiting. But I think that after you've done more shows, you realize that you might have been able to express everything you wanted to express within that previous format, without having to go and start something new and maybe never get the platform again.

MAG: *When you made the decision that your fifteenth season would be the final one, how did you imagine closing night going? What was your highest hope?*

STEVE: I experienced my highest hope with probably every audience during that last season. At least one person, if not several in the audience, would come up and say, "Thank you. Thank you for so many laughs and so many great times."

That was it. That was all I expected. That was the epitome. It was a great, fun thing that we shared, and we were all grateful. Because I *was* grateful, I still am grateful.

FAREWELL BUT NO REGRETS

MAG: *So you're pretty convinced that you won't miss doing the show.*

STEVE: I won't miss it. I did everything I could think of. There are no deficiencies anywhere for me in the whole project. I've had so many positive things said to me and written to me. It's just like, "Okay, that's good. I'm done."

I said to all of the guys in the show, individually, that this was not a time to be unhappy. We'd done something together that most people don't ever experience. We'd had so much magic.

There were moments there. And we talked about it backstage. Like Mike—Wayne Robson—on one episode where we did a telethon. There are three of the guys on the phones. I pick up a phone and I'm calling him, and he thinks I'm calling in a pledge. So I say, "It's *me*, you idiot!" And he says, "Dad?" into the

Once you promise to quit, everyone is so grateful.

phone. Before we tape it, I tell him, "That's going to get a huge laugh." And he says, "Oh, I know."

And when he did that line, it was such an explosion of laugher. I looked at him and he looked at me. And we went backstage and I said, "Regardless of anything, Wayne, that is the biggest laugh gotten from one word in the history of comedy."

Stuff like that is so great. And we've had so many of those moments during tapings—where I looked into their faces and it was just pure love. And the audience would start clapping just for sharing that with them. That was fabulous stuff.

How could it be bad? Was I going to cry? No. I got to go on the big Ferris wheel. I just kept up the same thing I'd been saying all along, which was that

Bob Bainborough paddles Steve and Wayne Robson to shore after taping a bucolic scene for the 14th season.

this is a celebration; it's a time for great joy. We got a chance to share something together. It's been great. Broke all kinds of world records.

Bob Bainborough said to me one night, "You know, this is so cool to be part of something that'll live on in the Canadian fabric."

Well, I thought, "There we go. Exactly. Isn't that fantastic? Who expected anything like this?"

MAG: *So you got through the whole thing with no regrets?*

STEVE: I haven't had a twinge. There's no negative in it for

Bob Bainborough, an experienced comic actor and writer, joined the cast of *The Red Green Show* in 1994 playing the character Dalton Humphrey, an unhappily married local store owner. In 1995, Bob also began contributing as a writer.

Red Green wrap party, 2005. (Left to right) Back: Mark Wilson, Jeff Lumby, Laurie Elliott, Bob Bainborough, Rick Green, Jerry Schaefer. Front: Graham Greene, Wayne Robson, Patrick McKenna, Steve Smith, Joel Harris, Peter Keleghan, Peter Wildman.

Jeff, Wayne, Bob, Patrick and Steve singing karaoke at the wrap party following the taping of the 300th episode.

me. There's no negative about the show. No "Thank God that's over with." I also don't have a negative about, "Oh my God, it's over and *now* what am I going to do?"

I don't have *any* negatives. It's all positive to me. I can't even remember the bad things—the whole fifteen years must've just been fun and easy all the way. It must've been because that's the way I remember it. Like bringing up my kids—I can't remember the bad stuff, you know?

And going on…I'm looking forward to that. My stress level's going to be so much lower because I'm going to be able to control so many more things than I could before.

MAG: *I once heard you say that with* The Red Green Show, *you feel you've been able to express everything you had to express.*

STEVE: Absolutely. Yes. And I got that award—The Earle Grey Lifetime

Achievement Award.

MAG: *Right. This has been your year, apparently.*

STEVE: This has been my year. That's what I say—once you promise to quit, everyone is so grateful.

MAG: *So, is there any chance that after a couple of years, you'll come back with a new television idea?*

STEVE: I'll never, ever, *ever*—and you can come and slap me around if I ever do this—I'm never acting on television again. I'm never doing it. I'm never going to put my face in front of the camera as an actor again. Ever, ever, ever. Forever. I'm done.

The Earle Grey Award is the Lifetime Achievement Award of the Canadian Gemini Awards (television awards similar to the American "Emmys"). The Earle Grey Award is presented annually to an actor or actress in recognition of their body of work in television. Steve received his in November of 2005.

Steve with a gang of well wishers at the 2005 Gemini Awards, after receiving the Earle Grey Award for Lifetime Achievement. Left to Right: Davy Smith, Sandi Richardson, Steve, Mag, Allan Foster, Graham Greene, Patrick McKenna.

MAG: *That's a pretty strong statement considering you've spent half your life on TV. What's the basis of that "never ever again" thing?*

STEVE: It would be a lie for me to go put my face on camera. Because in my mind I'd be saying, "How do you like me now?" Again.

And I just don't want to do that anymore. I don't want to play that game anymore. I don't want to feel that way. I don't want to have that feeling inside that I'm asking for approval. I don't even want to put myself up for the scrutiny. Enough. I've had thirty years of it. I passed my own scrutiny, not with flying colours, but I got a passing grade. I got my diploma. I can move on.

A QUESTION OF APPROVAL

MAG: *You say you're sending out the message, "How do you like me now?" But I don't think that's what you do at all.*

STEVE: But the basis of entertainment is, "How do you like me now?" Like if the court jester says something that isn't funny, they'll kill him. He's only being entertaining for his own survival. To me, that's the basis of the entire entertainment industry. It's not personal. It's just the nature of the beast.

MAG: *Now I know what you're talking about. It's the* role *you don't like.*

STEVE: It's the role. I put myself in a subservient role, and I don't feel subservient. I'm like the assistant who's making all the decisions while the boss is deciding whether or not he's going to let me come to lunch. Meanwhile, I'm thinking about whether I'm going to grant him the privilege of having lunch with me.

MAG: *If seeking approval from an exterior source is so stressful for you, it must make it hard for you to be in this business.*

STEVE: Absolutely. I can't imagine it not being a source of stress for anybody.

MAG: *Well, it's what business is about, usually.*

STEVE: Yeah. Selling. That is stressful. I mean, you get to the point where you can say, "Well, I don't need it. If they say no, so what? I'm okay."

MAG: *But you know you're talking yourself into something.*

STEVE: Yes, because you'd never ask the question if you didn't care about the answer. So as soon as you arrange a meeting or even bring up the subject, then you're asking, at some level, for some kind of approval. There's a stress involved with that.

MAG: *So in the future, the thing that would make you happiest would be getting to approve of yourself?*

STEVE: Yeah, that's got a ring to it.

You know, there was this thing I was thinking about. You get a job and maybe you're the apprentice, the trainee. And then you go through all those steps and eventually you're a tradesman, then you become a journeyman, and then a master.

If you apply that to your life—your first twenty years was your apprenticeship and so on. Well, I'm sixty and I should be at the master stage now. I shouldn't be doing stuff subject to approval, or having the tradesmen take a look at my work or tell me to go and get a left-handed screwdriver. I should be beyond that now.

So all of the training that I've had, the way life has informed me and guided me, that's all inside me. Whatever I am now is the result of all of that education. I should be ready to do a combination of accepting and applying that stuff rather than continuing to go back into a subservient role where somebody has to guide me a little bit farther along. I mean, there'll always be that aspect— things will happen that I don't expect, and I'll continue to learn things.

STRESS SIGNALS

STEVE: I'm dealing with lifespan now. My lifespan is probably somewhere between two-thirds and three-quarters done, logically, based on averages. So I've only got a quarter or at most a third of my time left. Therefore, those days are at least three times as valuable as the days I used to live. I don't want to waste too many of them.

So I'm starting with, "What are the situations that I find stressful?" And as often as possible, I'm going to tell myself, "Don't go into those!" I'm going to try and stop before I accept that invitation or sign up for something, or take on something. To stop, take a minute and say, "That's just going to be a whole load of stress for me to do that. Why would I do that?" And then say, "No, thank you."

And at the end of my life, what I want to be doing—it's very simple —I want to be looking forward to the next day. That's all. That's it.

MAG: *I wasn't aware that there was much besides work that was causing you that sort of stress.*

STEVE: No, and you know, we'll have to see if there is. Because I think we all have a certain tolerance for stress. If your work is taking up ninety-five percent of it, it doesn't take much for you to go over that line. But when you take away that ninety-five percent, those little things could still be there but they're so far below your level that they don't even bother you.

When you're maxed out, you're just out of it. You go into the house and something's not where it's supposed to be or you can't find something and you know *you* put it back where it belongs…that drives you crazy. But on another day, who cares?

So we'll have to wait and see. As I take away the major stress sources, we'll see what happens to the other ones. My stress level's going to be so much lower, because I'm going to be able to control so many more things than I could before.

MAG: *So control is a measure of your happiness?*

STEVE: Well, I think being able to avoid potentially stressful situations and circumstances is not a bad starting point, along with not having to ask for approval that you'd really prefer not to have to ask for in the first place.

MAG: *Sounds like you're going to have a big decompression.*

STEVE: Yes, it's a big change. I want to make a list, for example, of all of the things that I can think of that create stress for me. Some of them may be very specific, like, "When I'm with this person, it drives me crazy…I'm always worried about something." Or it may be something very general like being obligated to go to a social event where I was never involved in accepting the invitation—that's a lot more general than stress from a specific person.

Anyway, I'll list all of those things and then try to prioritize them in terms of how much stress is caused by each one. I'll deal with the biggest ones first because I probably won't get to them all. If I can get the top three out of there—boy, life gets a lot better.

Then I'm going to roll all my pennies.

MAG: *How many pennies do you* have?

STEVE: I have a lot. I got a parking ticket during the last month of taping the show, and I was yelling at the old man who was giving me the ticket, and I thought, "This is probably not my best moment."

I'm at an interesting point because I'm old enough not to need to start anything new, but I'm young enough to have the energy for it.

It was a thirty-five-dollar ticket and when I got home, I felt that I had enough pennies that I could pay it in pennies. I was going to put them all in a box—this is how bad I was getting—put the pennies in a big friggin' box and take it down to the city. And not just drop it off. No, no—I had to *see* somebody.

I told a friend of mine about this on the phone, and he says, "They won't take 'em. There's a limit to how many pennies they have to take."

MAG: *He's* tried it?

STEVE: I don't know. I'd think more of him if he had. Anyway, I've justified it. I paid the ticket. Wrote a cheque, paid it, it's done. But when I roll those pennies, then I'll get the thirty-five bucks back. It'll all work out.

See, in a less stressful year, like next year, I won't even bother. None of that would even fizz on me. Did a dumb thing, deserved to get a ticket.

BACK TO THE PAST

Fizz on me—Canadian slang, circa 1945, meaning, "It had no effect on me." Normally, bubbles fizz all over an object after you've dropped it into a glass of soda pop.

MAG: *If you look back over the history of the show, what would you say has changed the most about you in the fifteen years of* Red Green?

STEVE: I would say that life is a great leveller. I've been through some deaths and some illnesses and some financial setbacks. And there were times when I didn't think I would make it through those things, any of those things. But I did. Now I know I can.

I'm not afraid of those things now, whereas before I'd experienced them, you know, maybe I was a bit afraid. And then when each thing happened, I'd think, "There's no proof that I can get through this." But now there is. Now I have proof that I can get through those things.

So, it makes me feel stronger and more equipped to handle whatever's coming next, and therefore I can feel more relaxed. Kick back a little and not be constantly worrying that something's right around the corner. I think that's been the biggest change. I don't worry about life.

And my sons are on their feet now, and no matter what they choose to do from here on in, I think they're equipped to handle it. And I think that's really good.

MAG: *Do you feel like your sons have what you have now—that security of*

Steve after receiving the Order of Canada, with Governor General Michaëlle Jean, 2006.

knowing that they can handle a lot?

STEVE: No. I don't think you can get that handed to you. Max and Davy were aware of the problems I was going through at the time, but I think you have to be the one under the gun to get the full benefit of the experience.

The Order of Canada is the highest civilian honour awarded to Canadian citizens. The award recognizes a lifetime of distinguished service in or to a particular community, group or field of activity.

MAG: *So, it's been a big year. You finished* Red Green, *you got the Earle Grey Award and the Order of Canada. And you turned sixty.*

STEVE: Yes. And I've never felt better—physically or mentally. I just feel really…

secure. It's great.

MAG: *Secure? That's the top of feeling good for you?*

STEVE: Yeah. Secure's good.

MAG: *That's as high as it goes?*

STEVE: Well, yeah.

MAG: *Secure.*

STEVE: I think secure is a good thing because you can reach up. You know, if you stand on something secure you can reach up and not worry so much about falling over.

MAG: *Oh, so this security thing is a whole ladder analogy.*

STEVE: It's a ladder analogy. But using a good ladder. Because we have an old rickety wooden ladder that came with our house, and that's the opposite of how I feel right now, that ladder.

THE NEXT FIFTEEN YEARS

MAG: *What's your most optimistic idea of where you'll be at the end of another fifteen years?*

STEVE: I would really like another fifteen years of more laughs, more happy times, taking away the stress of having to generate a living. I think that should create space for having more fun.

I have enough friends now. I mean, you can never have too many, but I certainly don't feel like I need to go out and make a bunch of new friends. And I'd like to see my family happy and at peace. That would be really a nice thing.

But it's not bad now.

MAG: *Okay, but what about you, personally? What is your picture of yourself?*

STEVE: I hope that I continue to enjoy people. I know I'm demanding and I'm probably not the warmest person that people know, but I enjoy people. And very rarely do I talk to somebody where I don't get something of real value out of the conversation. That person would probably have no idea what it was, but I'll get some little kernel of something or other, or some new way of looking at something. And I'll be really glad that I spoke to that person, no matter who it is. It could be the guy coming to spray the lawn, but he's got something.

I just hope I'll continue to feel that way and not become the crabby old guy that you're supposed to become, where you wake up crabby and you look for something more to be crabby about.

And it would be nice to have a grandkid or two. I think I'd be a pretty deadly grandfather. I think the parents would have to step in. They'd have to have a word with me.

MAG: *They'd have to separate you from the young 'un.*

STEVE: Yeah, I think so. "Take back the Corvette." "What?" "He's a year old!" So that could be good. I have no trepidation about old age or decay or anything. Especially now. I'm not that old.

MAG: *Yeah, it's early yet.*

STEVE: My dad was sixty-eight when he died. And, you know, I was thinking, "Boy, that's eight years from where I am now. Like, that's a long time." I'm planning, believe me, on far outliving my dad. But even so, eight years is a long time.

I mean, if you look at the years that I've worked, I've probably put in so much time…a lot of days and nights. So I get all those back. Those working years were like human years, and now it's like I've got dog years—I really have fifty-six years left. So it's good.

And at the end of my life, what I want to be doing—it's very simple—I want to be looking forward to the next day. That's all. That's it. When it comes to the last day of my life, I want to be surprised. Because I'm looking forward to tomorrow now. I feel a lot better about tomorrow than I do about yesterday. And yesterday was fine.

MAG: *You'd normally be trying to make your deadline to finish all of your writing right about now. Do you even think of that?*

Rhythm is huge— huge in comedy, huge in music and huge in life.

STEVE: I have a range of emotions about the whole thing. The only emotion that I haven't had is one second of regret for either doing the show or stopping doing it.

I'm still searching for my new space. I don't know what it is. And it might be no space. I'm not rushing into anything. I'm not even rushing into *not* doing anything. I'm just kind of…

MAG: *…being?*

STEVE: Yeah. Just being. When we went to Florida a couple of weeks after the show ended, Morag and I would sit down. She had a notebook of things we wanted to get done. And I would just go at the list. I didn't realize that I was really just filling a space. It was a positive thing to get those things done, but I was really trying to get myself over a situation.

As I've tapered off on doing all these jobs, I started to get that fear—"Oh, man, you did all those jobs because you were afraid of being useless after being so productive for all those years."

MAG: *Maybe you were so productive all those years because you were afraid of being useless.*

STEVE: That could be. I hadn't thought of that. Maybe it's just business as usual.

MAG: *As we've talked, I've realized you generally seem to focus in one of two ways. You're either thinking about something that is happening right now in your mind, or you're leaning forward into the future. The past has very little bearing on your present, ever.*

STEVE: Oh, absolutely. I never reminisce. Ever. You'll never see me looking through a photo album from ten years ago or looking at old shows. It's gone. It's done. I've got enough occupying me right now.

Plus, I've always thought that as soon as you're looking back more than you're looking forward, then you're old. I want to keep going right to the end, you know? To me, looking back is a futile exercise. You're already living everything that could come out of your past. That gold mine is empty and closed. You got everything out of it you could.

Steve piloting his boat during a staff party on Hamilton Bay. "I'm still searching for my new space."

And it's funny, because Morag really loves to reminisce. She enjoys nothing more than putting on a couple of VHS tapes we have from 1980—Davy's *just* walking—and she'll watch them. I think she really misses the kids. When they moved out of the house to go to college, that was big for her. And, of course, I was working, I was away a lot. That was a big transition.

She loves watching those tapes. She'd probably watch them three times a week if she could. I can't take it, I've got to get out of the room. I'll put the tape on, but get me out of there. I don't know who those people are.

INTO THE FUTURE

MAG: *What do you think is next in your life?*

STEVE: I'm looking forward to getting into this new retirement phase. That's my biggest thing to plan…what am I going to do now?

MAG: *Maybe there's some desire in the periphery of your thinking that's magnetizing something new for your retirement.*

STEVE: Well, I'm at an interesting point because I'm old enough not to need to start anything new, but I'm young enough to have the energy for it. That doesn't happen to very many people.

MAG: *I know. Your mind is working with a huge range of options. Maybe that's why your thinking is so veiled, even from yourself, regarding what you're going to be doing after you retire. Only your deepest processor can construct the thing that you'll be doing, and it needs secrecy.*

STEVE: Yeah.

MAG: *Nobody else can know. Not even you.*

STEVE: No. I'll blab.

MAG: *I know you don't read the paper but we're in a bit of a recession right now. How does that affect you?*

STEVE: Not much. There have been a couple of other recessions in my lifetime—one in the early Eighties, one in the early Nineties. I thought the world would end, but I've gotten kind of immune to gloom and doom.

I didn't live through the Thirties when things got really bad and the stock market plunged and everybody was losing their shirts and everything. But I remember in the middle of those later recessions, I'd go on the highway and I wasn't the only car. People were still going places and doing things. And, yeah, it was tough, but we made it. The media exaggerates it, I think. Things are rarely as bad as they say. They need to pump you up. Someone usually has a political agenda—they're trying to change governments or something so they make it sound horrible.

My dad always used to say, "People are a lot nicer in a recession. Affluence brings animosity."

I kind of take it all with a grain of salt.

THREE-PART HARMONY

MAG: *Judging by recent events, it seems like you're back to where you started as a kid, when you said you were "kind of a singer." What is it about music that keeps calling you—can you remember making an emotional connection with music as a kid?*

STEVE: Certain kinds of music. A stirring song sung with extreme conviction, with no regard for what's popular—I seemed to respond strongly to that.

MAG: *Was it the music or the lyrics that got you?*

STEVE: The last thing was the lyrics. It was the music. Very strong melody lines, strong chord changes. That probably is one of those things that drew me to music. I really felt that music was always a powerful motivator.

I used to sing at little talent shows. If we'd go to a cottage or something, I'd get up and sing in the talent show. I actually volunteered for that for some reason. So there was always a musical connection. I always thought that music and comedy were very close anyway.

The Fabulous Miromars, 2006.

MAG: *How are they close?*

STEVE: There's a rhythm. Like, nothing drives me crazier than a video editor who can't dance. If you can't keep a beat, you can't cut comedy. Rhythm is huge—huge in comedy, huge in music and huge in life. Things have to happen right on the beat or it just throws you off a little bit.

MAG: *You know, this will sound weird, but I took an acting class once and they put us all in a circle and made us touch fingertips. Within a few minutes, all of our pulses started to match.*

STEVE: Ah, well, there you go. So if a person was upset and their heart was racing, you could calm them just by holding them. I never knew that. That's a good thing.

MAG: *So, in the past few months you've started a singing group called The Fabulous Miromars. What happened that brought you back to singing again, just when you thought you were retiring?*

STEVE: Well, when we're in Florida, we go to a karaoke bar about once every two months—Morag likes karaoke bars—and we take a whole bunch of people with us. Over the last two years we've gone maybe six times with a bunch of friends. There was one guy, Tom. He had been one of the Vice Presidents of Bank of America. He was the only one who consistently never got up, not even with a gang. He wouldn't go up.

So one evening we went out to the karaoke place and Tom was there. Then, two or three days later, he took me aside and said, "I think we should form a singing group."

I said, "Who?"

He said, "You and Morag and me."

I said, "Yeah, right! What have you done?" I'm kidding him, you know. I was making it difficult for him because I didn't want to do something lightly. It's going to take a lot of work if we're going to do it.

So anyway, I just let it go. But he kept persisting and I kept saying, "We don't have a star. None of us can sing well enough to be a star." I thought he was just being a goof. And I'm saying, "Who's going to arrange the vocals and everything?" Because he wanted to sing three-part harmony to karaoke tracks—that was the whole premise.

Turns out, forty years ago he was in a gospel group that toured all over the place and even made some albums. So I said, "Okay, we'll learn *one* song."

Steve, Morag and Tom Dawson rehearsing at the Smith's house before a gig at Fisher's in Hamilton, Ontario.

Steve and Ed Fisher, 2008.

Morag has this karaoke microphone with a memory chip that can store a bunch of songs, so we learned *What a Wonderful World*. I arranged the harmony and we learned it.

Then Tom had a party for me to celebrate my Order of Canada. Unbelievable party. So the three of us got up and sang that song and we had no microphones or anything, and it went over pretty well. I mean, it was just our friends.

So we got home and I thought, "Oh shoot." And the next day I buy a P.A. system.

MAG: *The next day?*

STEVE: Yeah. I said to Morag, "I've probably lost my mind." And then it's just been a whole series of things. I got into finding better karaoke tracks and I'm looking for all kinds of songs we can do. And it's just me—the guy who wants to do things on his own terms—taking over and being at the helm.

Then I found this on-line karaoke club that I could join for forty-seven

Above Left: Tom's wife, Nan, runs the sound mixer and lights at all performances of The Fabulous Miromars *Above Right:* Steve, Morag and Tom performing to a sold-out audience at Fisher's in Hamilton, Ontario.

bucks, and for that, you get this downloadable manual that gives you all the steps—about fifty pages of steps—to reconfigure your computer. That way, you'll be able to download karaoke songs from the Internet because they have a karaoke network on one of these Internet Relay Chat things. And they give you customer support. The only reason I bought it was because whenever I had seen it before it was ninety-seven bucks. This was March 28th and it was fifty dollars off until March 30th.

MAG: *How cool is that!*

STEVE: Well, it gets better.

I finally got through this incredibly complicated on-line system and now I have this ability to type in the name of any song I'm looking for, and they start coming in from all over the world. I mean, there are twelve million songs available in different karaoke styles and I can listen to different versions of the same song until I hear one that I like.

Then I put it onto my computer and it comes up as a sound file with a graphics file that has the lyrics on it. I get the words off that and then I have recording studio software that allows me to change pitch, change tempo. So, I'm doing medleys.

MAG: *Wow!*

STEVE: And the whole point of this is that when we sang *What a Wonderful World*, rehearsing it...the *joy* that I felt singing with those two. It's like, "Okay, that feels good. That's a *good* feeling."

And now when I'm arranging the vocals I get teary-eyed because I feel like I've got it and it's going to be so damn good.

When I emailed Tom that I'd bought the P.A. system, he offered to help pay. But I'm not allowing him to pay anything. I said, "I can afford the equipment but I can't afford your opinion." Because if he's going to help pay, he's going to start telling me what to do. He did buy a pitch pipe.

Steve doesn't let me pay for any of the equipment. The one thing I get to buy is our costumes. And the hats.
—Tom Dawson

MAG: *And then you're not free.*

STEVE: I'm not free. And it's just so fun. I'm really loving it. We call ourselves The Fabulous Miromars because Miromar is the name of the golf club we belong to in Florida.

And Tom, he's just a hambone. This is the joke—the guy who would never get up in the karaoke bar is a total hambone. He sings the lead on a lot of songs, and after the first few times, he says to me, "If I'm going to be singing lead, I think we should change the name to Tom Dawson and the Fabulous Miromars." He's just a little bugger.

ON THE ROAD AGAIN

MAG: *So your group wound up with gigs all over southern Florida, and then you played Fisher's last week. I'll just never forget that performance. You were on fire and the audience was just spellbound.*

STEVE: Is that fun, though? Is that just stupid pure fun?

MAG: *It was just…outside of time. Those people in that audience—the well-being was just rippling through them. And it was coming from you!*

STEVE: I know. It's so neat.

MAG: *And the three of you have such different energy. Morag is so lovely. And Tom is so glad to be there that it doesn't matter whether he's singing a hurtin' song or a happy song, he's got the same expression on his face—"I hope nobody finds out about this and tells me to stop."*

STEVE: I know. I look over at him onstage and I can see him at six years old, this little guy who's just kind of getting away with something.

MAG: *And you—you were so lined up with yourself. I have never seen you more…who you are. I've never, ever seen you like that before.*

Fisher's is a cozy and hallowed bar on James Street North in downtown Hamilton. Those who discover it are automatic regulars. Owner Ed Fisher is a proud supporter of The Fabulous Miromars, who perform in his establishment at least once every summer.

STEVE: I'm glad you came to see the show because I could never explain to you what that was like without you seeing it.

MAG: *No, you couldn't. You know why? You don't even know what it's like to be where I was. I would look around at the people watching the three of you. You don't see a whole audience in that state of grace very often, just in pure enjoyment.*

STEVE: Ah, that's great.

MAG: *The performance really affected me and I think it affected everyone in the audience. You know how people sort of sub-vocalize along with music? Well, I think something else happens…*

STEVE: At a deeper level.

MAG: *Yes.*

STEVE: Resonance.

MAG: *Yes. So when you get going on that level of being aligned with your own soul, everyone else comes along for the ride.*

Audience members taking in The Fabulous Miromars.

STEVE: Well, I have a theory about resonance. I always think people are like a piano keyboard. You've got the low notes and you've got the high notes. You've got the black keys and the white keys.

And *you* decide which ones you're going to play every time you talk to somebody, or put on a movie or a television show—whatever it is you're looking at—all of your experiences are just piano keys sitting there and you're playing. And every note will resonate; it's just a matter of which ones you press.

And you know, with our little singing group, there are going to be obstacles. But we've had enough audiences like that one the other night…I know that's our audience. And I know that if we can get to them, we can make it a good time for everybody. So nobody's going to keep me from my goal of getting to that audience.

I feel…I'm feeling really good right now. I feel like everything's really working out the way it's supposed to. It wasn't the way I planned, or the way I even imagined, but it feels like it's going the right way.

TWO THOUSAND MILES

MAG: *I think this music thing is enormous for you. It's amazing to see the creativity that's coming from you in a way that no one expected.*

STEVE: It's huge for me. You know, I was working on something today—and this has happened a few times… There are certain times when I…when I get so deeply into it, I get tears in my eyes from the music. I'll think, "Okay, if I get this line to do this and this voice to do *this*"—and I can hear it all. And…oh my God! It's just so…I just feel *so* lucky to be able to tap into whatever that is.

MAG: *Why do you think music runs so deep in you? It's a really core thing in you.*

STEVE: Well, I was at a golf club function the other night, and someone we were sitting with brought up the subject of Pier 21.

MAG: *What's Pier 21?*

STEVE: Pier 21 is like the Ellis Island of Canada in Halifax, Nova Scotia. It's where people who came over on ships landed. They'd come into Pier 21 and the authorities would process all their papers and send them somewhere, like Saskatchewan or whatever. And if the clerk couldn't pronounce their name, he'd give them another name and away they'd go.

Well, one of the women who was there at the concert the other night, Barbi, her mother, Ruth Goldblum, is a very dynamic woman. She lives in Halifax and she did a lot of research on Pier 21. The building had been turned into a warehouse after all that immigration stuff ended in 1971.

So Ruth Goldblum helped get government funding to turn Pier 21 into kind of a museum. Anybody who immigrated to Canada can go there and they've got all of the ships' manifests. You can see when your grandfather came over. And they've got videos that people recorded about their memories of coming over, and you go and sit in these little booths and you watch a video and it's just...oh man, if that isn't heart-wrenching.

Anyway, ten years ago when I was in Halifax, Ruth told me this story.

(pause)

Oh…it's just one of those I find very hard to tell.

Ruth said that when they were trying to put the money together, people from all over Canada were sending in money because they wanted this to happen. They wanted this warehouse to become a museum.

One day she got a call from a minister in Winnipeg—I think he was Ukrainian—and their church had raised money. They wanted to come and give her the cheque. In person.

So they all came by bus. From Winnipeg.

(pause)

So they arrive on the bus, and Ruth is there. The minister gets off the bus and he wants to go into Pier 21. And he's got an accordion.

Ruth says, "Well, there are rats in there, and seagulls. We haven't done anything yet."

Pier 21, Halifax, Nova Scotia, in 1957.

And he says, "I don't care." So they all went in there.

(long pause)

It's crazy...I wasn't even there and I have a strong attachment to this.

So they all stood in a circle. And the minister opened a case and took out an old accordion and put it on. And he began to play—and they sang *O Canada*.

And Ruth said she's just never heard a version of *O Canada* like that. In a dirty, old, empty warehouse. And then they gave her a cheque.

That's a hell of a story, isn't it?

MAG: *Yes. And I don't think it would mean so much to you if there weren't music in it.*

STEVE: No, that's right. Absolutely right.

He brought an accordion two thousand miles on a bus. *Phew.* Yeah.

STEVE ON HIS COLLEAGUES...

Wayne Robson—"Mike Hamar"

Number one, Wayne is a really solid performer. Really solid. Like, when he is in a scene and I look into his eyes, he *is* Mike Hamar. And there's so much joy in his performance. And I just love that. And he'll tell you that, too. He just loved doing the show.

In the last season we had a three-minute retrospective video that we played at every taping. And there's a thing in there that Wayne Robson does—it's a word game—and every single audience that saw that clip would *explode* at what he was doing. He's just a good performer doing a good piece of writing with tremendous conviction. And just...we're just having so much fun.

But all the guys are like that.

Jeff Lumby—"Winston Rothschild III"

Jeff's a guy who always looks forward. He fears nothing. He has progressed so much, on every level, it's just amazing. I remember he did a scene with Pat in one of the last shows, and after it was over I said to him, "You know, five years ago I would never have given you that scene. You've come along so far and you just nailed that thing." He was so good. And Pat said the same thing about him. Pat and I know. We're working with people who deliver. They come, and they deliver. *Deliver*. Amen.

With Lumby, it's funny because when he started he was the least experienced and you'd probably have seen him as the least likely to succeed, and now I see him as the most likely—honestly—to have a successful future in whatever he chooses. He's just got that thing—a lot of energy and a lot of drive. And he has emotion without getting down for long. At some level, negative feedback is just information to him. He doesn't take it negatively. I know, because I've been bugging him for years and he's now doing all the things I've been trying to get him to do. And there's no resentment or rancour from him, you know? And I think that's the way he'll approach whatever he's going for next.

He's great. Great attitude. The whole way through he just had a fantastic attitude. He's made some good choices for himself, and now he's living those choices. He just seems happy.

I probably have the most common ground with Lumby. I find him the easiest to talk to. And he's come down and stayed with us in Florida. There are some ways that he thinks similarly to me, so that helps. And then there are some ways that he thinks quite differently and then we can get into a discussion. That makes it interesting. So it's just that great balance with him and me.

Bob Bainborough—"Dalton Humphrey"

I was always a fan of Bob's from his early days performing sketch comedy. He was the perfect choice for the role of Dalton Humphrey. Bob, to me, is just a really solid human being. In contrast to the gruffness of Dalton, Bob is a very sensitive guy, probably the most sensitive guy in the cast. Like, if he's not working, he'll learn about how to grind his own coffee beans and make exotic coffees. He'd bring you flowers. He's just a really neat guy. And he's really good. Nothing would please me more than to see him get his own series or something like that.

Peter Keleghan—"Ranger Gord"

Back in 1986, Peter auditioned for the *Comedy Mill*. What struck me about Peter is that he was just a very oddly funny guy. He's either too good-looking to be funny, or he's too funny to be good-looking, but somehow it all works. In *Comedy Mill*, Peter did a character called Akela Gord, a sort of geeky, sensitive Cub Scout leader. It was an easy and effective transition to morph him into Ranger Gord for *The Red Green Show*. Ranger Gord was probably the most normal looking guy on the show, playing the most dysfunctional of characters. And despite his hectic schedule, Peter always found time to come and play.

Gordon Pinsent—"Hap Shaughnessy"

In the late Eighties, I had been trying to develop a sitcom with Gordon. He had gone to a million meetings with me and had put a lot of creative thought and energy into the script that I was getting paid to write, and when the series ultimately didn't go, I felt I'd let him down. So I sent him a cheque to make myself feel less like I had just used him. The cheque came back by return mail with a note saying, "Not every Newfoundlander will take money for not working." I called him with a compromise. I said I was doing this crazy new show and if he would come out and perform for one day I would overpay him as much as I could and that would make up for the sitcom fiasco. He agreed, and Hap Shaughnessy was born. The character became a fan favourite because Gordon is such a great actor, he made you believe that he didn't think he was lying.

Graham Greene—"Edgar Montrose"

Graham was in an airport passenger lounge and they were running an episode of *The Red Green Show*. A bunch of people were gathered around the screen watching, so Graham went over to see what the show was. He saw Gordon Pinsent doing Hap Shaughnessy. He thought it was a really weird show and he wanted to be on it. He came over to tell me so at the Gemini Awards, and I took it from there. The very first segment we had him do was making fun of *Dances with Wolves*, the movie Graham had starred in with Kevin Costner, which had also earned him an Academy Award nomination for Best Supporting Actor. Graham told me that his appearances on *The Red Green Show* are the thing his family has enjoyed most in his career.

Rick Green—"Bill Smith"

Rick is intelligent, knowledgeable and articulate. He knows a lot of stuff and has opinions on all of it. He is also the only writer I've met who is more creatively prolific than I am. He generates a lot of ideas, and a high percentage of them are winners. His unbridled enthusiasm and creative energy were essential components, especially in the first few years when we were finding our way.

Rick and I have worked together off and on for about twenty-five years, starting when Rick worked as a writer on *Smith and Smith*. Because we were a non-union show and Rick was a union member, I was hesitant to give him a screen credit for fear it would get him in trouble. On the other hand, I didn't want to imply that I was writing all the material myself, so we compromised by giving Rick the name Enrico Gruen in the credit roll. Rick subsequently wrote for the second season of *Comedy Mill*. He then co-created *The Red Green Show* with me, and for the first few years, he and I were the only writers. He left the show for several seasons to create and star in his own successful series, *History Bites*. He ultimately returned for the last couple of seasons of *Red Green* to finish off what he'd started.

Patrick McKenna—"Harold Green"

Back in 1989 when I was looking for a guy I could play off for *The Red Green Show*, I went to Second City in Toronto and watched their comedy show. Pat was in the show. I was aware of him and I knew he was a very talented guy. But I couldn't see him in the role, so I was really there to look at other cast members. Then they did this skit where a bunch of school kids were making a presentation and Pat did this character. And I knew right then that he *was* the guy. He was so great.

There's an innocent side to Patrick that is very endearing. And he's also a very good dramatic actor. Like when he played the Marty Stevens character in *Traders*—they were tapping into the dark side of him. And it was there. They knew it was there. I don't think you can manufacture that. But he's got really big eyes. It's awfully hard to be Satan with big eyes. It's as though he's been programmed to stay on the bright side.

The history of Pat and I from day one, for all those years—he was there heart and soul. And through the trials and tribulations…like him not wanting to be Harold anymore and going through some real conflicts internally about where he was going with his career, moving to Los Angeles and all that stuff… I really felt that for a couple of years there, he just did the show for *me*. He didn't want to let me down, but *he* didn't want to do the character anymore. So he left the show for a few seasons. But ultimately, he came back and we recaptured the magic.

In the later years of the show, Pat was having a lot of back problems. I always wondered if it was Harold's gyrations that had done in Pat's spine. After all, you always hurt the one you love.

Overleaf: Script #300—Do As I Do—The final page of the script for the final episode of *The Red Green Show*.

SHOOTING SCRIPT #1579
PRODUCTION DRAFT
EXTERIOR SHOT OF LODGE

<u>RED (V/O)</u>

The years that followed saw a lot of changes to the
Lodge members.

DISSOLVE TO PICTURE OF MIKE WEARING POLICE BADGE

Mike Hamar became the Police Chief of Possum
Lake. With Mike having a legitimate job, the crime
rate dropped to zero.

DISSOLVE TO WINSTON BY HIS TRUCK.

Winston got a job investigating government
corruption. He knew the territory.

DISSOLVE TO DALTON STANDING BY A WOMAN IN A BLACK DRESS WITH
A BLACK VEIL. DALTON LOOKS SOUR.

Dalton and Ann Marie took a second chance at
happiness by renewing their vows.

DISSOLVE TO ED HOLDING 'DON'T MAKE THEM MAD' SIGN

Ed Frid became the leader of the local Animal Rights
Group.

DISSOLVE TO SHOT OF HAP.

Hap Shaugnessy told us all he'd been appointed
Ambassador to Guam. We hoped it was true.

DISSOLVE TO SHOT OF SMOKING CHARRED RECLINER

Edgar K.B. Montrose attempted to make his own
heated recliner using plastic explosives. He hasn't
been seen since.

DISSOLVE TO SHOT OF HAROLD AND BONNIE WITH A FIVE YEAR OLD
DAUGHTER AND SEVEN YEAR OLD SON WHO LOOK EXACTLY LIKE THEIR
PARENTS.

Harold and Bonnie were slowly taking over the
community.

DISSOLVE TO SHOT OF STEVE IN TUX (FROM PLAYHOUSE)

In fact, everybody changed except me.

FADE OUT.
END.

CHAPTER
SEVEN

FAMILY AND FRIENDS

THE INNER CIRCLE

FAMILY AND FRIENDS

THE INNER CIRCLE

ADVENTURES IN FATHERHOOD

MAG: *You've had about thirty years to think about my next question—what's it like being a father?*

STEVE: The greatest emotional moments for me have been with the kids—the kids I said I would never have.

I remember with Davy, when he was little—he wasn't more than two—and I was trying to put him into the car seat. I wanted him just to sit in the seat. I opened the door. I've got him in my arms and I put him down on the seat. And he wouldn't sit down. I thought the seat was hot but it wasn't; I had touched the seat. So I closed the door.

Opposite: Steve supervises Max and Davy on their boat, Brigadoon.

Davy at two years of age.

And he's yelling and screaming inside the car. I'm saying, "It's not hot! It's not hot!" So I open the door again to pick him up and I'm mad at him. But I had closed the door on his finger. It wasn't really bad, but it was pinching him.

Oh God. I just felt so bad. And as I'm apologizing, he's kissing me, the whole time. I'd hurt him, and he's kissing me.

Well, that's just amazing. And his personality was formed at that time. I'll remember that forever. That's just a kid I will never, ever abandon. He's just so sweet at the absolute core of him. How many people would do that?

That's in the top ten moments of my life. I'd never known anybody like that. It's a hundred and eighty degrees from anything you'd expect. I certainly wouldn't have been like that. I mean, I would've been punching whoever did that to me. I wouldn't be kissing them.

MAG: *You've said that when you look back at the past, you never remember any of the bad things that happened. Do you remember any rough spots so far in being a father?*

STEVE: Sure. Davy was always the more difficult child in terms of being irresponsible and unreliable. Max was difficult in that he was just so headstrong. But Davy was always easier to discipline because he knew if what he'd done wasn't right or fair. He knew. He'd be the first one to tell you.

I remember a time when Davy had done something wrong in school and he got away with it. He was either cheating on a test or he'd copied someone else's homework. He was little—I'm going to say Grade Two or Three.

And he came home and he was feeling bad about it and telling us about it. He'd basically handed in a forged document. I made him phone his teacher and tell the teacher what he'd done. From home. That night. That was a killer for him. He did it, though. That was maybe a little heavy. That's tough to do to a seven- or eight-year-old.

MAG: *Did you stand there while he made the phone call?*

STEVE: Yes. And the teacher thought a lot more of him. I mean, he'd already gotten away with it.

And I remember another time with Davy. I don't think I was ever so angry as I was at him that night when he took me for granted.

It's going to sound like a little thing but it was a buildup of things. He was playing basketball in the schoolyard and I was very busy trying to keep things together. I took time out from whatever the hell I was doing because I knew he was going to finish about nine o'clock. And I made sure I got there about five minutes early.

He wasn't there. There were no kids there. There was nobody in the schoolyard. I didn't know what the heck had happened. Maybe he'd quit early and walked home or gotten a ride with friends. I didn't know what the reason was, but I just snapped. It drove me crazy.

I wasn't even in his mind. It wasn't, "Wait a sec—Dad's coming at nine. I better phone him and tell him not to bother coming or I'd better hang around here and wait." And it wasn't even that he'd thought of me and said to himself, "Oh well, so what, Dad has to drive over there and pick me up." I wasn't even on the radar with him.

Know yourself, figure out what you're about, then go out and be true to that.

I meet people like that in business. They can say something and it doesn't mean anything. You know they just said it—and maybe at that moment they even meant it—but ten minutes later it has now become negotiable. I hate that. I can't deal with it. I don't like people like that. I stay as far away from them as I can.

And to see it in my own son was just…oh, what a killer! I went crazy. I was just screaming at him. And he's such a sweet kid.

He doesn't do that now.

FINDING THE TRUTH

MAG: *What do you want most for your sons?*

STEVE: I want them to be happy. And to have a sense of accomplishment. I think that's a very important ingredient.

I recommend the route that I tried to take—Know yourself, figure out what you're about, then go out and be true to that. Find something to do that works for that, that encourages and supports that, rather than fight it or try to change it drastically. And not just in their careers, but with friends and personal relationships with spouses or significant others as well.

Below Left: Max and Davy as little kids, 1981. *Below Right*: Steve with the boys in 1985. "I want them to be happy. And to have a sense of accomplishment."

236

One time Davy and I were in the middle of a huge argument—because I was always on his case—and I said, "I'm trying to prepare you for the day when you realize that you expect more of yourself than I do!"

And that was our defining moment. Then he and I didn't have problems any more.

I mean, how many problems can you solve just by finding the truth like that? Let's not worry about solving the problem. Let's just find the truth. What exactly happened here? What's going on? What is actually at the core of it? And it works.

I do that with friends, and in my marriage and in work. I always try to figure out what is the truth of the situation. And then let's see how close we can get to that. The hard part is figuring out what the truth is. Because you're not always honest with yourself.

I have this thing that Morag did up in needlepoint. "To thine own self be true." But that's really the *second* step. You've got to *know* yourself before you can be true to yourself. Then you're okay.

The hard part is figuring out what the truth is. Because you're not always honest with yourself.

And kids. It's not easy raising children because sometimes you have things about yourself that cause you disappointment. So you try to project them onto your kids so that they'll make the correction on your behalf, so that somehow, inside your tent, it got fixed.

Sometimes your kids don't behave or dress in a way that you would like. So you might be tempted to get on their case or maybe even step over a line as to what you can say or do to your kids, particularly after they get to a certain age.

Well, whenever I find myself doing that, I say, "Okay, what is the truth?"

The truth is that there are no people more important to me than my kids. And I want to have a relationship with them for all of my life, and I want it to be a good, open relationship. Which means that *they* have to define some of the relationship. That's the truth.

So I'm better off to shut up and work towards the truth—what I really want in the long run—than making an absolute point with them today and then paying the price, maybe forever.

Because I had lived that one.

MAG: *Well, they've both turned out to be great human beings.*

STEVE: You know, as soon as you have a baby, you love them. You can't help it. It's a natural instinct. But what we tried to do is make them into kids that we would like. We wanted a child who we would like, not just love. That really affected a lot of our choices. And what we didn't realize was that while we were doing that, first of all, they wouldn't resent it. And, secondly, they'd end up liking each other.

We never thought of that. I should say, *I* never thought of it. I'm sure it crossed Morag's mind.

After high school, Max and Davy went to Europe backpacking and then they came back and roomed together. I thought, "Wow, those guys are bonded for life." And they're *so* opposite. Yet great friends.

Now that they're grown up, I realize kids have armour seven feet thick. You don't have to protect them. Just let them experience life. They'll figure it out.

MAG: *How did the boys react when you were going through some of your difficult times?*

STEVE: Davy was very…he tried to comfort me. After the show was cancelled in '93, he would say, "You know what? We've got a great family. We've got everything we need. We just lost our bonus." That's the way he would explain it to me. Max was just more like, "Whatever." It was no big deal. He wasn't really sympathetic, but it was helpful. There was no guilt from him. If he had to leave private school, so what? "Of course we will. We'll do whatever we have to do."

Max was never afraid. He's pretty unflappable. The more scary or unsettled things are, the calmer he gets. If there's something Max is afraid of, I haven't seen it. And I've seen him do incredible things.

Like, he decided at the age of twelve to be on a hockey team. Not a pickup game of shinny down on the corner, but go in there and sign up for the league.

Max and Davy at Disneyworld, 1991.

So we go to his first game. He's got this uniform on. And he's in with kids who've been playing hockey since they were four years old. He'd never played hockey. He'd hardly ever skated.

So he's coming down the ice, and he's on his ankles for the whole game. He was a little bit embarrassed. It's not that he wasn't aware. But the next week he's back there again. And three weeks into it, he got a goal! It didn't bother him or scare him. He knew he didn't have the experience or the ability. It didn't matter. He said, "I want to do this and I'm going to do it." I could give you a million examples of that.

He decided he wanted to ride a two-wheeler. He just hopped on, and away he went. He fell off a few times and then he didn't fall anymore. That's his method of doing everything. He just looks at it and then he goes and does it.

I was talking to him the other night about when he was six years old. He was taking swimming lessons. And the teacher has the little kids go up onto the high diving board. They go to the end and just jump off. Max goes to the end of the board and *dives*. The teacher can't believe it. Everybody is high-fiving him.

He says, "I forgot that I was supposed to jump."

Over and over and over again. His initial reaction is never fear. It's always whether or not he wants to do it. If he wants to do it, he just does it.

THE EVOLUTION OF PARENTHOOD

MAG: *You have quite a different relationship with your kids than you had with your dad.*

STEVE: My dad felt that I was lazy and he kind of convinced me that I was. So it's something I've really fought all my life. Like, last night it took me two hours to get home from a golf tournament because traffic was really bad. And I've got a trailer down at Lake Erie that I'd said I would pick up. It's an hour and a half each way, and the main road is closed because there's a truck flipped over.

Now, it would probably be natural and perhaps even sensible to let myself off the hook and just say, "You know what, I'm going to get the trailer tomorrow. I don't need it until Wednesday anyway. I'll get it tomorrow."

Well, I can't do that. I don't have that option. Because, in the back of my mind, my father's going to go, "See? See how lazy you are? You can't be bothered going down there and doing what you know you're supposed to do."

So I'm there; I just do it.

You get programmed from an early age. I don't think anybody who knows me would think I'm lazy. It really bugs me when people think that if you work in television, it's not even a job. Like somebody said to me today, "Workin' for a change?" Just a little comment. But because of my default position that I have a lazy streak, it's like, "Am I not pulling my weight here?" So it's funny. You get over-sensitive to those things. The guy probably couldn't understand the look on my face.

But I think people who know me and work with me know that I work pretty hard. I think I work as hard as anybody who works for me. And they know I would never ask them to do something that I wouldn't do.

My dad was always on my case, and now *I'm* on my case. I have a high expectation of myself. I don't need it from anybody else. Very few people do.

MAG: *When you think back, why do you think your dad was always on your case?*

STEVE: I think my father saw a spark in me, to be honest. I think when he would call me lazy and be on my case a little bit—that was his way, I think, of trying to get me to *not* be lazy. He wanted me to know that if I thought I was getting away with being lazy, I wasn't.

He certainly challenged me. I knew I was going to be a better husband and I was going to be a better father. I had to do that. I didn't see that as being particularly difficult, and it wasn't.

But he had it backwards. He was waiting for the stove to give him a little heat and then he was going to put some wood into it. But you've got to *start* it. You've got to initiate it and *then* it will come back to you.

My family knows that I love them. I not only tell them, I think I reaffirm it all the time. It's amazing what comes out of that. And I try to maintain that message. There are things that bug me about them, and I'm sure there are things that bug them about me, but we've chosen to pick our fights. We tolerate each other's flaws rather than striving for perfection. And when I get mad, I think, "Wait a minute, whoa, whoa, whoa. You're mad at this, but don't lose sight of the big picture. It's just this one thing; you've just got to get over it."

If you come up with a solution to a problem and it's a very complicated solution, it's not the solution.

I don't get mad very easily. I have a big temper but I use it sparingly. But there's never been any question that our family cares about each other—unless they're all great actors. I think it permeates through the whole family, with each other and everything else.

So there's an opportunity for me to feel that I've made something better than it necessarily would have been. I've been the beneficiary. My father did

Steve's dad, Howard, with Steve and Morag aboard Brigadoon, 1984.

half the work for me. I don't have to wonder what was down that path—I've seen it. He ended up dying alone with no friends, and me supporting him financially. Not good.

But here's one my dad told me. He said, "There's one thing in life that's above all else. It's above love, it's above sex. It's above everything. And that's a sense of accomplishment. If you have a sense that you've accomplished something, you'll have the greatest feeling you'll ever experience." And I've found that to be absolutely true.

So, you see, that's the kind of thing…out of that ridiculous dictatorship come these little gems that I've watched for, and they've proven themselves true.

MAG: *I know your dad was gone before* Red Green *came along, but what do you think he would have appreciated about it?*

STEVE: My dad would have really liked the philosophy behind the show. He would have really enjoyed those bits where I'm sitting at the desk and just talking to the folks. He would have seen that under the comedy there was kind of a peace—a sense that we're all going to be okay. And I think he would have liked that.

My father always had a chip on his shoulder, but the things I remember about him are the things that helped me. That's because I *choose* to remember those things. The truth is, he was a man who had an axe to grind with everybody in the world. There was always some reason—which had nothing to do with him—that whatever he was trying to do didn't work, or he wasn't getting the promotions that he was supposed to get…and, you know, the governments were all stupid. Everybody in the world was stupid. So there was a lot of negativity about life from him. But I don't *use* that.

MAG: *Were you and your dad ever able to get past the problems in your relationship?*

STEVE: You know, I say things about my dad, and we didn't have a very good relationship, but...he's my father. I only have one father. I don't feel bad enough about him to erase him from my mind or my thoughts. He's my *father*. I don't mind that. At all. My dad, my real birth dad, is my father. Despite all.

The way my dad would talk to me is not unlike the way I talk to Harold on the show. But I never got a chance to show that Dad was wrong. And he never got a chance to show that he actually had some affection for me. With the relationship between Red and Harold, I think I kind of corrected that.

I always feel like my goal in life is to be significant to myself, and I really feel that my father suffered from that same disease. I think he disguised it as wanting to be significant to others. But I really feel that he never felt significant to himself, and that's why he was always fiercely independent, to try to accomplish that.

He and I were out of touch for about six years, and then in 1971 I got him to come to my house. I was married by then. He was on my mind a lot. I was having a lot of dreams about him.

And he came to the house. He came in the front door and he was just an old man. I think his first comment was critical—I can't remember what he criticized—I probably had a beard or something.

But I said to him, "You know, you've been on my mind a lot. I just wanted to get together. Thank you for coming. I want you to know

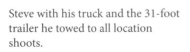
Steve with his truck and the 31-foot trailer he towed to all location shoots.

that I feel pretty good about myself. And I have you to thank for that."

And that really disarmed him. There was no bitterness.

MAG: *Well, you empowered him. That's the gift of what you said to him.*

STEVE: I like to empower people because it expands both of us.

THE GREATEST WEDDING

MAG: *You said earlier that the greatest emotional moments for you have been with your kids. I know Davy got married recently. What was that like for you?*

STEVE: Oh my God. That was just the greatest wedding of all time. Before the ceremony, I had been kind of Mister Nonchalant around everything to do with the wedding. But when they came up the aisle, oh my God, it was just…phew! First of all, Morag and I were the last ones to come in before the bride—and Davy came out to get us. The groom comes out to get us…

The two of them, Davy and Kelly, were just beaming. It was one of those weddings where I didn't sense that anybody thought either of them should be marrying anybody else.

> *I grew up with lots of laughter and love and warmth, and that's what I want for my family.*
> *—Davy Smith*

It was unbelievable. And the speeches…they were either sort of mildly sarcastic but incredibly funny, or they were sentimental but bang on. For both of them, for both sides.

The guy they had as emcee is the shyest guy. He was Davy's roommate in college. And I thought, "Why would you pick him? This is your wedding. This is it. Why would you pick him?"

But Davy has a way of sensing something about people, and he will give them faith. He'll trust them in a position they thought they could never handle. And then they do well with it. The guy was fantastic.

And for Morag and me, it was just…Holy Cow. Max and Davy, the two of them, the things they said about each other. I just said to Morag, "What more *is* there for a parent?"

Davy said in his speech that when he was a teenager, his family life was such that he would prefer to stay home than to go out to a party or a dance or something, and then he met Kelly who was the same way. She had a really close family and they'd play games and she'd just stay in. And he said, "I grew up with lots of laughter and love and warmth, and that's what I want for my family."

Hearing that from your son. Fantastic. And even Max, Mister Cool, he was absolutely impressed with the whole thing.

It was a great wedding. Anybody who was there was damn lucky to be there as far as I'm concerned.

MAG: *What do you think Davy is looking for in his life?*

STEVE: He definitely wants to have a meaningful life where he's helping people. There's no doubt about it.

He's into the church thing pretty big and Kelly's the same way. Her parents

At his wedding, Davy escorts Morag into the church.

never go to church. They're like us—we're the agnostics. We were kind of hoping the kids would get into drugs, but oh no.

At the end of this year Davy is going to be leaving the company. He's been offered the position of youth pastor at his church. His leaving the company is not something I would've chosen. But the way he talks about what he's going to be doing…and his eyes are shining…that's what I *definitely* would have chosen.

> *I can say something that's half-funny and people really laugh because they give me the benefit of the doubt on it.*

He said to me, "I know it's probably a little disappointing that I'm leaving the family business. That's not what you wanted. But I'm following something I really love. And I think that's what you did. So I *am* kind of carrying on the family tradition."

Davy will always want to help people. He does it with his youth group. When he meets some guy, he's already thinking, "What can I do to help this person?" A very giving…a very giving guy.

MAG: *I can see you've had some stirring times lately.*

STEVE: Yes, if I was being emotionally moved once a month or something, I would just take that in my stride, but because it's kind of rare…it wells up. I don't know what it is.

I think because of the way I approach life, having emotional upsets is counter-productive for me, so I just keep my eye on what I'm trying to accomplish and keep working on that, thinking that the emotions get pushed to the side. But they don't. They get pushed somewhere else and then…

MAG: *Something hits you hard.*

STEVE: Yeah.

Anniversary dinner, 1985.

WE'RE ALL IN THIS TOGETHER

ON BEING VULNERABLE

STEVE: I resent being vulnerable. I'm not afraid of it; it's absolute, pure resentment. If I do everything, I should not be vulnerable. I don't think I should do everything and still be vulnerable. I don't think that's right. I don't think that's fair.

MAG: *What do you mean "do everything"?*

STEVE: Well, you know, do everything that you can. Like, everybody tells you what to do and you do it all. But you still get nailed. I just don't like that. I'm not happy about that.

For example, when Morag got cancer a few years ago. I didn't think that was very nice. I didn't think that was an appropriate response, for everything she's done in her life, for her to get cancer. That just seemed kind of punitive to me. Randomly punitive.

But she never questioned it. There was never one second of, "Why me?" It was, "Okay, this is what we've got to do."

In fact, the way all of that happened was an example of my addition to the Golden Rule. Morag was trying to get me to go and have a complete checkup. I never do that. So she said, "I'll tell you what. Just because you're such a big baby, we'll both go. We can do it together and then we'll go out for a nice dinner." She was only going in order to get me to go. And then she ended up being diagnosed and it really saved her life. She thought she was doing it for me, and ultimately it was really good for her.

"Do unto others…because you *are* doing it to yourself." That's really what that was. She was treating me the way she would hope that she'd be treated.

She handled it really well. She gained a lot of points in my book through that whole thing. That was huge.

And—they told me this at the cancer centre—some husbands don't take it well. They don't even stay. They just can't handle it. I guess they're thinking more of their own reaction rather than their wife's reaction.

But if I had been one of those, if I had left her, she would still have been okay. She was more concerned about *knowing* what my take was going to be than what it *was*. She just didn't want to get fooled—that I would be supportive for a while and then just couldn't take it anymore. She's a very strong person.

MAG: *How did you get through that time, mentally and emotionally?*

STEVE: When Morag got sick, I couldn't find any rational, logical reason for that to happen to her. My emotional response was to conclude that this cancer was a random act of cruelty. But I wasn't satisfied with such a depressing view of the world. So that led me to theorize that we live in a form of chaos. For a while, I railed against that chaos and wondered why it would exist.

That led me to realize that it is our function, as people, to bring order to the chaos. The chaos creates a need for order and the need for order creates a need for *us*. So although chaos creates difficult challenges in our lives, it also creates a reason for our existence. Then I started feeling better because I had turned chaos into a natural and essential component that validates human existence.

MAG: *You simplified the situation.*

STEVE: That makes it even more credible. If you come up with a solution to a problem and it's a very complicated solution, it's not the solution.

THE NEED FOR SOLITUDE

MAG: *How important is having time to yourself?*

STEVE: Really important. Really, really important. If I'm at somebody's cottage or something, about a day and a half into it there's going to be an explosion of biblical proportions. And this is with people I *like*.

I don't know what it is. I would say that I have so many thoughts going on in my mind all the time that I like to see where they're going. Sometimes I just find it such an effort to *not* be doing that. So it's like a pressure cooker and I've got the lid on, and I don't have any safety valve. I can only hold it for a while.

It's not a rejection of anybody, it's just my nature. I really need time alone—and we will all suffer if I don't get it. I'll suffer, you'll suffer, our friends will suffer. I don't know what that is, but I know that it's there and it's always been there. Like, we've gone on cruise ships and I really enjoy that—but you know, on that second or third day, boy, you can't find me.

I seem to be a little more open these days, talking about things and sharing my thoughts.

MAG: *Even now you still need to be by yourself, even though you don't have the excuse of writing anymore?*

STEVE: Yes.

MAG: *How do you manage that?*

STEVE: I just go off by myself. We have house guests coming up on Saturday and they're here for a week. Morag will say to them, "Don't worry. He's just like that." Because I'll just get up and you don't know where I am. I do it with Morag. She's just used to it.

I need to be with myself, probably more than I need to be with other people. I just know I need to do that.

MAG: *It keeps the motor engaged.*

STEVE: Yes. I usually have a lot of things that I'm concerned about—I'm not necessarily worried, I'm just interested. And when I'm with other people for an extended period of time, they keep bringing me back to the things that *they're* concerned about. I try to go with that for a while, and then it's just...I need equal time. Or I need a little bit of time for myself. So, no, that hasn't changed.

Probably never will.

At the same time, I feel the need to engage with people. I was thinking the other day that one of the biggest problems in the world—from the very simplest level of two people trying to have a relationship, to countries and civilizations trying to get along—is that people don't engage. They don't truly engage with another human being. They avoid it, or even when they're in a situation where it would be natural, they do stuff so they never quite hook up. Between husband and wife, or father and son, or friends.

I don't really feel like I've got a whole lot more mountains to climb, either personally or in my career.

I see it all the time. I see guys...they're trying, they're kind of dancing around it. If you're going to spend an evening, wouldn't you rather be with people you engage with? It's just so much better.

MAG: *Do you find it easy to engage with people in a social situation?*

STEVE: No. When I was a kid, I was always more comfortable with one or two friends than I ever was in a class doing something, or in a group of people or at a birthday party—whatever the social environments were. That may just be an innate, instinctive thing. That's just the way I prefer it.

I've told you about how I went to a different school, so I was taken out of my own environment and, after that, if I had any sense that I was a little bit odd, that clinched it.

I was always small for my age. I don't think I was over five feet tall until I was maybe twelve or thirteen. So that made me feel that I was physically incapable of competing in sports or whatever was going on.

I remember a number of times in high school when something would be presented, like a Shakespearean play or a book or some piece of creative work that we were examining. And I'd have some ideas, some impressions about it, how it hit me. But I wouldn't necessarily raise my hand first.

When I heard what the other kids were saying, it was like, "What?" I didn't get their point of view at all. And, you know, a large majority of the class all felt the *same* way about it—and here I was with a completely different opinion. At that time, I was just a little odd guy. So I wasn't going to push my own opinion through. But it really makes you feel like you're odd. It's like you don't like French fries—"What's wrong with me?"

But I think *that* part of me is really the whole reason that I've had any kind of success. It's *because* I see things differently that I've been able to get into comedy. There's no bigger asset in comedy than to look at things differently than other people do and surprise them with it.

But, socially, I think it's a bit of a handicap. I *can* make people laugh. And my success has made it easier because people expect me to be funny. So I can say something that's half-funny and people really laugh because they give me the benefit of the doubt on it. On the other hand, I can go into a room full of strangers and make *them* laugh too. But in many ways, I envy normal people.

MAG: *How do you mean?*

Steve listens attentively to *Happy Birthday* sung by friendly passengers as he celebrates his 50th birthday on a cruise in 1995.

STEVE: Like me at a cocktail party. Oh my gosh. It's just *awful*. It's excruciating for me. I'm spending at least a hundred percent of my energy not letting them know that I don't want to be there talking to them, ever. Especially now. So once I've got all my batteries doing that, how much do I have left to say, "So, how's it going? What are you doing now? Oh, really?"

There's a real talent to that. I see people who are really good at it. And I think to myself, "Ohhh, why can't you just do that, Steve? It's not that hard, I'm sure you could learn."

About two years ago I picked up a magazine and it had a little ad in there from some woman—you send away for a videotape and she tells you how to *do* that. How to do small talk. I almost sent away for that...

But it's not doing it that's hard, it's pretending that you're *interested*. I'm not that good of a liar! Can you imagine me with a talk show? My first question would be, "What do you want to ask me now?"

A NEW STEVE

MAG: *For the past ten years or so, you've spent your winters in Florida. When you first went there, did people know you from television?*

STEVE: No.

MAG: *So it's not because you've been on TV that people gravitated to you. I mean, you found your way into a social group there without too much effort, didn't you?*

STEVE: Yes. I'm just not as intimidated anymore. I can go into any *small* group and I'll just have fun. I know I can make people laugh. I can go into a golf foursome, and if I'm playing with new guys, I know by the third hole they'll think I'm kind of funny. And then everything warms up and it doesn't matter whether they know me.

In fact, I prefer that they don't know that I've worked in television. Because they think, "Boy, for 'just a guy,' he's pretty funny." Whereas actually for a guy on television, I'm really not very funny at all.

MAG: *You talked earlier about feeling like you're two people. The world meets one of them, and the other one is pretty private.*

STEVE: Yes. But that seems to be changing a little bit.

MAG: *How so?*

STEVE: I seem to be a little more open these days, talking about things and sharing my thoughts.

Like, I did something today. A friend of mine just had a heart valve replaced four weeks ago. They use a heart valve from a pig.

This guy is a great guy. I really like him. But he's so strict—"Don't come and see me in the hospital; don't come and visit me." He just wants to recover. And he's the kind of guy who wants to entertain you if you're there. I didn't want to add that burden to him, so I've been ignoring him. And then finally I went over to see him and I took him a piggy bank that said, "You Owe Me HUGE" on it.

Anyway, he phoned me last night and said, "I'm home now." And I know him well enough that what I did today was take a whole bunch of flowers and a card for his *wife*.

MAG: *That's good. Because she has to put up with him while he recovers.*

STEVE: Absolutely. She's out on the riding mower just to get away from him. So that was kind of neat. I enjoyed that.

MAG: *And how is that different from what you used to do?*

STEVE: I think that years ago, I wouldn't even have bothered going to see him. You know, I'd find a way to rationalize it. I'm really good at that. But now I've made things like that important where they weren't important before.

I feel less afraid now than I ever have in my whole life. And I think that some of the things, like that example, are things that I probably might have done, but I was so afraid of…of everything. Keeping the wolf from the door and not delivering on something I promised to do, and not being good enough and all that. I always felt that whatever it was I'd taken on, if I didn't give it every waking moment, then somehow I'd be cheating the person who'd asked me to do it.

But now I'm feeling, "Wait a sec—that guy's friendship is at least as important to me as everything else on my agenda today."

MAG: *Any idea why that shift occurred?*

STEVE: I think there's some sense that I've done a lot of the things that I set out to do, and more. I don't really feel like I've got a whole lot more mountains to climb, either personally or in my career. At least, I haven't thought of them yet if I do. The boys are out living on their own. The company's surviving.

I mean, certainly, Morag's bout with cancer was a key component in that. I think I've been more social in the last five years than I've ever been.

MAG: *Do you ever find you outgrow some social relationships?*

STEVE: Yeah. We have had some people that we've seen socially for a while and then it's just—no. I don't want to do that anymore. I'm not trying to stop everybody from seeing everybody; it's just…I don't want to do it and I don't want to wait until it's all set up and then at the last minute pretend I'm sick or say that some meeting came up. I'd rather tell you today that whatever you're thinking about doing from now until forever, I'm not gonna do it. And I don't change my mind much.

Like salmon. I'm done with salmon.

MAG: *Salmon, the fish?*

STEVE: Yeah, the fish. It's over. I loved salmon. Did love. Past tense. It's over

Throwing out a little ray of hope—Steve does comedy between songs during a performance of The Fabulous Miromars.

with me and salmon.

MAG: *Have you told salmon?*

STEVE: I haven't told salmon, but I've told anyone between me and salmon.

MAG: *You're hoping that salmon gets the message. Is this Atlantic salmon?*

STEVE: Any salmon of any kind. I'm done with it. I feel like I had a lifetime salmon quota and I hit it about eighteen months ago. And now we're done. All of a sudden, I don't like the taste of it. And I'm just stubborn that way because that's it, I'm not having salmon. If salmon's the only thing for dinner, I don't have dinner. I'll be okay, I'll do something else.

But I'm *not* eating the salmon.

FRIEND FOR YOURSELF

MAG: *So you're particular about fish. And people.*

STEVE: I'm very defensive about who I spend my time with. I won't go to a party just to be nice. And if somebody says or does something that offends me, I can't seem to be able to just let it go. I'm missing that gene.

Like, I'm in Florida and I go into this Mail Boxes Etc. store. And they're so slow and there's a line. Six of us in line. I'm just about to the point where it's my turn and this woman who had come in and was walking around the store looking at envelopes or something, butts in front of me. And it was just like —"No, no"—but all I said to her was, "Excuse me—I'm just curious. How did you get in front of me?"

She started crying. She's seventy and she's bawling her eyes out. I feel terrible. Oh God. I said, "No, no, never mind."

She went right out, right out of the store.

I thought, "Okay, Steve. Shut up!" I felt horrible. But then yesterday in the Tim Horton's coffee shop it was a very similar thing. A guy butted in front of everyone and I pointed out to him, "We're all standing here. We all saw you come in. Did you see us come in? That should be a clue."

That's bad, isn't it? I need to get some medication for that.

MAG: *Finally you'll take some medicine for* something.

STEVE: That's right. I don't take any medicine.

MAG: *I know. But there's going to come a day when they won't let you into Tim Horton's.*

STEVE: Yeah. No shirt, no meds, no service.

MAG: *You seem to have a lot of friends these days compared to twenty years ago. How do you choose your friends?*

STEVE: I guess it starts with wanting to have friends, no matter what. So you try to give yourself a lot of choices by meeting people and being open to new people. Everybody is flawed, so it's a matter of where you set the bar. You can set it high enough to exclude as many people as you want—including yourself. If you want to have a certain number of friends, you can't set the bar too high, or you won't have any.

And then, you know, it's something way back in my head. When I meet somebody, something gives me the "thumbs up" or "thumbs down." Then we either become friends or we go our separate ways.

I have so many friends whose company I really enjoy. My Canadian friends are good-hearted. Same thing in the States. I mean, everybody has their flaws and their peccadilloes. But they're good-hearted people, I think. And they're the kind of people I enjoy being around. And the things that are wrong with them hurt them more than anybody else. They're their own victims.

MAG: *Are most of your Florida friends Americans?*

STEVE: Yes. I think that with the Americans—and I've got some really good American friends and this does not describe *them*—but for most, the initial surface-y thing is so much easier; they're really good at it. You're instantly a warm acquaintance. They're happy to see you. They shake your hand. They're polite, they're pleasant, they think of what you would enjoy and they try to look after that. It's not a deep friendship. This is not going to be a huge blood bond between you, but on that surface level, man, it's pretty darn nice. And if you're not looking for a lifelong friend, they make damn good acquaintances.

But I find with the Canadians, that surface-y thing is really tough. There's a huge reluctance to talk or be open in any way. I've got a friend here in Canada and he says, "I just don't want to meet any more people. I've got too many people in my life now." And yet, when you get friends here in Canada, they're solid. You know, if I was in trouble I would call a few of my Canadian friends. Canadian friendships are like Lake Ontario. They're cold, but they're deep.

But when you're going into a new community, Americans sure know how to break the ice. They act like they like you and then you have to change their mind. With Canadians, they act like they have no use for you and then you've got to change their mind. And sometimes you just can't be bothered.

MAG: *But once you do, you're solid.*

STEVE: You're gold. You know, I tend not to be open to people. And Morag is. She'll make that initial opening but it's hard for her to take it to the next level on her own. So I can come in and do that because I find out that she was right—these are good people, they're fun to be around. I end up a huge beneficiary of her ability to make instant friendships. And then I think she benefits, because I can maybe entertain the people and they have a good time, too, so it warms up the whole thing. It works really well.

If you go with hope —if you actually act on it—you'll be rewarded.

I appreciate my friends because I know they put up with a lot from me, because I seem—I was going to say I seem self-sufficient, but I *am* pretty self-sufficient, so it's awfully hard to be a friend of someone who doesn't really need you. Or at least you get the feeling that they don't need you. And yet, I really appreciate my friends. I like being with them.

I think it's hard to be my friend. I regret that. I wouldn't change it, but I regret it. Losing all of my friends, that would bother me.

MAG: *Is there anything else that would bother you at this stage?*

STEVE: Certainly losing the love of my family—that scares me—because I think I'm a little wacky, a little obsessed.

MAG: *Why do you say that?*

STEVE: I have this thing about fairness and I think that sometimes I will make a decision and take action based on what I think is the fair thing to do, rather than the thing that may be pleasing to a relative or someone who I care about. And it hurts them. My path hurts them.

And they wonder why I wouldn't just do what wouldn't hurt them. So what if it's not fair? I'm supposed to be prejudiced on their behalf. But I've never been able to do that. So there's always a risk that they'll interpret that as a lack of love, affection or respect. But it's actually love, affection and respect for something a little bit bigger than that transient thing, and a year from now I'll still feel the same way about them. And this thing will be in better shape than it would have been if I'd let it slip away.

SO FULL OF HOPE

MAG: *So you think your reactions are a little eccentric?*

STEVE: Yes. That's where Morag is a good balance for me. She's so sensible and level-headed. The kids really know that they're going to get rational, common sense opinions from her. They won't necessarily do what she suggests, but it's always nice to hear, so you know what the common sense way is.

And when they don't do what she says, they know that they're going to be fighting everybody else in the world because her response tends to be normal. Mine tends to not be.

Steve and golf buddies Bob, Karl and Brendan, wearing Elvis sunglasses. "The glasses were left over from an episode we did about Elvis impersonators coming to town. I took four sets of glasses to Florida as a joke. We'd wear them to play and then forget we had them on. We'd show up at the snack bar looking like middle-aged Elvis wannabees and freak out the cashier."

Morag's much more in tune with what the outside world thinks and how they'll respond to certain actions. I'm not. And I'm less interested. I'm more concerned about how I internally respond to what it is I'm thinking—"Does that excite me? Does that feel like the right thing to do?" And then I'll do that.

Then sometimes I stand there in absolute awe of another person's reaction. Like, I think *Nobody's Fool* is the greatest movie ever made, but I say that to people and they look at me like, "Are you out of your mind? You think that's better than *Star Trek*?"

Well. Yeah.

Nobody's Fool is a 1994 character-driven movie starring Paul Newman as a 60-year-old construction worker.

MAG: *I haven't seen* Nobody's Fool *yet. What did you like about it?*

STEVE: I just love it. I've watched it about twenty-five times. It's such a warm movie. I mean there's this guy who's divorced, he's living in a rooming house, he's got a bunged-up knee, he's working for minimum wage doing horrible jobs. And it's so full of optimism.

I've always had—and this is probably just me saying I'm an optimist—I've always had a tremendous sense of hope that there's going to be something good. Something's going to be good. And a lot of that is because of comedy. Because when you say something that you think is funny, that is so full of hope.

I've had so many experiences where I've thrown out a little ray of hope, and people have responded. So that sets up a pattern in your mind. If you go with hope—if you actually act on it—you'll be rewarded.

A FEW WORDS FROM DAVY SMITH...

I'll always remember my dad getting introduced at *Red Green* tapings—walking out with his hands in his pockets and then bursting into song. He has a way of walking out like he owns the place, and he's in his element. Seeing your dad come out there to thunderous applause—that sticks with me.

Whenever I think of my dad, mostly, I think of laughing, and I think of really happy family times. He makes you laugh. He just has that way about him.

But I remember when we were in Jamaica years and years ago. We got the call that my dad's father had died. My dad brought my brother and me into the room and told us that he loved us and wanted to make sure we knew. And he cried in front of me. I was nine or ten. It was the first time I'd ever seen him cry. I'll never forget that night.

When my dad gets hit with something, he won't share it until he's sharing his plan on how to make things better. It's so not like him to be down and not have a plan on how to get back up. When my mom got sick, we went to the hospital with her, and then my dad, my brother and I went to a pub across the street while we waited for her to have her surgery. And my dad was just saying, "This sucks." No plan for how to...no control over how to make it better, no... no nothing. Just the feeling that this was awful, this shouldn't be happening.

My brother and I felt that way too, but it was sort of like we didn't know what to do because we weren't used to seeing Dad like that.

I think he's more emotional than when we were growing up. I think of him as a combination of a really fun guy and a really hard guy. By hard, I mean putting a principle above people. It was more important, for example, that a principle of honesty be held intact than how you as a person might be doing as he's talking to you. I think as he's gotten older, he's maybe let go of those things a bit and thinks more, "How is this person doing?"

He's definitely said to us over and over again or in different ways conveyed that you've got to be true to yourself. If you look at my parents' lives—they were school teachers who would rather be in a band. That was more fun for them, so they did that. And they became a success.

They've learned the lesson that if you go after the thing you're passionate about and you work hard at it, you'll succeed. My dad wanted to do *Red Green*, so he did. As parents, they're saying, "Look, go after what you're passionate about and everything else will work out."

I feel like I'm doing that, leaving the family business to go work at a church, for less money, and who knows what

Davy helps Steve play guitar, 1985.

the future is in working at a church these days. But it's where my heart is. And it's what fulfills me. My parents support what I'm doing because they want me to follow my dreams and my passions, even if they're not their own passions. That's a tough lesson to learn for both sides.

I admire my dad a lot. I think he sees himself pretty clearly. I think he has faith in himself and what he can do and what he can't do, and I don't think he backs down. He doesn't give the power over defining himself to other people, not to critics, not to fans. He holds onto it himself. I think that's a really good thing.

And he's fast, man. The fastest comic. I mean, the guy is *old* and he still beats me to the punch every time. He comes up with a better line in half the time, every time. I can't believe it.

CHAPTER EIGHT

TURNING POINTS

THE MAN BEHIND THE CHARACTER

TURNING POINTS

THE MAN BEHIND THE CHARACTER

KIND OF LIKE A BULLDOZER

MAG: *We've talked about a lot of things over the last few years. What would you say is the most unchanging thing about you?*

STEVE: Everything. I don't think I've changed in any significant way since I was twelve. I think the same way now as I did then. I feel way better because I've had a lot more positive responses to the way I think and do things. Maybe I'm not as abrasive as I was and I seem to make friends more easily and I can fake small talk a lot better than I could at twelve. But, generally, I don't think I've changed much.

Morag would tell you that I've changed a lot since we got married, but she's

Opposite: Red Green bobble-heads are a popular décor item for the Possum Lodge brotherhood (120,000 members).

only talking about the social graces, I think. And maybe I've gotten a little better at meeting people and being with people. But the basic core of me—I don't think that is going to change.

I do think I've become more considerate of people. If we have people over, I try to think, "What would a nice person do here?" I have a sense of what a nice person does—that's progress!—and then I actually *do* it. That's a good thing, because I *want* to do it. It's not like I'm abrasive on purpose. I would only be abrasive by accident or in self-defence, or when I just thought I was somehow unworthy of being with a group of my peers. I don't feel that anymore, so that helps me relax a little bit.

> *When I've got something bothering me, the first person I sit down and talk to is myself—and I get right down to the absolute honesty of it.*

I try to be really honest with myself. When I've got something bothering me, the first person I sit down and talk to is myself—and I get right down to the absolute honesty of it. And then I try to choose a path that reflects that.

Like my sons…they are two of my favourite people in the world. And, you know, last week I told them that. There's no reason not to tell them. We've been through a lot, working together and all that stuff. The way I treat them and deal with them is based on that feeling. I'm sure they sense it anyway, but I figure they might as well know it.

Once in a while, it's interesting to tell somebody what you really feel—it's like handing them a gun to see what they do with it.

MAG: *You've mentioned a few times that guarding your control over your own life is important to you. Is there anything else that you want to protect?*

STEVE: Well, I certainly have some people that I try to protect—actually, I try to protect a lot of people when I think about it. If I sat down to write out a list of people that I make a conscious effort to protect, I think it'd be a pretty long list.

And I really like it when I have a sense that somebody's doing well, that they're okay. It makes me feel good. I can take them off my list. From people who work at the company to friends to family members—everyone. They're all on the list.

On the other hand, if somebody's trying to do something that I don't approve of, I don't mind them doing it to themselves or, to a certain extent, doing it to people I don't know. But if they're doing it to me, then it's not going to go so good. It's probably a horrible attitude to have. I mean, it sounds like I'm a disgruntled postal worker or something.

MAG: *Are you usually aware of when you're being stubborn?*

STEVE: Usually. I remember in the early days, when Dave started at the company, I used to apologize to him because I knew I was being stubborn. I said, "I know I'm kind of like a bulldozer." And he said, "You have to be. Don't ever apologize." And then I was okay with it. But I am aware of it, yes.

I mean, half the time, with Morag or the kids, I'll try to think of another way to say something because I've already said it four times this week and it still isn't done. And I can't *not* say it, but I also understand that maybe they don't really want to hear it. I mean, that can't be much fun.

MAG: *Do other people's rigidities bother you? What do you do when you notice them?*

STEVE: I laugh. I just find it funny when other people are rigid. I try to do exactly what they want and really exaggerate it. And then I usually end with, "So you must be happy now." That kind of thing. Just so we both know that we both know.

MAG: *And none of them has ever wanted to kill you, as far as you know?*

STEVE: Not as far as I know. But I would only do that to someone I like, and they know I like them.

If you want to be successful, you need to live like you're successful, act like you're successful, talk like you've already arrived where you're trying to go, and you'll get there.
—Kevin Hunter

POSITIVE ATTRACTION

MAG: *You seem like someone who gets what he wants a lot of the time. How do you do that?*

STEVE: When I decide what I want, I believe somewhere in my mind that I already have it. So if I don't get it, somebody's taken it away from me. It's not that I didn't get it. I have it as soon as I think of it. And once I have it, how could I let someone take it away? If it was important enough to want, it's important enough to keep. So, for me, I'm putting my energy into keeping something, not attaining it.

Kevin Hunter was managing Jason along with The Bells and Natalie Cole, among others, and later Peter, Paul and Mary.

MAG: *That's…very upside down from the world.*

STEVE: Yes, it is. In the early days of our band—*Jason*—we had

a manager who said to me, "If you want to be successful, you need to live like you're successful, act like you're successful, talk like you've already arrived where you're trying to go, and you'll get there."

I thought that was interesting. That resonated with me because that's kind of the way I would approach things too. The important side of that for me is putting a lot of energy and effort and deep thought into what it is that you want. Because if you think you're going to *get* whatever you want, you better be sure you're picking the right thing. You know—that "be careful what you wish for" thing. That was key to me.

MAG: *Have you had the sense of good things being in store for you all your life?*

STEVE: Oh, absolutely. Every person I meet, I feel they're going to help me somehow. They're going to say something to me, they're going to do something, they're going to show me something, they're going to teach me. They're the shortest distance between me and where I *need* to go, not necessarily where I *think* I'm going.

How could you be happy if you *didn't* feel that way? What would be the point? There'd just be a whole new set of disappointments tomorrow. When you're born, I think that you've got to be programmed for optimism at some

Opposite: Steve's golf swing bears no resemblance to the superior technique of Red Green (*Below*).

level. Or hope.

Like golf. Only an optimist would play golf. I mean, everybody saw that shot. You're going to hit it *again*?

MAG: *You have a sense of expectancy. More than optimism, you actually expect your optimism to* deliver *to you.*

STEVE: I do actually. Yes.

MAG: *Has it ever failed you?*

STEVE: Yes, so I try to be careful about what I'm optimistic about. Because it's that same thing again—once I want something, I assume I already have it. If I'm optimistic about it, if I have an expectation for something, then I'm kind of assuming that's the way it's going to go. Then if it doesn't, I'm not happy. So I'd better be careful about what it is that I do set my sights on.

You just work hard and try to do something that has some value.

But, you know, I've had a long time now of experiencing the freelance approach to life in terms of trying things. Even if you get something, it's usually short term and you always have to re-invent yourself and see what you're going to do next. And it's probably a braver existence in some ways than hoping you're going to get that lucky job and you can see the ladder leading up to the executive offices and all that stuff.

I don't think I've ever met somebody in a corporate position where I've thought that person should be out on their own because they've got it going for themselves—they don't. They're exactly where they should be. I can't think of anybody who I believe would have been better off on their own, as an independent.

It's usually the other way around. You meet a lot of people who are trying to be independent and you think, "Boy, you need to be protected inside some kind of a corporate structure with safety nets and all that kind of stuff." And that's usually where they end up.

So, for me to go that long and to have had that much good fortune, you can't help but feel that that's normal. That's the way it goes. You just work hard and try to do something that has some value, and it works out.

Bad things become inconsequential. That's a huge lesson because then you don't worry anymore about obstacles or bad things, or somebody who's stopping you from doing what you want to do. There's probably some reason why you shouldn't be doing the thing anyway, but you can't even see it. And it all becomes inconsequential.

MAG: *How conscious is that positive outlook for you?*

STEVE: I still need to remind myself because I think my initial reaction to things is that I'll get mad and want to strike back, or at the very least, let them know that I don't approve. So I have to remind myself that it's not always the best course.

Usually for me, time is a good friend. If somebody could stop me from reacting—like, if something happens and I'm out of the country and can't get to the situation—that's a huge advantage for everybody, especially me. By the time I get there, I've had a chance to think about it and cool down a little bit.

So I need to delay my reaction and make sure I'm giving the right one, because I have a quick temper and I may react in a way that's not really how I feel. It may be how I feel at that moment, but I want to react in a way that reflects how I'm going to feel forever.

Decide who cares the most about this, and who knows the most about it—and let them make the decision.

MAG: *When things aren't going your way, how do you hold onto your original vision?*

STEVE: You know, I was thinking about this the other day. We have some silver in our house. Morag got it. I don't know where it came from, but it's black. It's just been black forever. So I'm sitting there thinking, "You know, I don't like seeing it black."

And I have energy to make it silver again. So I think, "Why don't I just, when I'm sitting there watching television at night, why don't I clean the silver?" I'll clean it and polish it and then I'll keep an eye on it, and I'll see how often I need to polish it. Maybe once a month would do it. I don't know how often you clean silver.

MAG: *It's like, twice a year.*

STEVE: Well, that's nothing! It's *black*, you know? We've been in the house now for nineteen years and it's been black all that time.

Anyway, there was some of it that was pretty old, and then there was some other stuff that was obviously newer. And I cleaned it all the same way. But the old stuff was really good stuff, and when I cleaned it, it just came out like—Holy Cow! And the other stuff I cleaned exactly the same way, and it's just junk.

> *The world would be so much better if people were very careful about giving their word.*

It occurred to me that something of value like that will wait forever for you to come around and polish it up and reveal it. And it'll still be as pure as it ever was. But the other stuff, it doesn't matter what you do to it, it's not ever going to shine.

So I'm thinking that applies to a lot of things. You look back in your life and find a basic truth that could have gotten all corroded and turned black for ten years. But as soon as you clean it up again, it's fresh. And the only person who was hurt by not cleaning it was the person who could've used it. The thing itself doesn't corrode, it doesn't decay.

That just really struck me. Things of value don't need recognition today or even tomorrow. When you're ready, they'll be there.

DUE VIGILENCE

MAG: *Is there anything you have to remind yourself to be careful about?*

STEVE: I'm a very strong person. There's no reason for it. Physically, I'm a small person. And I kind of have an easygoing approach. I'm a guy who can usually say something that breaks the tension or whatever.

But I know that I'm very strong. Anybody who has known me for a while or works with me or anything, they know that it's going to end up pretty much my way. They defer to me or just do what I want and don't ask about it. And that really can be dangerous because if you're not aware that you have this power, you may push through a bad idea—which can be bad for everybody.

So that's something I consider a really dangerous trait. Sometimes, if I'm tired or I didn't put a lot of thought into something, I'll just make a casual remark, "This is what we should do," and then everybody will do it because it's coming from me. Whereas it shouldn't have come from me because I didn't care enough to put a lot of thought into it.

To ignore your own happiness, to not even figure out what makes you happy, or if you do figure it out, to not do anything about it— that's a dangerous way to go.

At that point, I need to decide who cares the most about this, and who knows the most about it—and let them make the decision. Then I'll see how I feel about it. If I don't like that decision, I still might say something, but at least we're not starting from my point of view. My opinion carries more weight than it should a lot of times, and I have to be careful about that.

MAG: *And what would you say you are really trustworthy about?*

STEVE: My word. If I give you my word on something, you're not going to be surprised. I'm either going to keep my word, or I'm going to come back to you with incredible lead-time advance notice as to why I can't keep my word, and what I'm prepared to do to make up for that. I define myself mainly around my ability to keep my word.

And it goes right down to—if tonight's garbage night and it's my responsibility to take the garbage out, that garbage is going out. I don't care if I didn't sleep, or if I broke my arm. It doesn't matter. I'll drag the garbage out. It's going out. To me, that's a key thing.

To me, the whole social order is based on people keeping their word. The world would be so much better if people were very careful about giving their word—and they *would* be more careful if they were planning to keep it! It would force people to be very hard on themselves in the short term, but they would actually be the greatest to themselves in the long term.

I'm really, really proud of being somebody who keeps his word. And that's a direct benefit from all those times in the past when I couldn't be bothered, when I let people down. "Yeah, I said I'd do that...," but you know, on the day, it's like, "Oh, come on, I've got a headache and I didn't expect these phone calls and blah, blah, blah"—a million excuses. But I don't let myself off the hook on those now.

My family will tell you. It drives them crazy. If I say I'm going to do something, I'm going to do it. There *are* no extenuating circumstances for me.

TURNING POINTS

MAG: *What gives your life meaning?*

STEVE: I do. I'm totally responsible for giving my life meaning. It can't come from outside. If it's an internal problem, it's an internal solution. I think that's the obsession with keeping my word. I don't want to be a meaningless person, so if I say something and don't do it—"Oh, I didn't mean that"—wow, what a horrible thing to say! You didn't *mean* that? What are you then? And what are you going to say *next* that I need to ignore?

MAG: *Do you ever wake up in a fit of regret about something you've done?*

STEVE: I've said things and done things that I regret, but generally when I do something, I do it from the perspective of, "Am I going to feel good about this a couple of days from now?" rather than just doing something in the heat of the moment. So that's a really big motivator for me. I do judge myself.

I have regrets. Regrets about being mean to people. And those people probably wouldn't even remember; it wasn't a big moment for them.

But I suffer because I did the wrong thing and time hasn't made it any better. That wasn't the right thing to do and I did it. And I *like* remembering it, because maybe it'll stop me from doing it again. I don't want those memories to go away easily.

MAG: *Do you never experience a softening of difficult memories?*

STEVE: No. Sadly, I have a tremendous memory. It's brutal. I can wake up in the night and think of something I said twenty-five years ago that was cruel. And I think, "Oh, why did I have to do that? I wish I could have taken it back when I had the chance."

Or sometimes I think to myself, "Boy, I wish I'd told that person how much I appreciated their company and their friendship." But it seems kind of stupid to phone them up now when I haven't seen them for fifteen years.

But I don't think it's bad to carry the bad memories with you a little bit. Because I'm sorry I missed opportunities, it makes me do better now. So that's the good side, that's the benefit to regrets.

So, yes, I've had those moments where I've just said the absolute wrong thing, or done the absolute wrong thing to someone. I knew it was wrong and they knew it was wrong. And sometimes I wish I could go back and erase those moments, but I can't. And I've had so many other moments that are just unbelievable—just so much joy and happiness and fun and goodwill and love.

MAG: *The good far outweighs the bad.*

STEVE: Yeah. Whenever I get myself kind of stymied—where I feel like I'm at a dead end and I can't see anything, or I start thinking about something that I have a real big regret about, or we've got a family issue or a business issue—I always have the same reaction. I take a huge step back and try to look at the whole thing.

So if I'm looking at regrets, if I can step back and look at all of the positive things, then the problem is such a small speck on the horizon compared to all of the positive stuff. I find that really helps me.

To me, you can never be a happy person if you don't know yourself.

And the same thing if it's a business problem. You think it's a huge problem but it might not be. A deal going bad or something that you hoped would go through that didn't—you may have just dodged a bullet there.

Anything that doesn't go the way you wanted it to just means that what you thought you were going to do tomorrow is not happening. But that means tomorrow is available—suddenly your datebook opens up! Ten years ago, would you have thought you were going to be doing what you're doing today? Probably not. So what the hell? This could be *good* news. You had the horrible burden of knowing what you were going to do tomorrow. That's been removed!

MAG: *What's the process in your head with this stepping back and trying to see the entire horizon line, the big picture? Is it a matter of discipline that you've trained yourself to step back?*

STEVE: I think it's self-preservation. If I don't do that I will spiral into an abyss from which I will never return—and because I believe that, I can't *not* do it. I can't just let it happen and pretend I didn't know.

MAG: *How do you know it's an abyss from which you'll never return?*

STEVE: I see it all around me. So many people seem depressed. Most days I think the natural state of humanity is depression, and then they have these odd little times when they come out of it. I hate to say it, but that's what I see. I don't think that most people are happy, and I think *not* being happy is a dangerous route to take. To ignore your own happiness, to not even figure out what makes you happy, or if you do figure it out, to not do anything about it—that's a dangerous way to go.

In my mind, it's not honourable to be a martyr, to be a person who takes on the woes of the world and puts themselves last. If you're not happy, it probably has to do with something way back in the past, when you came to a little turning point and you went towards what *didn't* make you happy, instead of what did.

FINDING YOUR HAPPINESS

MAG: *I would call you happy. And you're saying that it's because you refuse to go towards what makes you unhappy that you end up with happiness as your baseline?*

STEVE: Yes—and my default mode is optimism. The other day I was playing golf with a friend of mine and we were both having horrible rounds. At the end of the round, he's got his clubs and he's thinking about smashing them all and quitting golf—he's that serious. And he can't find me. I'm on the driving range. I've got to figure out what's wrong, because I know I can fix this.

So optimism is my natural state. I might get upset and I might slam the door and sit in a room for a while, but don't ever worry about me. Give me twenty-four hours and I'll figure a way out.

> *We're instinctively looking for a rhythm. And if we don't have a rhythm in our lives, I think we're all kind of lost.*

MAG: *Do you ever get depressed about anything?*

STEVE: I have this huge fear of being worthless, of not making any difference, so I recoil from anything that takes me down a path to worthlessness. Which I think is what depression would do. I think that would cause a huge withdrawal, and I would go down into a hermit-like state.

Finding out at sixty that you're worthless would be way worse than finding out at eight. Maybe at eight you could turn it around. But if I'm worthless at sixty, it means I've always been worthless. So instead of thinking that, I pull back. And when I pull back, I can see that whatever I have been viewing as a problem is just one small part of the whole. There are a bunch of other things going on.

MAG: *How do you work with your thoughts to get that kind of perspective?*

STEVE: I actually zoom out and zoom in at the same time. I zoom out to put the problem into perspective in terms of there being a whole other big world. And I simultaneously zoom in to find the absolute core elements of that problem. Let's get down to the absolute core of this—Is it a power issue, a status issue? What actually is the problem? What's creating the complication?

I find that if I have a problem with somebody—or if I'm in a situation where people are having problems with each other—when we tap into that core thing, the lights go on everywhere. Even if we don't solve it right away, we suddenly *think* there's a solution.

If somebody can identify what's bothering you, you feel like you can come out of it, whereas when no one has an idea, it feels absolutely hopeless. Because you need a plan, and you can't have a plan if you don't have the starting point.

MAG: *It takes a lot of awareness to identify problems. Do you have any blind spots?*

STEVE: Absolutely. I don't think you could ever accomplish anything if you *didn't* have blind spots. I think it's really important to have things that you don't see. Like, you don't see that you're not as prepared for your future as your competition is. It's better not to know that.

But when it comes to knowing your own *self*, you can't have any blind spots. To me, you can never be a happy person if you don't know yourself. And the best thing about knowing yourself is that every day you live, you have a little more evidence. If you can't figure it out, just watch—see what makes you happy, and what makes you unhappy. That gives you a sense of what kind of basic person you are—and then don't let anybody mess with that. Because then you're lost, you're gone.

MAG: *Have you ever had experience with feeling that loss of self?*

STEVE: Oh sure. And then I'm really, really lost and it takes me a while to get back, but then I say to myself, "You know what? Don't *do* that!"

I read about guys who get these million dollar contracts and they end up in the weirdest situations—they're either suicidal or on drugs. It's because they're lost. So, to me, that's a really key element—to really know yourself.

I hoped I didn't have any blind spots in the area of knowing myself. Then a while back you pointed out that things have to be "on my own terms"—and that was a huge revelation. So I went home and told that to Morag and she said a couple of insensitive things that would imply that I do have a blind spot in *that* area!

BORN WITH A RHYTHM

MAG: *You seem to remember so much detail about things. Would you say that your memory is more visual, or is it auditory?*

STEVE: I don't remember things visually. I don't consider myself strong in the visual department at all. I see well enough to function, but I'm actually legally blind in my left eye. Funny thing is, I see almost as well now as I did twenty-five years ago, so I can read a paper without glasses—if I ever did read a paper.

But it is a chore. I have to *will* myself to see. I don't do a lot of reading because of that—well, I'd like to blame it on that rather than think that I'm just a cretin. But because seeing is a weakness in me, I don't feel that I'm strong with visual stuff.

Whenever there's a choice to be made about photographs or set design, I always defer to somebody else. It's just not my forte. I do remember the sounds of things. I mainly remember things by the emotion. I'll remember how I felt, and that's my memory of that event.

Like my memory of high school. For me...a lot of people talk about high school being a big deal or whatever, but I was just kind of numb for most of high school. There was no emotion there, so it's not a big memory for me. I remember events where I was really happy or really sad. Those are the things that stand out in my mind, as opposed to a mental picture or the words being said.

MAG: *Yet you seem to remember conversations and stories well.*

STEVE: I remember stories. I have a lot of stories. And I always look for some meaning in stories.

MAG: *So once again, it's an emotional connection.*

Whatever it is that you see as your purpose, that's what you turn into.

STEVE: Yes. I can learn something from a story. So I remember those. And I like people who have stories. Because you know, I think we're all trying to figure out how this all works. And sometimes you can hear a story and it will help you avoid a mistake. That's always a good thing.

Morag's father has always played the stock market, and one time I was asking how people invest. He said, "Well, if it was raining yesterday and it's raining today, it's probably going to rain tomorrow."

I thought about it for a while and I said, "Yeah, but it's probably not going to rain the day after." In other words, there's a pattern, but it's short term. So, if you're going to invest short term, take a look at what's happened historically over the last little while. But long term, look at bigger cycles, and invest totally differently.

MAG: *What did you take away from that?*

STEVE: In my world, this conversation had nothing to do with investing; it was just kind of seeing a pattern or a rhythm.

The other day I was thinking about that friend of mine who had heart surgery. He's having this thing where his heart is skipping a beat, and it's driving him crazy. And there's nothing wrong, it's just…it's normal after surgery. It's nothing to worry about, but he's been to about five doctors. And he says that when he's alone, he can feel it and hear it, and it's driving him crazy.

Well, I just started thinking that we're born with a rhythm. There's a rhythm, and without that rhythm, there's no life. So we have these wild ideas that everything is kind of random and floating and it just happens serendipitously. But, in fact, all of the things that have been successful, all of the things that have moved humanity forward, have happened in time, in rhythm.

My job is to make people's lives happier. That's the purpose of my life.

Whether it's music we relate to, or the timing for an idea, or a certain development or a conversation—we are predisposed to connect with a rhythm, and the rhythm needs to be there. We may not even know what it is, but we're instinctively looking for a rhythm. And if we don't have a rhythm in our lives, I think we're all kind of lost.

And people try to go against it—"I'm not going to do that. I'm just going to be a free spirit. I'm not going to follow a rhythm. If I want to do something, I'll just go out and do it." But they work their way back to wanting the rhythm.

That thought came out of my friend telling me about his heart. And I thought, "You know, we all have that." We need that. I need that four beats to a bar. I'm not a 5/4 guy. I can listen to one song by Fleetwood Mac and then I need to go back to Toby Keith.

I think we only have about one percent of who we are to work with in our lives—ninety-nine percent came with the package. You know, "It's not my fault. I didn't design the machine, I'm just the current operator." The package that defines who we are has its limitations, it has its tendencies. I don't feel bad or apologize for that. But it sure makes you want to make the best out of the one percent that you're adding.

MAG: *I think it depends on the quality of your intentions. You may only have one percent control, but one hundred percent purity of intention can have a huge impact on the other ninety-nine percent.*

STEVE: Right.

MAG: *How do you make the best of that one percent?*

STEVE: Well, I've got a neighbour who does motivational type work with companies. So when they're having a big changeover, downsizing or whatever, he goes in and helps. He doesn't get rid of anybody. He just goes in and tries to get them around to the new way of thinking.

We were at a dinner party with him one night and I said, "I have this theory that people become their intent." That led to an about an hour of conversation. I still believe that. Whatever it is that you see as your purpose, that's what you turn into.

MAG: *That's really funny because I was going to ask you that question.*

STEVE: Really?

MAG: *Yeah. If you could think of yourself as an idea or an intention made incarnate, what are you?*

STEVE: First of all, I do believe that you become your intent. That makes your intent hugely important.

In my case, I think that my purpose—my intent—is to teach. I think I know something that a lot of people don't know. But the problem is, I don't know what it is that people need to know. I think my job is to teach, but it's not like I have a textbook or even a curriculum. But I feel like I know something. And people treat me like I know something. I just don't know what it is.

I also think that human beings are instinctive animals, and the first thing that they look for is intent. When they meet somebody, they're trying to assess that person's intent. They're not looking at how they're dressed or how they look. It's, "Is this person a threat to me? Is this person here to help me? Hurt me? Or just be a nondescript bystander in my life?"

So I think this sensitivity is operating. That means some people can be terrific salesmen, because their actual intent is to help, and a customer can sense that. The customer goes in to buy a car, and they're thinking, "Ugh, this is going to be awful…" but then it's like, "You know what, I think this sales guy is trying to prevent me from making a mistake, or buying the wrong thing."

Somebody can have what looks like a threatening position, but their *intent* is not threatening at all. Other people can be in a seemingly benevolent position, but you're getting all these danger signals that their intent is quite the opposite.

I think people really pick up on this. When I'm on TV, I think people can see what that "me" is like—I don't have a malicious intent. I'm not a threatening person. I'm just goofing around. The reactions I get from people—in email and in person and in letters—that's the feeling I get.

There've been lots of situations where humour really was my only tool.

There's some connection there that I don't completely understand. It indicates that we're connecting at a different level. It's not just that they think the show is funny, or they think I'm a funny guy and I make them laugh. There's always more to it than that.

HAPPINESS IS...

MAG: *Have you ever struggled with the question, "What is the purpose of my life?"*

STEVE: Well, you know, I've always judged my purpose by what was being told to me. I don't really have a good internal answer to the question.

MAG: *How do you mean "what was being told to me"?*

STEVE: By people in general. I could go to a party and my attendance and participation at the party would maybe enhance people's enjoyment. So that would be my purpose on the social level.

On a professional level, I would get direct feedback from an audience, and I'd also get a lot of mail. And it was the same kind of thing, where people were very appreciative of what I was doing, that I would make them laugh, that I would bring joy to their lives.

So, I mean, if I ever got to seriously addressing that question, that would be the answer—my job is to make people's lives happier. That's the purpose of my life.

Now, I also think that the purpose of my life is to make *myself* happier, but there's a double edge to that. Because what I've found out is that the things that make me happy also make other people happy. And that's a huge bonus, because if the things that made me happy made everybody else miserable, I would have had quite a different life.

But there's something in there, there's some ingredient that makes that whole thing work. I don't know what it is. I don't enjoy hurting people at any level. I wouldn't ever hit a person. I never have.

MAG: *Not even pounding out your brother when you were a kid?*

STEVE: No, I never have. I've never punched a person, or hit anyone. Ever. I mean, I've done it verbally, but only when I felt it was hitting *back*. I've hit back verbally, but I don't think I've ever been the aggressor in a situation, even verbally.

If I'd ever been beaten up physically, emotionally or mentally, it would introduce the possibility—if not probability—of being hurt on my way to wherever happiness was. But since I never had been beaten up, I always felt it was extremely possible—and most often probable—to be happy. So I was very fortunate.

I think for someone who went through a more difficult childhood and had all those things happen…it's awfully hard for them to get happy because they're just waiting for that sucker punch every day. I never am because it's never been my experience. I don't worry about somebody hitting me in any way because they never have.

So I've managed to be happy without hitting anybody. If I hit somebody now, I think it would make me really unhappy.

I remember one time when I was at that gifted school. All of the brainy kids were just put into two or three classrooms within another school. We didn't know anybody. But all the normal kids at the school knew we were the brain-kids, so they weren't too receptive to us.

There was this one great big huge guy—of course, everybody was huge to me—and he comes up to me at recess. He's got a whole gang of kids, and they all kind of circle around me. And I'm like, eleven or something, and he's about fourteen. That year the Yankees were playing the Dodgers in the World Series, and he says, "Who are you rooting for, the Yankees or the Dodgers?" And I say, "Well, I'm cheering for the Yankees, but I really hope the Dodgers win."

It took him the rest of the year to figure out what the hell I had said. Meanwhile, I just walked away.

The second year, that same guy cut his fingers off because he reached under a lawn mower to grab something. So, the brain that would circle people and pound them out is the same brain that would put a hand under a running lawn mower.

And humour is always helpful. Something in me defaults to looking for the humour in things. I really appreciate what being funny has allowed me to do. There've been lots of situations where humour really was my only tool. It wasn't that I came in as the boss, or came in with some kind of authority to do what I wanted. I actually ended up getting control of a situation through being funny. I mean, who doesn't like a funny guy? I don't care how bad you are, how rotten you are, everybody likes a funny guy.

So, I think that's part of it, that my intentions are not to put somebody down or hurt them. And maybe that comes across, so that helps me in pursuit of my own happiness. It helps me to make *them* happy too. I don't think it's as simple as just making myself happy.

...A CHOICE

MAG: *I think it is that simple. When you make yourself happy, you make other people happy.*

STEVE: And I do like being happy. I have no shame in that. And people like to be around people who are happy.

I've been very blessed because know what ma me happy.

MAG: *I think it's only the people who want to be happy who like being around a happy person.*

STEVE: You're right.

MAG: *Somebody who is disappointed or angry can't be around you because you can't see their point of view, and they can't make the jump to where you are. Neither of you can really hear each other.*

STEVE: You're exactly right, and it's a huge problem.

MAG: *Whose problem is it?*

STEVE: Well, it's not *my* problem!

MAG: *You just spent fifteen years doing* Red Green. *I know there were times when you must have felt burdened, but you never seemed unhappy. Is that because you were* choosing *what you were doing? And as long as you're choosing, you're happy?*

STEVE: Yeah.

MAG: *So it really doesn't matter what you're doing? It seems like you automatically swing to being happy no matter what. And when you feel like you're out of control, you make sure that you find a way to think differently, so you don't feel like you* *have no choice. So you feel you're more at the helm of things.*

STEVE: You're absolutely right. And that hasn't changed.

MAG: *So the* actions *that you take don't necessarily mean anything—it's the* state *of* being. *Because if you're not happy, then you're in "scan" mode looking for happiness.*

STEVE: Yes. And I will scan infinitely.

MAG: *That, I have finally figured out, is your particular…*

STEVE: …approach.

MAG: *Power. Your particular power.*

STEVE: There's probably a naiveté involved.

MAG: *You use the word naiveté like it's a bad thing.*

STEVE: Well, naiveté isn't always realistic, and some people would be critical of that. But it's part of choosing to be happy.

You know, I'm incredibly aware of when I'm happy. But I'm not often aware of when I'm not happy. Somebody has to draw my attention to it when I'm not happy. And then I'll see the symptoms and think, "Oh, I guess I'm not happy."

But when I'm happy, boy I'm telling you, it's hitting a button in me. "Okay, this feels *good*."

How motivated can you be if you don't even know what direction to run in?

MAG: *My perception is that most of us are more aware of when we're* not *happy. And then we think, "I've got to figure out what is making me so unhappy," and that makes us even more unhappy! But you don't seem to give unhappiness much thought.*

STEVE: It's like mining slag. Who wants to mine the slag? Don't you want to go for the diamonds?

MAG: *This desire to find* only *what makes you happy—where did it come from?*

STEVE: My grandmother was a very positive influence. She got on my nerves sometimes, but ninety-nine percent of the time she would lighten the tension of a situation. She would make things magical.

That reminds me, I want to show you something. I saved it. You remember I told you my addition to the Golden Rule—"Do unto others…because you *are* doing it to yourself."

And you know my grandmother was my favourite relative. Well, at

Steve's grandmother, Nan, August 1979.

"This music...brings me so much joy that sometimes I wonder how people can live unhappy."

Thanksgiving my mother gave a little speech, and she said that my grandmother always said this. Now, I never heard my grandmother, in my whole life, ever say this in my presence. And this is it:

> There is a destiny that makes
> us brothers,
> None goes his way alone;
> All we send into the lives of
> others,
> Comes back into our own.
> (Edwin Markham, 1852–1940)

And I thought, "That's exactly the same thing as, 'Do unto others because you are doing it to yourself.'"

MAG: *That* is *exactly the same thing.*

STEVE: I just thought, "Wow." And Mum said that whenever my grandmother had to give a toast or anything, that's what she would say. But I'd never heard it. So I asked my mum to email it to me so I could keep it.

The idea that anything you do, you *are* doing it to yourself—that's been a key component in my choices. I had a great connection with my grandmother, and the fact that this quote was an important enough element in *her* life, so that it was the one thing she would say whenever she was asked to give a toast—it wasn't just one of a hundred little homilies she had—that was neat.

CHAIRMAN OF THE BOARD

MAG: *You've got a lot of years ahead for doing whatever you want to do. Are there things that you still want to understand? Do you have any big questions that you wonder about?*

STEVE: This music thing that Tom and Morag and I are doing—The Fabulous Miromars—that brings me so much joy that sometimes I wonder how people can live unhappy. How can they put up with that? I don't understand how they can go on, day in, day out. I meet them every day, and they seem to have basically unhappy lives with moments of some kind of happiness, rather than the reverse of that. They're living the negative of their lives. It seems illogical to me. It boggles my mind. I'm curious about it, but I don't have the patience to do anything. If I asked, they'd probably just say, "What're you talking about?"

You know, when my friends in Florida had that Order of Canada party for me, I had to give a little speech at the end…and I didn't prepare anything. I just said, "I've been very blessed because I know what makes me happy, and I'm the type of person who is willing to go after that." And that is so huge for me, because I don't think most people know what makes them happy. And how motivated can you be if you don't even know what direction to run in?

I got thinking about this the other day. When you're born, it's like you're a start-up corporation. You're the Chairman of the Board and you have to put together your Board of Directors. So all of your life lessons—things people tell you, what your parents teach you, what you experience—all of that stuff goes into little packages that you could call the members of your Board of Directors. And you also have this whole range of human behaviour, including envy, sloth, honesty and so on, as part of the Board.

Now, picture yourself sitting down every day—in fact, every moment—at the head of the table. The table is really long because everybody around it, every one of your life lessons and behavioural choices, is one of your Directors.

And in many cases, when things have gone wrong in your life, what's happened is that the Chairman has deferred to at least one of the Directors.

He's abdicated his role as being the guy who makes the final decision.

So sometimes when you read about somebody or you meet someone, you've got a pretty good idea which of the Directors is actually running that company, rather than the central figure balancing everything out. And that's what started me thinking.

I heard about some guy who just got carried away with his dalliances and lost everything. Self-respect, everything. So, my thought was, "Okay, how many decisions do you want your genitals to make? All of them? Half of them?"

Then you see somebody who's incredibly obese or someone in business who's very aggressive…one of the Directors is running the company. That's never going to give the best results. You always want the Chairman, the central person who has the whole vision, to be managing. You want the Chairman to be taking advice from the Directors, not giving them control of the company.

It makes more sense to manage all of those influences than to deny them as if they somehow don't exist. They *do* exist. But you've always got to put them into perspective. You've got to realize that they're going to make a suggestion and you're going to have to *evaluate* it. You can't just pretend that those bad things don't exist, or take the approach that as long as you don't make any contact with the outside community, you're good.

It just gets better, the whole thing, all the way through.

Well, baloney. Those impulses are hard-wired in and they're going to make suggestions, but you have to manage them.

MAG: *Okay, as long as we're talking about choices—if time and money were not a factor, what would you choose to do now to make yourself insanely happy?*

STEVE: I would pack up my golf clubs and I'd go around the world. I would play as many of the great courses as I could—I'd start at Number One and I'd work my way down to Number One Hundred or something. That would be a huge thrill for me.

MAG: *What else?*

STEVE: I'd have a very intense time with Morag, the boys and their wives. I'd take them somewhere that was really spectacular and yet had a bit of isolation to it. I'm thinking like a resort—where you get the spectacle, and yet you also get those times of…something that will stay with you. It's always difficult to manufacture life moments, but I would take a crack at that.

Also, I probably would like to do a one-hour presentation of me just talking about life. I mean, any humour that was in it would just come out naturally. It would not be a yuck-fest. I might enjoy doing that. And I wouldn't do it with any worry about whether there was an audience for it or not. It would take a lot of work, but I think that's something I'd like to do.

And I'd probably fix my house. Get my house right up to code. I can't afford to. But if I had the money, I'd do it. It's a great old place.

MAG: *And all of those things are probably within reach if you really wanted to do them. So it seems like you're pretty close to being insanely happy.*

STEVE: Twenty years ago I would have had a longer list of things I wanted to do. But now I'm living most of the things that I wanted to do. I feel more independent now than I ever have. And since that's a priority for me, since it doesn't scare me to be independent, that's a good thing. I don't see any reason for it to diminish.

Honestly, this is the happiest I've ever been in my whole life. And it's just so encouraging to be able to say that at sixty years of age. That's the kind of thing I'd say in my one-hour talk because I want some twenty-three-year-old to know that it gets better. It just gets better, the whole thing, all the way through.

CHAPTER NINE

STEVE SMITH

NEW AND IMPROVING

STEVE SMITH

NEW AND IMPROVING

DECIDING TO CHOOSE

MAG: *Over the last few years I've asked you questions about growing up, your career, your family, the creative process and dealing with obstacles. A lot of this stuff we've covered has been personally helpful to me. For example, learning about your truth-seeking process and finding out what makes you such a decisive person.*

STEVE: Well, my experience with indecisive people is that they're just so full of fear. They're so afraid of being wrong, in most cases. It's not the ridicule of the outside world. They just can't live with themselves if they make a mistake. So, they become indecisive.

Opposite: "I feel like there are whole new experiences out there waiting for me."

MAG: *When I'm indecisive, it's not fear of making a mistake—it's that I start factoring in what other people want. That complicates everything and brings the whole process to a halt. But I've finally come to the understanding that I cannot truly please anyone but myself.*

STEVE: Yes.

MAG: *I spent fifty years trying to please everyone else, but it's simply not possible—I was kind of shocked to realize that. When I'd try to please people, I'd inevitably disappoint them. And then we'd all be unhappy. I guess I got trained into pleasing others at an early age.*

STEVE: That's normal. It's normal to be raised in an environment that teaches you to try to please others first, and put yourself last. And the truth is, I think that if you're a *kind* person with a decent moral code, then there's no harm in pleasing yourself because you'll be hitting the right buttons to please others as well.

To have a mind that can think about anything you want to and nobody can stop you—how much power is that?

You'd think that if you're not spending all your effort pleasing other people, you won't have any friends. You'd assume people would just think, "Well that person's completely self-absorbed and selfish." And yet, I think it's the opposite.

People are drawn to people who have peace and contentment. Your feeling good is not a negative to other people. There might be some jealousy, but generally, it draws more people *to* you than it ever pushes away.

You know, I'll be playing golf with my friend Bob, and I'll hit a bad shot. And he goes, "Oh, geez." And I say, "Yeah, but you know what, Bob? I'm still happy."

And he'll say, "Well, if you're happy, I'm happy." And I'll say, "Bob, my happiness will never be your responsibility."

MAG: *It's a rare man who can stay happy even when he's playing bad golf. But your perspective is often unusual. What is it you see that other people don't?*

STEVE: This is going to sound really naïve—but what I see is the incredible power that each individual has over their own life. I don't think most people see that. They feel pretty much like victims. I hear them complaining about everything—the taxes, the price of gas, the potholes in the road—they miss the point.

I never knew one kid who was as boring as half the adults I know.

You have *so* much control over your own life—how you spend your days, what you want to do, what you want to *think* about. Holy Cow—to have a mind that can think about anything you want to and nobody can stop you—how much power is that?

Most people don't have any control over anybody else, and very few get to run a company or a country. But that's all external stuff. To me, anybody running a company is really just trying to run themselves. They have a vision and a goal they've set for themselves, and they decide that anything below that is not satisfactory. But we all have the ability to manage *ourselves*.

I think most people who don't take much control of their lives as adults used to take control, or tried to, when they were kids. They've let it slide somewhere along the way. But when they were little kids, when they were seven, eight, nine years old playing in the park or down on the beach—even playing hide and seek, they picked a place to hide and thought, "This is going to be the greatest spot."

They were making choices and acting on them. And then...it somehow slips away. They let it slip away.

I meet people now who are just going through a routine every day of moving back and forth between where they live and where they work, and that's about it. And I think, "They couldn't have been like that as kids." I never knew one kid who was as boring as half the adults I know. So, where did it go?

I don't know the answer to that one. I think they give up. Maybe it fills their day just to exist, just to make money and pay the bills. I don't know.

MAG: *So you look at people and you see the power of the choices that they could be making?*

STEVE: Yes. And I really enjoy people who are aware of their choices. They might not put it in those words, but they're doing things with their lives that bring them a lot of pleasure, and they don't care if it's a waste of money or whatever. I mean, if a guy is building a car or a rocket ship—I don't care what he's doing—there's an expression in his life of something that is completely driven by himself. He's just saying, "This is something I want to do and I've put a lot of time and effort into it."

You need to put a lot of thought into how you help people. It's not as easy as giving them money or property.

And people who do those kinds of things—regardless of their educational background or social or economic position—I find them to be more interesting. Because I've noticed that if people know a lot about one thing, they know a little bit about a whole lot of things. And because they've had to solve problems in whatever it is they've tried to do, it's not that hard for them to talk about other subjects because there are similar problems in everything.

Mainly, they're truly alive.

MAG: *A while back we were talking about how sometimes you set out to do something and then at some point it's not feeling right anymore. You said you keep going anyway because you know that achieving the* goal *is going to make you feel good.*

Well, I was thinking that there are two kinds of people. There are goal-oriented people, like you. Even though they might not feel good on the way to the goal, the goal is going to be enough of a payoff that it doesn't really matter.

Then there are people like Morag who are journey-oriented. As long as the journey feels good, they figure they're in the right place at the right time. If the journey stops feeling good, it doesn't matter whether that particular project ever gets done. It's totally about the journey.

STEVE: Yes. Absolutely right.

MAG: *And* both *are right. It's just two different points of view for two different kinds of people.*

I think it's good to not like losing because if you like losing, you will. But it needs to be tempered.

STEVE: Yes.

MAG: *A journey person can say, "Well, you're not on the right path if you have to push and if you keep hitting obstacles." But that's simply not true for a goal person. In your mind, you're still on the right path. So one person can't say the other person is wrong.*

STEVE: Well, my response to that would be that it's not wrong for someone who's just focused on the journey…it's not wrong for *them* to change their path, because the goal is secondary, or may not even exist. That's fine.

But for somebody where the goal is the thing—where they've put a lot of thought into the goal—that's what they've *got* to go for.

MAG: *Right. But then the journey person isn't accurate in saying that you're off your path when they notice that you're hitting some obstacles.*

STEVE: Well exactly. Exactly. They can do their thing and you can do your thing. But I think trying to do each other's thing is…

MAG: *Disastrous!*

STEVE: Right.

GIVE AND LET GIVE

MAG: *Is there anything you're afraid you'll regret not doing in your life?*

STEVE: I think there's a danger of me not being very generous. With friends and family. I think there's a danger in that. I think that's something I have to watch for.

MAG: *What do you mean?*

I wouldn't mind being taller, but it's not a big issue.

STEVE: I've got friends who are generous. I watch their behaviour and that gives me a measuring device. I'm not saying that I would necessarily go to the trouble that they would, but at least I can see that that's what they do, and this is what I do. And I see that I'm way low in generosity compared to them and what they do for their friends and family.

But I have rules about how I would help. You need to put a lot of thought into how you help people. It's not as easy as giving them money or property. At least, I don't think it is.

As a kid growing up, I didn't get things given to me, and I think it's been really good for me. I wouldn't want to deprive somebody of that sense of accomplishment, but I don't want to be a crabby old miser either.

So, being low in generosity is definitely a weakness.

But I am *trying* to be more generous. In the last couple of years, I've made a real effort to identify my friends and make time for them. And I try to *be* a friend, be the one who initiates getting together. I never did that before.

MAG: *I think it's the things that we* don't *see about ourselves that we have to be careful of, because they will run us without our even knowing it.*

STEVE: Yes, and that's why it's good to have a partner, just to live with somebody. They see things that we wouldn't necessarily notice.

MAG: *If you were allowed to augment your character with any three elements—to supply something that is perhaps missing in your nature—what would you choose?*

STEVE: I'd like to be able to speak more easily to strangers. I also have this competitive thing that I don't think is very good. I mean, it's okay when you need it, but I'd like to be able to shut it off and not be upset when somebody else wins. When people that I *like* beat me, it shouldn't bother me, but it does.

MAG: *In business, you mean?*

STEVE: In anything. I don't like losing, and I think it's good to not like losing because if you like losing, you will. But it needs to be tempered.

When you look at a person's lifespan —it's more relevant to count how many times they were in the moment than to look at how many years they survived.

I'd also like to be more comfortable with people. That may be related to the competition thing—I feel that I can't possibly compete in a crowd because I don't know enough. I don't have enough information to go in there and be one of the more interesting people.

And I wouldn't mind being taller, but it's not a big issue. I'd put that a distant third. That'd be it.

MAG: *You say you'd like to be more comfortable with people. Who are you comfortable with now?*

STEVE: Well, the other night I had a thought about that. It was the end of the season for our Tuesday golf foursome, and the guys always have dinner together to finish off the year. So there we are sitting around this table, and it was a very pleasant time for all four guys.

And for one person in particular, it struck me that it was the first time I've ever noticed him actually being in the moment. Being really comfortable with the present moment. Not worried about what had happened yesterday or this morning, not thinking about what he was going to do two hours from now, or the next day, or the next week.

I felt really good. I felt really comfortable. And I started thinking that probably our most comfortable place *is* to be in the moment, and yet it's also the most vulnerable place. We know we want it, but sometimes we're so afraid. Or even if we try it and sense something isn't going well, then we'll quickly escape into talking about what we're going to do in two weeks, or at least thinking about what we're going to do in two weeks. Getting away from the *now*, you know?

And I thought, wow, there's something there.

MAG: *How do you keep yourself in the now?*

STEVE: Think of your life as a movie, and let's say it's a hundred thousand feet of film. It's just a whole bunch of still pictures, and as they go by, you perceive them as "moving." And you can look at any point on this movie of your life, you can look back at any scene you want. You can even kind of sneak forward and at least take a peek or make a conjecture as to what's going to happen a little while from now.

There's no more limiting factor in a person's life than fear.

But when you *watch* a movie, the projector only shows you the *now*. So, if we live our lives like we're looking through a projector, we're only able to see that one frame at a time. When you're sitting there watching the movie, you are living in that *moment*. You're so focused on the present. And people enjoy that experience! It's not necessarily *their* now, but they like the feeling of that. There's something exhilarating about it.

You're most alive when you're in the moment. And, you know, when you look at a person's lifespan—it's more relevant to count how many times they were in the moment than to look at how many years they survived. Some people may have lived a long, long time and never have been in the moment, never have been, by that definition, alive. I mean, I think you start out that way—every kid is in the moment.

It's funny. All of this occurred to me from four guys who've spent a lot of time together, just enjoying the moment. I think it's a natural feeling to enjoy the moment when you can get there. You want to get there, and yet you avoid it at all costs because you're so afraid of what's going to happen when you arrive!

MAG: *Why do you think that is?*

STEVE: Well, it goes back to the guy who couldn't find his car keys. He'd looked in every pocket except one. He didn't want to look in that one last pocket, because once he looked in there, either the keys were there or they weren't. But as long as he didn't look, he could *hope* they were there! If they're not there, *now* what?

FEAR FACTOR

MAG: *We've talked a lot about fear. Fear of failure. Fear of engaging. Fear of living in the now. I want to go back to something you mentioned a while ago. Your father told you that there are two things that motivate humans. One of them is fear of loss and the other is hope for gain, and out of the two...*

STEVE: Fear of loss wins every time.

MAG: *Right, but he didn't make a distinction that I think is really important. Motivation is* always *fear of loss. Motivation is* acting *to prevent loss. Hope for gain doesn't belong in the same category as motivation because hope comes from a place of inspiration.*

Your dad muddied those two things together and ended up cheating you—because we get to choose *whether we're going to be motivated by fear of loss, or inspired by hope for gain. And that gives us two very separate platforms from which to act. But you were only counting fear.*

STEVE: That's very, very good. Thank you.

MAG: *You're welcome.*

STEVE: I was thinking a lot about fear after a recent experience. There's no more limiting factor in a person's life than fear. It's the biggest obstacle we'll ever face, and if we don't believe we can conquer it, we're right. And we'll have a life that never realizes its purpose.

What's more important than what you find is what you're looking for.

Fear is not only destructive—it usually brings the worst possible results. The nine-year-old standing at the plate so afraid of striking out that he can't swing the bat. The lonely person so afraid of strangers that he never gets to know anyone. The hypochondriac so afraid of obscure random diseases that he gets one from worrying. Fear is self-fulfilling and self-perpetuating. Most fearful people get the results they fear, which makes them feel that they were right to be afraid.

Scientists might ultimately come up with a bomb that can instantly kill half of the people on Earth, but it'll pale in comparison to the one weapon that's been at our disposal since the beginning of time. That weapon is fear. It may even be the devil itself.

I think the use of fear as a weapon or tool is the worst crime against humanity. Jealousy, theft, murder, even war are usually crimes of fear. Let me go out on a limb and say that the root of all of the world's problems is fear. We're all concerned about Iran or North Korea having nuclear capability, but most of us are using a much more powerful weapon on a daily basis. Fear is used regularly every day—by parents, teachers, employers, even friends. We've gotta find a way to stop doing that.

Fear kills. Figuratively, spiritually and literally. So people who live in fear don't live. Death isn't the opposite of life—fear is. Death can have meaning; fear makes a person meaningless.

MAG: *What got you started thinking about all of that?*

STEVE: Golf. I was trying to play golf and just couldn't hit the ball. I'm thinking, "What the heck's going on?" Then it struck me. I was so afraid of the results that

I couldn't execute a golf swing. It had nothing to do with preparation or focus or commitment. Fear erases all those, negates everything positive.

How many times has it happened in my life, where I've aborted my plan as a result of fear? And I've seen it in others.

The way that we used to raise kids—using fear as a controlling device—in the short term, it gets the job done. You can discipline them and they'll do what you want. But long term? What are you doing to those people? They've got to get over that to move forward.

I think that's why sometimes it's the most rebellious kids that end up being the most successful. I don't think permissiveness is a parent's answer either, but

Steve and Morag enjoying an annual weekend get-together with friends from high school, 2008.

you're better off—much better off—to go with offering love and support, and then react with disappointment when the kid screws up, rather than terrorizing them from the get-go.

You know, we just spent a weekend with some old high school friends up in cottage country and we had some really great conversations up there. One night, we had a dinner with lots of wine and we just sat at the table and talked for about four hours.

MAG: *Sounds pretty mellow.*

STEVE: It was. And we got talking about when you first go out into life, you don't know what you're going to find. You believe that you have no control over what you're going to find.

Emotions trump all thought and action.

And through the conversation we concluded that what's more important than what you find is what you're looking for. What you're looking for will absolutely determine what you find.

Then we got into the whole business where, as a parent raising a kid, you really can't control what *they'll* find. But you do have some input into what they're looking for. The way you raised them will help shape what they're looking for.

And then we went further into the whole parenting thing. The idea came up that everybody is a parent, because we all have at least one child, which is our Self. So there's a part of you that's parenting the child in you all the time, shaping what *it's* looking for.

THE LANGUAGE OF...

MAG: *Okay, so if we don't use fear with kids, or with anyone else, what do we use instead?*

STEVE: We have to communicate using a whole different kind of language—a different way of communicating.

The challenge is to get people to reveal their emotions. We don't want people to see our true feelings, so we mask them. There's this odd human condition that makes us so proud of our knowledge and so ashamed of our feelings. When it's an emotional issue, even pragmatic people will present shaky logic in an attempt to cover their emotional involvement. When emotions run high, words cannot be trusted—language was created to convey information and emotion, to reveal the former and to mask the latter.

Emotions trump all thought and action. They sure add to the challenge of human interaction, when the prime motivator in each person is the one thing they're least likely to reveal.

MAG: *Can you give me an example of how you've seen people's emotions behind their words or actions?*

When you think back through your memories, you remember the emotions.

STEVE: I've been watching people I know. Some guys have a lot of money and they have to convert that money into something that has an emotional resonance for them. They have to buy a four-hundred foot yacht or do something with that money, something they can show off, rather than just having a bank account or saying, "I'm worth ten million dollars." A number is kind of cold. There's no feeling in quoting the amount of money they have.

So they've got to somehow turn that number into something that gives them an emotional response, and also gives other people something to respond to emotionally. They've got to let you know somehow. They need emotional feedback from their success.

MAG: *It all comes back to emotions?*

STEVE: Yeah. I really believe that emotions are key. When you think back through your memories, you remember the emotions. Then you build around those. Like, I remember picking strawberries at my grandfather's farm. But

From: Kevin St.Laurent
Sent: Friday, April 07, 2006 9:59 AM
To: red@redgreen.com
Subject: Steve, You have touched our lives!

Dear Steve,

You may not know what an impact your passion for good wholesome entertainment has made on your viewers, so let me tell you it is very large
and runs very deep. I am speaking for three people in my life that you
have personally touched and have made a positive life change. Shane
Rezmer was a sick boy diagnosed with cancer at a young age and led a
life filled with medical challenges. One of the positive forces in his
adolescent life was Red, Harold and the Possum Lodge. Each episode was
an avenue that offered a youngster an opportunity to leave all of his
reality behind and for a half hour, become part of the Possum Lodge.
For many years his love for all of the characters and the lodge grew
stronger. In his last year, you Steve, sent him some gifts, an auto-
graphed photo and a little note wishing him well. This thoughtful gift
came in the post after a long hard day of medical treatment and as his
mother related to me "he was giving up on that day, he cursed life and
had one of the worst days of his life, but when we came home, there was
a care package from the Possum Lodge filled with gifts and he later ex-
claimed that it was one of the best days of his life!" Steve, how could
you have known? Shane was buried wearing his Red Green tee-shirt that
he purchased from a studio visit, and your gifts of love were there as
well.

My sister Ann is the second person who has had her life filled with the
enjoyment of your wholesome show. Living here in Bay City we had the
luxury of being able to travel to Toronto in a simple day trip. She was
so excited to come home from one of these trips with the stories of
your kindness and you gave her a hug during this visit, this made her
day!

I am the third person. I have enjoyed your wholesome show, one that I
could share with my kids knowing that I wasn't exposing them to the
questionable behaviors I find so prevalent in today's cinema and television industry.

Tonight, my sister is having a Red Green party for all of us who have
enjoyed the show for so long and we are all going to watch the show
together on CBC. This final episode will make her cry and we will all be
sad to see the end of an era.

I don't know how I can do it but I wish I could thank you somehow for
all of those years and all of the love you have given us personally!
It will be sad for us because we won't have an avenue to check up on
ole Red and the gang, but more importantly, that man who has such a big
heart and took extra steps to make our lives richer. You, Steve Smith,
are a man who can look back, take a deep breath, smile and know in your
heart that you have made life meaningful for yourself, three individu-
als here in little ole Bay City and I'm sure millions of others as
well.

Steve, Happy Retirement, enjoy. And remember - because of you we will
always keep our sticks on the ice!

Kevin St. Laurent
Bay City, MI

what I really remember is the *feeling* that I had picking the strawberries.

If you can nurture your emotional side instead of shutting it down—I mean, don't let it get in the way of your life, but don't let it be something that doesn't exist either. At least make it an equal partner with the intellectual side, maybe even a little bit ahead—like five percent ahead. That would be a good thing.

So then I'm thinking, which people make emotions more important than intellect? And the answer is creative people. Creative people have a very strong emotional component. It makes them difficult to deal with, and it makes them sometimes overreact up or down, depending on the situation, because their emotions are so much a driving part of their lives. Emotion is not just something they use socially. They actually use it for their career. They use emotions to make their living.

I think the number one way that emotions communicate is not through words, it's through art. Whether it's sculpture, painting, music, writing—all of these things transcend time because they still speak to people emotionally.

I think the whole appeal of the Red Green character...is that he gives people hope.

We don't have fact galleries, where you can just wander in and look at old facts and say, "That's an interesting fact from 1804." But we have art galleries where there's a painting from some guy in 1804, and you think, "Wow. Oh, wow."

I think that art is such an effective and meaningful way to communicate, and yet…art is seen as secondary. If we have enough money, *then* we'll support the arts. Whereas if we don't *have* the arts, there's no amount of money that will satisfy our emotional needs. And I'm saying that our emotional needs are driving the whole deal.

I've never, ever felt this way before. I used to think that the whole arts thing, including my feeble attempt at it, is a dessert that you can either have or not have, and the intellectual stuff is the meat and potatoes. Now I think it's the opposite. The art is the meat and potatoes, and the factual stuff, the intellectual stuff, is the dessert.

I don't think comedy is an unemotional avenue. No matter how dry it is or how deadpan the delivery, comedy is an emotional presentation hoping for an emotional response, with the intellectual on the side. That's the bonus, because comedy can be smart too. Your main reaction is emotional, and then you think, "That's smart."

So now I'm trying to figure out where the heck does that leave me? This could be the thread for me. This could be close to the core.

MAG: *What do you mean by "close to the core?"*

STEVE: The core is the recurring theme for me, right from day one through my life. It never occurred to me that this is what I've been trying to say all along. It feels like this is such a huge thing, this elevation of the emotions. I look back at it now and it's like, "Holy Cow, you idiot." I kept getting the feedback, and I kept not seeing it.

Children remind us of who we're supposed to be. The kids are the upgrade.

I mean, especially with the *Red Green* audience. Guys who are sensible guys, and should know better, are hugging me. That should have been a clue to me that the emotional connection is very, very strong. Far stronger than an intellectual one.

I think the whole appeal of the Red Green character—and I've never said this to anybody—I think the whole appeal is that he gives people hope. Here's a guy who can't wait to get at that lawn mower. Who says, "We're going to make a blender that'll make your head spin, figuratively and literally."

I think people think they can be like that, look like that, think like that, and absolutely leap out of bed in the morning. That just gives them options for the future.

Otherwise, maybe they'd be thinking, "When I get to look like him, think like him and be his age, it's like—well, just put a gun to my head."

MAG: *How do you pick up on the hope that people feel?*

STEVE: Yesterday I played in a golf tournament, and there was a little person—a lady who was really, really tiny—working at one of the booths. She came around to meet me. I thought she wanted to speak to me but she just wanted a hug.

And I've had six-year-old kids who just wanted a hug.

So I think there's some kind of optimism, a good-spirited thing. I think it gives people hope.

WE'RE ALL IN THIS TOGETHER

MAG: *A long time ago you quit the band to see if you could find where you were "supposed to be." And then you found television, but even then you had many ups and downs. With* Red Green *coming to an end, do you still have a sense of being where you're supposed to be?*

I think to myself, "How can I be of the most value tomorrow?"

STEVE: You know, I had a thought during a conversation the other night. People around the table were talking about their kids, some good stories, some not so good. It occurred to me that children remind us of who we're supposed to be. The kids are the upgrade. Like, we've got all our software, but they're the upgrade.

I think we're all born with a deep inner sense of what we're supposed to be. Our parents and others may think they're teaching us, but the only lessons that resonate are the ones that remind us of what we already know, what we're born knowing.

There's nothing more peaceful or satisfying than being who we're supposed to be. But we don't know it until we get there, and sometimes getting there seems too difficult.

Because if nobody provides that resonance, it's very difficult for the child to stay true to his inner self. Even if we grow up in an environment that does reinforce those inner truths, it's not always an easy path. There are lots of reasons to stray. And almost all of the time, the resonating messages we get from our parents and teachers and life are mixed in with so many non-resonating messages. We get tired of sifting through the data and making choices, or we secretly want to ignore those truths. So we just let it all slide.

At best, the resonating messages from children are pure and clear and relentless, which makes those messages much harder to dismiss. The child reminds the parent of who he's supposed to be, and the parent accepts the message and alters his words and actions to achieve that goal. The parent's behaviour then resonates with the child and reinforces the child's commitment to be who he's supposed to be.

Throughout life, the parent and child have this mutual gravitational pull that keeps them both in orbit. Take it away and, most of the time, one or both go hurtling off into space.

There's even a religious context in the sense that whenever you repent and get around to being who you're supposed to be, like good silver that's been tarnished, the truth will be waiting.

MAG: *Your concept of parents and kids helping each other to become who they're supposed to be sounds a lot like, "I'm pulling for you. We're all in this together"— which Red says on every episode of the show. That statement conveys such a feeling of well-being and innocence. But how do you remain innocent through your life?*

You think, "I just need to go harder, faster, higher." No! You've got to throw those tools away.

STEVE: I feel that whatever it is I'm about to do, I'm innocent going into it. I have the ability to remain that way, or get guilty.

That's just the whole optimism thing, looking forward rather than looking back into the past. I don't see any reason why you have to be guilty in the future. You haven't done anything yet. And if you're guilty in the past, it informs you, it teaches you something, so now you're more educated and have a better chance of remaining innocent in the future.

I think to myself, "How can I be of the most value tomorrow? How can I achieve my goals most successfully?" If I spend my time licking my wounds over something that happened before, or feeling horrible about something that I did, even though I would never do it that way again—I'm going to waste another day.

I don't think there's any purpose in being pessimistic. We're all going to die—it can't get more pessimistic than that. So get over it and move forward. Or get a good parking spot in the cemetery now and just wait it out.

To me, it's a very easy choice, "Let's see how much we can get out of a no-chance situation, just for fun." That's where the optimism kicks in, and the innocence.

That "I'm pulling for you" thing—it's like the audience thought I knew something. They would come to me after the tapings—every night—they would come up and shake my hand. These guys were looking at me like I know something. I could see it in their faces. I think I'm supposed to know something. I don't know what it is, but those guys see it in the show. They'd be better at identifying what it is than I am.

Maybe it's that optimism thing—I would usually make some sexual reference at the end of the show. And I think the audience likes that, because here's this old guy and he's still got a lot of life force.

The journey becomes more of a priority when you don't have as long to live as you used to have.

MAG: *That's it—life force is what you know. That's what they want from you. You're always looking for life force, and you draw it through others. People who like to be around you aren't ashamed to have their life force read by you, or to share it with you.*

STEVE: Yes. That *is* what I know. That's exactly what I know. That's funny. And my family and my closest friends are loaded with life force. I see it and appreciate it in them, and I think they appreciate it in me.

MAG: *And maybe that explains your emotional connection with your audience, because they like that about you too. You respect the life force in yourself and in them.*

CHANGING YOUR TOOLS

MAG: *I don't know about you, but I've enjoyed this whole process of discussing your life and ideas. It's made me think and feel differently about how I approach* *life. And now that we're almost through the interviews, I'm wondering if there's anything else you want to add?*

STEVE: I have this new thing that's sort of revealing itself to me. I haven't got it figured out yet. I'm not going to rush it, but I think it's important that I figure it out, because at first, it seems like it contradicts a lot of things that are important to me.

It all started with golf. It was getting to the point where I just accepted that I couldn't improve. I wasn't even disappointed anymore. I just accepted that I couldn't do better.

Then it occurred to me that golf, from the time you take it up until you reach some kind of proficiency—like, where you don't embarrass yourself every day—requires a tremendous amount of focus and dedication, and a certain amount of aggression. Because even when you fail, you get out the next day and you go to that practice range.

And you have to be extremely conscious of what your hands are doing, what your arms are doing—everything that your body is doing. I practised all of that for ten years. I'd reached a certain level and I wasn't getting any farther. It seemed that the more of those approaches that I kept using, the farther away I was getting.

There's got to be a purpose in everything for me. But it doesn't have to be the only reason to be doing something.

So, it suddenly occurred to me that those tools—the focus, dedication and aggression—won't work anymore. They were only useful to get me so far. If I want to go any further, I have to abandon those tools and use other ones.

The last thing you want to have in your golf swing is aggression. You don't even want to be *aware* of what your hands and arms and body are doing. You've got to let them all go, completely. The only thing that you keep is your focus on the golf ball. So, the core reason that you're there doesn't change, but the way you get to it, the way you maximize it, changes a hundred and eighty degrees.

I had been hesitating to enter the club championship last weekend, but after that realization, I decided to play. I tried not being aggressive at all, not being in any way aware of what any part of my body was doing. Just focusing on the ball and trying to stay as calm as I could.

I had my career round on the first day and I beat it by seven strokes on the second day. I couldn't get over it! It was such a personal victory for me.

I've really been looking at the same principle in other areas. And I think it holds true. It seems to me that once you use a particular group of tools to get to a certain level of success or satisfaction or accomplishment, those are the tools you habitually reach for. And it's so frustrating when they won't take you to the next level.

Now it's important that life is more of a shared experience.

You think, "I just need to go harder, faster, higher." No! You've got to throw those tools away. You made choices, tools that you put aside and other tools that you chose to get you where you wanted to go. Now you've got to reach way back to tools you've never used before. I'm thinking that if you had used *all* of the tools coming right out of the gate, you might never have gotten anywhere in life.

So I've been applying that to my personal life in terms of how I deal with people. I'm trying to use different tools. Whatever I'm doing, where I would have been aggressive before, I'm now saying, "Okay, you know what, let's just back off and see how that works."

MAG: *Are the different tools working?*

STEVE: I think so. Another thing that flashed through my mind when I was going through all of that…I used to sailboat race with a guy. He was older than me and he had done a lot of racing. He told me one time that he was so far ahead in a race that he came about and *backed* over the finish line. Just to be a goof. And I thought, "That relates somehow to what I'm talking about. You're doing a one- hundred-and-eighty-degree turn to go forward! It's a new kind of mindset."

For me, even though I'm happy, I think what will bring me to the next level of happiness or contentment is the feeling of being more complete, across the spectrum, rather than having more success in a *specific* area that I've chosen.

I think that before I retired, I was oriented toward succeeding at whatever goal felt right to me. It was vertical, like putting up the CN Tower. And if you picture that structure as having one fundamental supporting member that carries on all the way up its height and supports this tall, eighteen-hundred-foot-high thing—that's the kind of vision I had.

And now I see a structure more like…the Royal York Hotel. Not nearly as high, but built on a much wider foundation that includes all kinds of levels of human interaction and activity. So now I've got time to interact with people, to share things, to learn from them.

When I was working, I had to put blinders on and say, "I really don't have time for that right now." Or "I don't see how that serves my building-the-CN-Tower career thing."

When you retire, you're automatically saying, "I've chosen to lower my profile." Sometimes that's hard on the ego, if your ego is being fed by your profile. For me it's not, but that's why I say that for happiness to come to me now, I need to broaden out. Even though it'll be a much lower structure I'm building now, it'll be a lot wider and deeper. I would never have gone in that direction ten years ago.

The CN Tower, built by the Canadian National Railway, 1973–1976, is a communications tower and tourist attraction located in downtown Toronto. It stands 553.33 metres (1,815.39 ft.) tall and is currently the tallest free-standing structure in the Americas.

MAG: *Why did you resist it for all those years?*

STEVE: This broader spectrum—I never *knew* that was what I wanted. And if what I want is to be broader rather than higher, then that's where the new tools come in. The reason I'm so narrow is because there are a few tools in my toolkit that I've never used; they're untouched by human hands. So, now I've got to start using those new tools to broaden out.

MAG: *Are you saying that maybe the journey is worthwhile now, whereas in the past, only the goal seemed worthwhile?*

STEVE: Absolutely. Particularly when life is shorter. For me, the journey becomes more of a priority when you don't have as long to live as you used to have.

When you're younger and you set a goal, you don't even think about time. You just think, "I have plenty of time to acquire that. I don't need to achieve it in the next ten years." But when you may not have ten years or twenty years, then naturally it focuses you on the journey. Because you do have a journey, right now, today.

So becoming more focused on the journey is a natural change that comes with retiring, but it didn't occur naturally in me. I had to think about it. But at least I'm noticing it! I feel good about that.

The most incredible thing for me is realizing that the patterns I've picked up that have brought me success in the past are now the patterns that are most important to abandon. Without losing the core.

The Royal York, a landmark hotel in Toronto, was officially opened in 1929. It is now The Fairmont Royal York.

THE BIG DADDY OF IT ALL

MAG: *We're back to the core. You can't lose the core because the core is you.*

STEVE: The core is me. But the methods I use to get what I want—these are crucial.

I could define the things that have worked for me in my professional career and just apply those exact same things to my personal life. But I'd get the same result. Nothing would change. I'd still sense a certain amount of "something's missing here."

But if I go at things a whole different way, even if they don't get me anywhere, it has a far more positive effect on the whole picture for me.

MAG: *So when you were focused on building the vertical structure in your career, you had a feeling that something was missing?*

STEVE: When I got to the top of my own personal CN Tower, I still felt like something was missing. Because in a way, I had created my own world, so it was like being in a roomful of mirrors at the end of it. Whereas…it's a lot more interesting to be in a roomful of people.

Whenever I've done this one-eighty, it's been very satisfying.

I mean, geez, sixty years of, "If it's not working, you're not working hard enough!" If whatever I was trying to do wasn't working, I'd feel I wasn't holding up my end. That all went away with me saying to myself, "No, you're going at it the wrong way!"

When it came to me, I thought, "Holy Cow, this is mind boggling." And people aren't aware of this. I haven't even figured it out for myself yet, but after I do that, I've got to figure out how to present it to people in such a way that they can have some understanding of what I'm talking about. Because it's so *crazy…*

MAG: *It's not crazy, but it is the reverse of what our culture rewards.*

STEVE: I think it's a big one; I think it's really key. I haven't really figured out all of the nuances, but I'm not going to do that this time. I'm going to let it slowly unfold. I think it could be very helpful to people, so I want to get it right. Even if I don't get it quite right, I want to get it right *enough* that they can take it the rest of the way.

MAG: *So your old tools were aggression and focus. But now you seem to be developing a gentler perspective.*

STEVE: First of all, this change just happened. Like I opened a door and now I'm in another place. I don't think the change can be managed by the people who are going through it. It's like getting teeth or facial hair—you can't plan for them, they just happen.

You get to this level and now it's important that life is more of a shared experience. There's a lot more sharing. It's the timeline of life. Some time before you pass away, you want to…you want to…it would be great if you could pass on everything.

Well, this is the way you do it. You don't do it by standing at a lectern pontificating. You do it by actually backing off a little bit. I mean, earlier on I talked about how, if you want to have a good relationship with your kids, you've got to let them define that relationship to a certain extent. This is the same kind of thing.

You've got to let your friends define the friendship a little bit. And you've got to let the people you're talking to define the conversation a little bit. All the way down the line, you've got to do a little more receiving than transmitting.

And then what happens is that *you* actually end up learning something and developing.

So that is the bigger picture. It's more of a sharing thing than just being so self-focused that you're just going to hammer forward no matter what.

MAG: *So would you say that you're changing into a blend of goal-oriented and journey-oriented person?*

STEVE: I can probably never get away from all of the goal stuff. There's got to be a purpose in everything for me. But it doesn't have to be the only reason to be doing something. There's value in things that don't necessarily take you directly towards that goal.

MAG: *It seems like what you're saying is that you aren't setting goals in the way that you used to, which is kind of a mind-bender because that used to be what filled every moment.*

STEVE: Well, the fear is gone.

MAG: *The fear of not meeting the goal?*

STEVE: Yes.

MAG: *So the goal was torturing you all along?*

I feel like there are whole new experiences out there waiting for me. Brand new, because I've got a different approach.

STEVE: Absolutely. If you feel that your goal is your destiny, that it's what you should be doing, and that you'll let yourself down if you don't achieve it...well, once you take that out of the equation, you see how much it was colouring the drive.

And again, a lot of this is a factor of chronology. It's a lot more comfortable to do this one-hundred-and-eighty-degree change at sixty than at thirty. I welcome aging.

It's just a new adventure, and it's a *big* adventure.

And I personally know a hundred guys who would be shocked out of their shoes to find out that *that's* the next step—to do a one-hundred-and-eighty-degree change with the way you *do* things.

You know, I have friends who are retired and near retirement and some who are not near retirement, and they all think that I'm happier than they are, so they would listen to me. So, I better get it right!

MAG: *I think you can afford to relax about that because when you say, "I better get it right," that's an aggressive stance on your new easier thing.*

STEVE: I know. I still have setbacks. I get aggressive. I get controlling. But I never have a setback that works—and I don't get *positive* feedback when I have one. Like, I'll be golfing and all of a sudden it's, "What the hell was that?"

But the new pattern is definitely there. Morag said to me last week that I'm a completely different person.

So that's the big change. That's the start of it. That's the Big Daddy.

All those years, I would never let it go.

MAG: *Let what go?*

STEVE: Anything! If I wasn't on top of something—hammering at it, checking its status every hour, making sure that I was constantly moving and repositioning—then it wasn't going to work out.

After sixty years of believing that, to then say, "You know, what would suit this situation best would be to let this go and see where it ends up"—and then just give up and toss the reins, see what happens—it definitely is coming from a place of freedom. From being at a certain level where I can afford to do that. I don't see myself getting hurt. I don't feel vulnerable letting it go.

I've had setbacks, like I said, but whenever I've done this one-eighty, it's been very satisfying.

NEW AND IMPROVED

MAG: *Well, a setback, as you describe it, is pretty important to feel, isn't it? Without those negative feelings to measure things against, you would have no way of knowing that you were moving forward.*

STEVE: That's right.

MAG: *And the truth is, you can look at any subject and find a way to feel either good or bad about it. It's your choice.*

STEVE: Everything is double-sided. You always try to take the best option, but there are bad things in every option that you take. And even the options that you thought were the worst have some good things in them.

Chances are it's not all bad in those options that I rejected over the years. There's probably something good in there that would help build my overall sense of well-being at whatever level I'm at now. So I'm going to find new options, but even the old ones that I've rejected, when I revisit those—it's like a guy revisiting his son. I'm going in from a different perspective.

So I find it exciting that there are all kinds of value-added things out there from my own past *and* from things in the future—even options that I would not ordinarily pick. I would go that way now, just to see how that works out.

You know, when I think about it, there are so many things in nature that support this. Like the Law of Diminishing Returns. You keep doing that same thing and then eventually it'll be meaningless. It doesn't just keep getting better and better into infinity. You've *got* to go somewhere else to get those returns that you're looking for, so that you have some significance and a sense of accomplishment.

I feel like there are whole new experiences out there waiting for me. Brand new, because I've got a different approach.

MAG: *Because* you *are different.*

If I can focus on being in the moment, things work out a lot better.

STEVE: Yes. I've got this new paradigm going on. It's absolutely bizarre. And the only bad days I have are the ones where I slip back and I try to control too much, go against the flow.

It's like reincarnation without dying. It's moving on to another life form. For me, it's a huge change. Talk about recalibrating your instruments.

So, I'm not sixty. I'm like six months old! But it feels right to me. Whatever's happening feels absolutely correct. I'm not worried about it and I'm not excited. I'm not frenetic like, "Oh come on!" and needing it to happen right now. I like the pace. In fact, I don't have to have anything to do with the pace.

MAG: *So do you have a clearer picture now of what the new tools are for this segment of your life?*

STEVE: Well, it sounds like a cliché, but I think the main tool is being in the moment. I think if you're a goal-oriented person, you're always living in the future. And you miss a lot of what's happening right now. When people are in the moment, it's a neat thing, so I think that's the most important tool. And I don't do it very well.

But if I can focus on that, if I can focus on being in the moment, things work out a lot better.

MAG: *Can you give me a recent example?*

STEVE: Sure. Sitting around last night on the boat with seven other people, talking about our lives. And instead of thinking about the phone calls I had to make tomorrow, I'm actually listening to what they're saying and seeing how I feel about it, and then reacting just enough to get them to say something else. Rather than me defining the conversation so we can move on to the next problem and solve that. That's what I would've done in the past. "Let's move on to something else." Or I'd leave the room.

Or even if I stayed in the room I wouldn't be thinking about this conversation—I'd be thinking about something I'm doing a week from now, or some deadline I've got coming up. Rather than just thinking, "This is good enough right here. This is an interesting opportunity. And these people—their lives can teach me about my life." That kind of attitude, rather than feeling, "If you're not talking about something that I see as being directly related to my goal, you're really wasting my time."

You end up liking people more, because you gave them a chance.

MAG: *So, on an emotional level, you used to feel anxious a lot of the time?*

STEVE: Yes, absolutely. Whereas the feeling of last night was just more…natural. It's like, that's the way you're supposed to interact with people.

If you're there with people, or even worse, if you've invited them to be there with you, that implies that you're going to be there too. They didn't think you invited them to *replace* you.

So it feels more honest. And then at the end of the conversation you feel like something happened here. You shared something. You end up liking people more, because you gave them a chance.

MAG: *So this could solve all of your problems with feeling uncomfortable with people.*

STEVE: Yes, that's exactly right. That was always my discomfort with the moment—wanting to be anywhere else at any time else, rather than be there in that particular moment. If I would've just accepted being there, it would've been fine.

MAG: *What a breakthrough. And you can look back and know that your path was perfect because it brought you to here.*

STEVE: That's so true. It's funny, you know, as I get a better sense of this, and then I look back at things—I mean, how long have we been having these conversations now? Three years?

And to go back and see how some things are still valid, and other things have fallen by the wayside...

I just have to keep my eyes open and hope I'll know the next thing when I see it.

MAG: *Yes, when you think about the earlier sessions we had, you were a different guy.*

STEVE: Yes, and it's so funny that this big change came out of golf. You know? I'm thinking that I was attracted to golf because I knew subconsciously that it would give me this—because there's something very spiritual about golf.

MAG: *Where you do want this new paradigm to take you?*

STEVE: Well, if I do figure this out, I'm going to want to tell everybody. Particularly people my age. And I'll be right on the edge of obnoxious. I'll be just...obnoxious. That's what I'll be. I'll say to people, "This is good for you. You don't know it, but you've got to hear this. Hey, you know what? You know what I'm thinking?"

People will say, "Oh no, here he comes."

I'm afraid that if I do figure this out, I'll really want to tell everybody and I won't be able to. I won't be able to find a way to tell everybody that doesn't either turn them all off, or get me killed. I'm worried that I just won't get the platform to do it.

THE BEST IS STILL AHEAD

MAG: *You're at a really interesting crossroad.*

STEVE: Well I feel—mentally and emotionally—younger than I am. So that's encouraging. And I have a reasonable golf score.

MAG: *Don't start.*

STEVE: I'm now—

MAG: *Here we go.*

STEVE: I'm so glad you brought this up. I'm now the long hitter of my foursome.

MAG: *Oh, please.*

STEVE: Well, it needed to be said.

MAG: *It didn't need to be heard.*
   Well, we're now at the end of our last session and you still haven't figured out what you're going to do with the rest of your life.

The Canadian Radio-television and Telecommunications Commission (CRTC) is an independent agency responsible for regulating Canada's broadcasting and telecommunications systems. It reports to Parliament through the Minister of Canadian Heritage.

STEVE: I don't need to. Two years ago I was really concerned about what I was going to do. I thought maybe I'd go into politics or become head of the CRTC or get into the broadcasting side of television. I didn't know what the hell I was even talking about.
   I just have to keep my eyes open and hope I'll know the next thing when I see it. It's already worked a couple of times.

MAG: *It has?*

STEVE: Yeah. The first time was when we started The Fabulous Miromars in Florida. That's still going strong. And the second time was this book. This book has everything in it that I would want out of anything that I would ever do.

MAG: *One thing I've never asked you and I'm not sure you can answer—What are you hoping to get from this book?*

STEVE: Well, you know, I've already got it. This whole process has helped me to clarify things and prepare for the next phase.

And if it becomes a book that somebody reads and it helps that person in the way it's helped me, that would be fantastic.

NOT THE END

EPILOGUE

THE LAST WORD

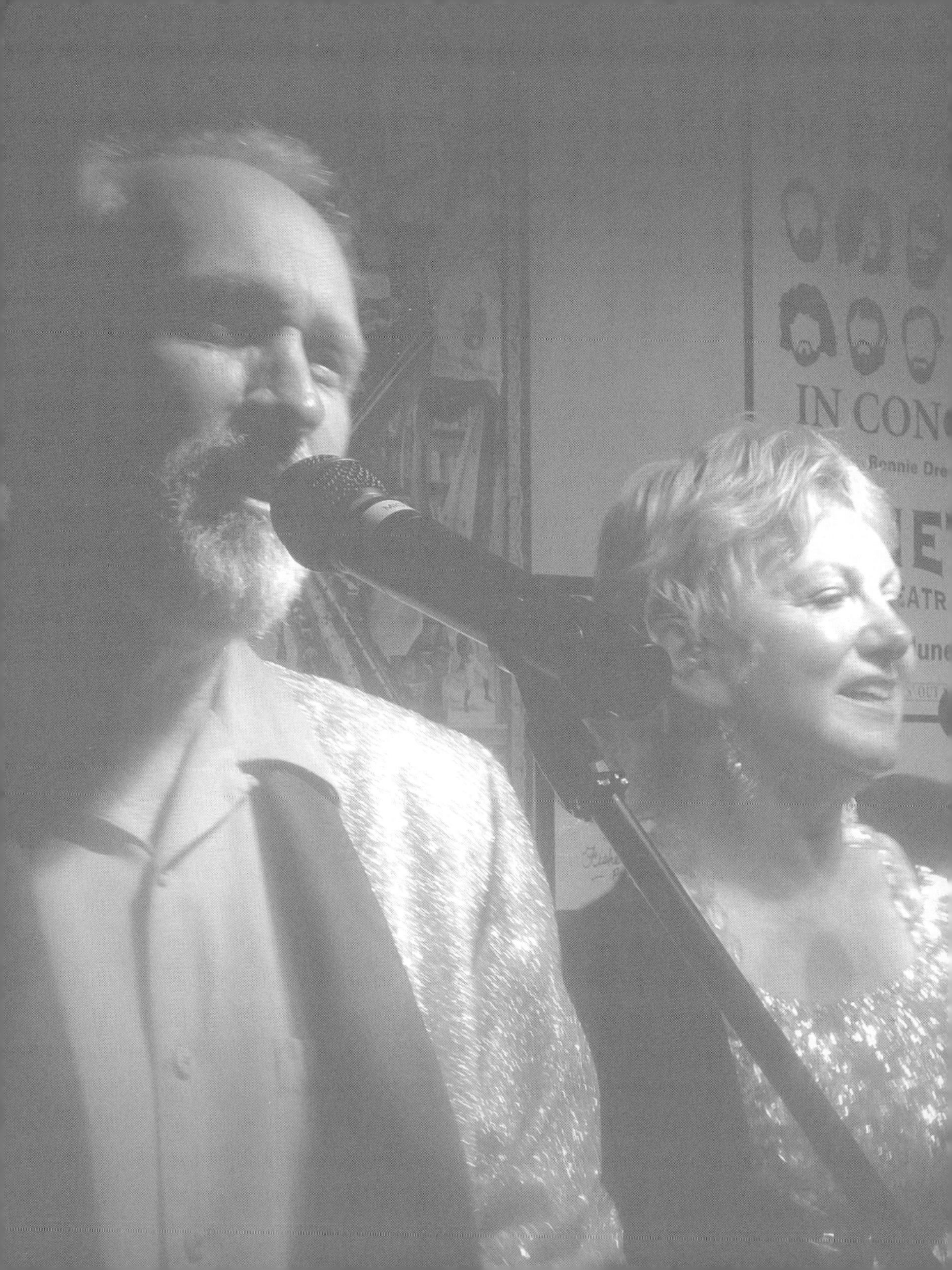

EPILOGUE

THE LAST WORD

FROM MORAG...

Boy, I did the right thing when I realized Steve was the person for me. Because even qualities I didn't think I would need, later on in my life I found out he had them. And later on I thought, "Holy Shoot, I was just a kid. I didn't know what my life would be." That's the whole luck part of finding someone and marrying them. Or maybe it's trust. Maybe it's just a feeling of safety and home and caring. "Okay, this feels really comfortable. I think I could live with this."

Shortly after we got married, we were in a folk group, The Unpredictables, and after that the rock group, Jason. My memory of being in the band is that it was really busy. I taught full-time, and then we'd work two nights a week in the band—loading up the equipment ourselves, going there, setting it up, playing

Opposite: Steve and Morag enjoy singing with The Fabulous Miromars.

all night, tearing it down, then bringing it back and storing it.

I absolutely loved the onstage part. Before the show I was always nervous. I'd go and throw up in the parking lot. Steve would calm me down ahead of time and then I would get him through the night. Once we were on the stage, I loved it.

But the living together…it was hard. The band members all bought a house together as an investment so we ate, slept and breathed the band. Everything we did, we did together. It took its toll, and I wasn't sorry when the band ended.

When Steve and I formed our duo, it was a laugh. I liked it—except that we were so desperate. We didn't have any money. We didn't have any work. We were selling equipment to pay the rent, so that made it a little stressful.

Steve wasn't all that interested in having kids. But when we decided, "Yeah, okay, we're going to," you just couldn't have gotten a better father than him. It's not that he gave the boys everything they wanted. He was able to say, "You know, if we do that, they won't learn such and such a thing."

He's just…just a really good dad. We're so proud of Max and Davy. It's not that they've become neurosurgeons or something, but they're people we really like, and like to be with. That's important. I would hate to have a kid and really not want to be with them.

It's absolutely sacrosanct to Steve that you keep your word. If he says to someone, "I'll meet you at 10:00 in the morning," he'll do whatever he has to do to make sure he's there. But that's not one of my great qualities. I just kind of go, "Oh yeah, I'll do that." And in my mind, what I mean is, "*If* it works out, I'll be there." Because to me there's a difference between casually saying, "Oh yeah, I'll do that," and it not working out. So that's a big difference between us that I have to respect.

Steve loves to make sure that all the details are together. When he was working, there were a million of them and he felt that he was ultimately responsible. He tends to get a bit frantic when he's got a lot of things going on. So he'd be going over these lists first thing in the morning and last thing at night. I'd

often accuse him of living in the future, not in the moment. And I'd say to him, "How about right now? It's pretty good right now."

I think that compulsion has really waned since he retired. He doesn't have to do that anymore, so he can be more relaxed. And I think he's more comfortable with himself.

I really want his life to be less stressful and just more enjoyable —that's my dream for him. Whether that's something he *can* do, or *wants* to do…I'm not even sure. He'll do what he feels is right.

Above: "What a wonder he is." Steve with first grandson, Luke, 2007. *Opposite:* Three generations of Smith men, 2007.

FROM MAX:

My brother and his wife having a baby—that evoked a lot of emotions for my dad.

FROM DAVY:

With having a grandson…oh man. Dad…he *loves* Luke.

Usually my parents are together when we talk to them. A lot of times my mom is the super-emotional one. And my dad is like, "That's great. Wow." Big smile on his face. But he almost tries to counteract Mom a little bit by not going crazy—someone's got to stay grounded here. But then he'll go off with his buddies to play golf, or he'll go to work or wherever, and that's when he'll get emotional and that's when he'll be giddy about it. And then we'll hear about that through other people. That's how we know.

And he's always emailing me and calling to ask how Luke's doing. He loves having a grandson. Loves it. Loves it.

AND ONE MORE FROM MORAG:

Having a grandson was huge for Steve. It's like, boy, you're just one of the links in a chain, you know? It minimizes what you are, and yet it connects you.

Every so often you get to work with an inspired leader, someone
who retains a calm, assertive demeanor when everyone else
around her is punchy, panicky or paralyzed, and who keeps
her own sacred focus against all odds. We had that leader
in Mavis Andrews, our supervising editor and designer.
Without her, this book would not be.
Thank you, Mavis. You're a beauty.

—Mag and Steve

Design and Layout: Paula Gaube, Victoria, BC

Design Assistants: Dave Murray, Red Deer, AB, and Sue Mitchell, Toronto, ON

Editor: Harriet Cooper, Toronto, ON

Proofreader: Tracey D. Hooper, North Saanich, BC

Supervising Editor and Designer: Mavis Andrews, Victoria, BC

PRINTED IN CANADA BY FRIESENS